"Happy Holidays" from

Bette + Desiree Leal

CENTURY 21 Consolidated

December 2005

MIRACLES HAPPEN

YOU CAN BET ON IT!

THE STORY OF LAS VEGAS

Author & Photo Editor
Rex M. Oppenheimer

Published by: Heritage Media Corp., 100 East San Marcos Blvd., Suite 400, San Marcos, CA 92069

ISBN: 1-886483-85-x   Library of Congress Control Number: 2004103685

Author & Photo Editor: Rex M. Oppenheimer

Profile Writers: Jenny Bengen, Allen Gardiner, Julie Gengo, Will Lerner, Victor Menaldo, Rex Oppenheimer,

Steven Osborne, Tony Parks, Carol Patton, Alexis Pedersen

MIRACLES HAPPEN—BET ON IT!

CONTENTS

CONTENTS

Partners in Las Vegas

INTRODUCTION

When astronauts orbiting through the dark reaches of space gaze homeward to Planet Earth, the first signs of life they report seeing are the amazing lights of Las Vegas. These far-reaching beacons, with their beckoning sparkle and promise of excitement and good fortune, reportedly draw 35 to 50 million visitors to the city every year — making it the world's top tourist attraction.

More people are also making Las Vegas their home. Long America's fastest-growing metropolitan area, between 1950 and 2000 Clark County, Nevada, grew more than 25 times in size, its population increasing from 48,000 to 1,375,765. How did this "miserable, dinky little oasis town," as Meyer Lansky called it, become what some reporters are describing as a paradigm for success in the 21st century?

Some observers say it's no mystery — gambling is the fuel that sent this rocket to the moon. Others praise the city's metamorphosis from the home of gangland vice to the world's greatest showplace for mainstream entertainment. Some commentators tout the rise of nongaming revenues, the broadening variety of the city's expanding business base, and its increasing sense of community and normalization. Other analysts have argued that the primary force behind the city's astronomical ascendancy is crime.

These critics assert that nefarious powers from all points on the globe use the city to acquire and launder ill-gotten gains. They claim that besides gaming, premier entertainment and plain old opportunity, it is drug money in the billions, political payoffs and massive corruption that have helped turn this artificial paradise in the middle of nowhere into the world's most popular destination.

Crime is part of every city's story. Las Vegas is no exception, and the city has specialized in activities that most other communities have deemed, or used to consider, immoral, offensive or sinful — gambling, drinking, faithlessness and unbridled hedonism. Yet, Las Vegas' brand of recreation reportedly takes in six times more revenue than all spectator sports and other forms of entertainment in the United States combined.

Rather than gambling, gangsters, entertainment or enterprise, perhaps the one element most responsible for the phenomenon known as Las Vegas is the very thing people come to Las Vegas to find — luck.

For many years Las Vegas skidded along, just another town seeking to survive far from the centers of commerce and sophistication. The city was lucky and it didn't even realize it. It benefited from its geographical situation and natural resources. Las Vegas began as an oasis that offered refreshment and hope in the middle of a burning desert. It was lucky when good people came, such as the early Mormon settlers and ranchers who helped make it hospitable to settlement. It was lucky when the railroad came, and it was lucky when federal dollars flowed in and buoyed the city through the Great Depression upon a reservoir of wealth as big as Lake Mead, which was created by Hoover Dam, the largest of the government projects.

Las Vegas was lucky when the bad guys came. The mobsters turned it into a goldmine unlike any other — one that attracted prospectors who filled it up with gold. People brought the gold and the gold brought people.

They come to Las Vegas for a chance. Pundits have proclaimed that many come to Las Vegas to escape a dark past, to make a fresh start or a new beginning. Today, many individuals come seeking the city's seemingly limitless opportunities, not to hit a jackpot but to build a good life.

Yet, what people have historically sought in Las Vegas is a release from care, the end of woe, the wide-open gates of endless paradise. They came to find luck and drink at the fount of transformation. They sought its power to reverse an aberrant fate, right past wrongs and wipe the slate clean. They hoped luck would pour forth like those artesian springs on the desert, the fountains of destiny that marked Las Vegas and began its journey through history.

It was an ironic journey. For while people came to characterize Las Vegas as Sin City, but what this caldron of desire and desperation actually became was a cathedral. A house of worship where the walls, floor, ceiling and very essence are made out of the object of worship — luck.

The rich, the poor, the young, the old, a multitude of races and nationalities, all come to worship at the altar of luck. They bring their offerings of bright, shiny gold, and they create opportunity. In Las Vegas, the streets are paved with it.

CHAPTER ONE

OASIS

Deserts have long been the refuge of exiles. For time immemorial outcasts were banished to their harsh, barren terrain.

Deserts have been the birthplace of revelation. Dwelling in isolation among the daunting distances imposed by a parched, almost endless landscape, jagged peaks and a beautiful but unforgiving sky, people have drawn out of themselves a link to spiritual salvation.

And so it was for millennia. But in 20th-century America, a desert was given a new definition, never before conceived or realized, and it was — Las Vegas!

Yet, the area that is now known as Las Vegas wasn't always Las Vegas, and it wasn't always desert. Between 10 to 15 thousand years ago southern Nevada was lush. Glaciers flowed from snowcapped mountains, vivid blue lakes and fresh running streams were abundant. Mammoths, native horses, giant buffalo and huge, tank-like ground sloths were among the wild creatures roaming the region's green valleys.

They named this gentle valley in the middle of the burning desert Las Vegas, Spanish for the meadows.

Many successive ancient cultures populated the Las Vegas Valley. *UNLV Special Collections*

Long before it became an entertainment mecca, a fountain of wealth, or America's playground, Las Vegas distinguished itself from its barren surroundings. Ancient people who hunted and foraged in the hot deserts would establish camps in the hospitable valley where water, once trapped in the geological formations beneath the earth's sun-baked crust, rose to the surface through artesian springs.

Many successive ancient cultures populated the Las Vegas Valley. In addition to the Clovis people, there were the Lake Mojave people who lived in the area between 10,000 and 7,500 years ago. The Pinto Basin culture evolved from the Lake Mojave people as the area became more arid. The Gypsum culture followed and remained until about 1,500 years ago. Archeologists have found stone weapons and tools, including leaf-shaped points and millstones for grinding seeds, made by the Gypsum culture. The Gypsum also left puzzlingly poignant petroglyphs carved into sandstone cliffs and canyon walls. While some archeologists debate the meaning and purpose of the carved pictures and designs, the petroglyphs do document some facts of these ancient's lives, such as the progression from spears to bows and arrows as a more efficient method of hunting.

There were people, too. Nomadic hunters and gatherers, probably part of a river of humanity that had flowed across the land bride connecting the tip of North America to Siberia and down through the generations into what would one day become present day Las Vegas. Based on finds, such as the ancient residue of campfires, charred animal bones and stone tools, some archeologists believe that nomads, thought to be the Clovis people, camped at Tule Springs just two miles west of modern Fremont Street about 11,000 years ago.

Beginning about 9,000 years ago, the once lush valleys and forests in what is now southern Nevada grew arid and barren. Lizards darted and snakes slithered. The sun's fierce heat baked the earth hard and dry. Conditions were less hospitable to life. The large, lumbering beasts had gone, but human foragers still wandered the territory.

The Basketmaker hunters are named for the tightly woven baskets that have been found in archeological digs. Pit-houses discovered in the area suggest these nomads, ancestors of the Paiute tribe of Native Americans, whose descendents still inhabit the Las Vegas Valley, were in the region between 300 B.C. and A.D. 700.

The Virgin Anasazi appeared in the area about 1,500 years ago. Related in a distant way to the more complex culture of the Anasazi in the Four Corners region, they built small, single story pueblos from adobe. Unlike the hunter-gatherers that had come before, the Virgin Anasazi also practiced agriculture, raising corn, beans and squash. The Virgin Anasazi lived in the Las Vegas Valley and the Muddy and

Baskets woven by the Southern Paiutes, who came to the area sometime after A.D. 1200, are today prized by collectors. *UNLV Special Collections*

Virgin River valleys until about the 12th century when for reasons not entirely clear, they abandoned the area and left it exclusively to the ancestors of the Southern Paiutes.

The Southern Paiutes came to the area sometime after A.D. 1200. They comprised 16 bands, each an independent economic cluster made up of several camps of families. Although they engaged in some agriculture, the Paiutes were primarily hunters and gatherers, roaming their vast territory, which included southern Nevada, southeastern California, southwestern Utah and northwestern Arizona, according to the natural cycle of ripening plants. They also trapped and hunted game, including rabbits, wood rats, lizards, desert tortoises, birds and occasionally bighorn sheep and deer. The Southern Paiutes made a variety of baskets. Originally created for use in the preparation, storage and transportation of food, today the baskets are viewed as a symbol of Pauite culture and are prized by collectors.

Loosely governed, the Southern Paiutes had no central or political authority. The bands were relatively separate economic entities comprising several camps of families. Most bands did have a head man, or pakwinavi, "big talker," but his power was more advisory than real.

The Las Vegas band, known as the Nipakanticimi, meaning "people of Charleston Peak," had camps at Las Vegas, Indian Springs, Ash Meadows and Cottonwood Island on the Colorado River. They occupied the largest geographical area of all the Paiute bands.

Petroglyphs found in the Las Vegas area document various aspects of the lives of ancient peoples. *UNLV Special Collections*

European – American Presence

The Southern Paiutes had lived in the Las Vegas Valley for centuries by the time the first Europeans arrived. Although there are differences of opinion among historians, they generally regard Father Francisco Garces, a Franciscan missionary, as the first European to enter the territory. His interaction with the Paiutes in 1776 was peaceful. Garces' expeditions, from what is present day Yuma, up along the Colorado River and west across the Mojave Desert toward Los Angeles, blazed what would later become part of the western leg of the Old Spanish Trail.

Future Las Vegas would come to depend on travelers' contribution to its economy. It was 18th-century travelers, traders and explorers, seeking safe and quick passage to and from California, who established the Old Spanish Trail and discovered Las Vegas as a traveler's oasis.

The same year that Garces established part of the trail's western leg, another Spaniard, Father Silvestre Velez de Escalante, led an expedition west toward California from Santa Fe. Escalante's expedition ran into heavy snow in Utah that forced their return. Their journey, however, pioneered what would become the eastern portion of the Old Spanish Trail.

The Spanish had traveled the new world searching for fabled cities of gold. Fifty years after Garces, fur trapper Jedediah Smith, also seeking wealth, helped further establish the western leg of the Old Spanish Trail. Pursing the profits from beaver pelts, Smith headed a party of trappers through the Salt Lake Valley down to Mesquite in what is now southeastern Nevada. Next, they moved on to the Virgin River and down to the Colorado River, crossing it near Needles, California, and finally arriving at Mission San Gabriel.

Just three years after Smith's journey, Antonio Armijo, a Santa Fe merchant, established the final leg of the Old Spanish Trail to California. In 1829, seeking a less dangerous and shorter route than the jornada de muerte, or journey of death, across the burning Mojave Desert, he decided not to follow Smith's path. Instead, at the northwest corner of Arizona, Armijo headed westward and north of the Colorado River to the Las Vegas Wash.

Rafael Rivera was the first non-Native American to set foot in the Las Vegas Valley. A young scout, who was part of the Armijo expedition, he wandered from his camp and discovered an oasis. Rivera gazed upon a valley swept with flowing grasses and graced by that desert miracle — water. They named this gentle valley in the middle of the burning desert Las Vegas, Spanish for the meadows.

Armijo was one of the first persons of European descent to reach California from New Mexico. His route through the hospitable Las Vegas Valley shortened the journey by several days and finally completed the Old Spanish Trail. Armijo's path through the Las Vegas Valley became the preferred way to California.

The Old Spanish Trail bore increasing traffic over the next two decades. Travel along the rough, rustic route could be a gamble. Caravans of wool and horse traders had to deal with thieves and bands of ruthless raiders. A thriving slave trade also traveled the trail. Slavers shipped Paiute women and children to New Mexico in exchange for goods, guns and horses. Slavery

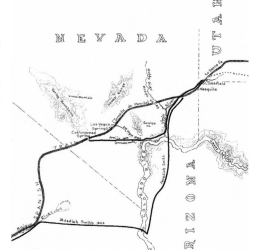

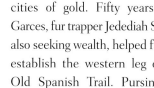

The fur-trapping expeditions of Jedediah Smith helped to further establish the western leg of the Old Spanish Trail.
UNLV Special Collections

Jedediah Smith's route

was illegal under Mexican law, but it was virtually impossible to police the wild frontier trail between New Mexico and California. It wasn't until 1860 that the slave trade was eradicated.

While journeying the Old Spanish Trail could be risky, Las Vegas was a safe bet. Its artesian streams provided precious water to weary desert travelers. By the mid-1840s, Las Vegas appeared on many Spanish maps. The area was still Mexican territory, but the U.S. Army Corps of Topographical Engineers had begun a systematic mapping program of the region. John C. Fremont, a young officer in the Corps, who had previously mapped the south pass through the Rocky Mountains in Wyoming, was leading his second expedition, including scouts, scientists and observers, on their return trip from California to Kansas City. Somewhere south of Death Valley, two of Fremont's men, famed scout Kit Carson and Alex Godey, got into a violent confrontation with some Indians.

Fleeing the area, Fremont's expedition took off across the Pahrump Valley and camped at Las Vegas Springs on the Spanish Trail. The desert oasis was a welcome respite. Fremont described the campground named Las Vegas

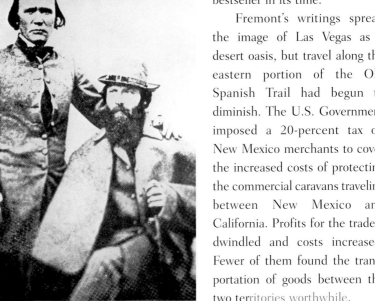

in his journal entry for the day they arrived, May 3, 1844, "…two narrow streams of clear water, four or five feet deep, gush suddenly with a quick current from two singularly large springs."

Fremont published his full report in 1845. Considered a valuable reference, it contained scientific observations and maps drawn by the German cartographer, Charles Preuss. The report also narrated the story of their adventures, which the public found fascinating. Although bearing the prosaic title of "Report of the Exploring Expedition to the Rocky Mountains in the Year 1842 and to Oregon and North California in the years 1843 – 44," it became a bestseller in its time.

Fremont's writings spread the image of Las Vegas as a desert oasis, but travel along the eastern portion of the Old Spanish Trail had begun to diminish. The U.S. Government imposed a 20-percent tax on New Mexico merchants to cover the increased costs of protecting the commercial caravans traveling between New Mexico and California. Profits for the traders dwindled and costs increased. Fewer of them found the transportation of goods between the two territories worthwhile.

Mormon Settlement

Las Vegas' evolution from obscurity to one of the world's great entertainment capitals has resulted from many factors. Among them were its geographical location and natural resources. Water had placed Las Vegas on the map. About the time that the Old Spanish Trail was drifting into disuse, Las Vegas was to become a rest stop along a new passageway, the Mormon trail. It began when Mormon missionary Hosea Stout, traveling with some companions to California in 1852, stopped for water at the Las Vegas Spring.

Stout, an early convert to the Church of Jesus Christ of Latter-day Saints and former officer in the Mormon militia, had been the law enforcement chief

Brigham Young, leader of the Church of Jesus Christ of Latter-day Saints after the death of its founder Joseph Smith
UNLV Special Collections

charged with keeping order on the Mormon's long trek to the Salt Lake Valley in 1847. Brigham Young, leader of the church since the death of the its founder, Joseph Smith, considered the valley, then still part of Mexico, as the Saints' Promised Land.

After the Mexican American War ended and the treaty of Hidalgo was accepted by the Senate in 1848, all the land north of the Gila River, including what would later become Utah and Nevada, was ceded to the United States. Brigham Young had planned a Mormon state, called Deseret, for this same area, and he had chosen Hosea Stout to be its attorney general. However, with the land absorbed into the U.S. territories of Utah and New Mexico, Brigham Young instead became the Utah governor.

By the time Hosea Stout stopped in Las Vegas, he was on his way to China to win over converts for the church. He always, however, had his eye open to extending Mormon influence closer to home as well, such as in New Mexico and California. The church had plans for a string of settlements between Salt Lake City and the California coast, and in 1851 the Mormons had acquired a large ranch at San Bernadino for this purpose.

Las Vegas' location at about the midway point on the route between Salt Lake and the coast, its abundant water and welcome refreshment made an impression on Hosea Stout. He wrote in his diary, "This is the first stream, since we left the basin, which I have seen that could be used for irrigation, or where the soil would produce anything for the use of civilized man... Here we found... grape vines in abundance... Like the oasis of Arabia, the weary traveler can here set down a calm repose and rest himself, after passing the parched desert."

Of course, by the time Hosea Stout wrote those words, the Las Vegas Spring was already fairly well known as a haven along the otherwise harsh trail. Less than a month after Stout's visit to the area, Las Vegas became a regular stop on the winter mail route between Salt Lake City and California. The U.S. Congress established a regular monthly mail service along the route in 1854 and appropriated $25,000 to build a military road. Las Vegas' strategic location would continue to play a significant role in its development.

The Mormon settlers built their fort using adobe bricks made onsite at the southeast corner of today's Las Vegas Boulevard and Washington Avenue.

Brigham Young decided the time was right for the Church of Jesus Christ of Latter-day Saints to have a settlement at Las Vegas. In 1855 the Mormon leader assigned William Bringhurst to lead 30 men to Las Vegas. Their mission was to "build a fort there to protect immigrants and the United States mail from the Indians, and to teach the latter how to raise corn, wheat, potatoes, squash and melons."

This statement was an example of the chauvinistic attitude that many whites had toward the Native Americans. The Paiutes had been sowing and harvesting crops in the region for centuries. Still, although somewhat paternalistic, the Mormon settlers were prepared to treat the native inhabitants fairly. Bringhurst sent regular reports back to Salt Lake. Less than a month after their arrival, he wrote of the Mormons' first encounters with the Paiutes:

"Shortly after we arrived here, we assembled all the chiefs and made an agreement treaty with them for permission to make a settlement on their lands. We agreed to treat them well, and they were to observe the same conduct towards us, and with all white men. Peace was to be preserved with all emigrants traveling through this country, as well as with the settlers...They recount many instances of unprovoked murder committed by white men who have traveled this road, but are now willing to bury all animosities and to once more try the conduct of white men."

Relations between the Paiutes and the settlers were generally peaceful. The Mormons converted many of the Indians, and other firsthand accounts, left in diaries or journals, convey a kindly, if somewhat superior, attitude toward the Native Americans.

Mormon settlers cleared acres of mesquite to plant crops. They chose a location for their fort and built it using adobe bricks, which they made onsite. Today, the site is a historical landmark on the southeast corner of Las Vegas Boulevard and Washington Avenue.

The 30 settlers who had come with 40 ox-drawn wagons, 15 cows and several horses cleared a wagon road to the nearby mountains. They felled trees for logs and hauled them down the road to construct cabins near the fort.

In many instances the Paiutes worked alongside the Mormon settlers, as in this account by George W. Bean, who served as the mission's clerk and interpreter, "The Indians were soon partially converted to the habits of industry, and helped us to grub the land, make adobes, attend the mason and especially to herd the stock. They were fairly honest and soon joined the Church."

As Bringhurst trusted deputy, Bean corresponded with Brigham Young. When some of the settlers returned to Utah during the first winter, Bean was one of the 17 who remained. He received instructions to take a census of "all Natives within the boundaries of our Mission field." While conducting this duty, he observed and reported some valuable discoveries. Bean sent word of tall ledges of crystal salt near the Virgin River, good timber in the mountains and what appeared

Octavius Decatur Gass

to be extensive lead deposits less than 20 miles west of the fort.

This last item particularly interested Brigham Young, who sent Nathaniel V. Jones to Nevada on a "lead mission." Young's intention was to mine the lead and ship it to Salt Lake City. Bean noted that Young hoped it "would be useful for tools and bullets."

Although the lead mine produced ore, Jones reported that it was "very hard to smelt." The settlers poured the ore into molds to make bullets, but the results were unsatisfactory. Many of the bullets cracked. The miners persisted, but the ore remained problematic. Little did they realize that what they thought was pure lead was in fact galena ore laden with silver. This they never discovered.

Problems with the lead operation weren't confined to the quality of the ore. Friction developed between the original settlers and the newcomers. Whether the mission's priority should be mining or agriculture was part of the problem. In addition, N.V. Jones and the lead workers' more liberal views clashed with Binghurst's strict rule.

Brigham Young called George W. Bean and three other missionaries to Salt Lake City to report on the situation. After hearing them out and asking many questions, Young delivered his opinion. He thought that the spirit of the mission had been broken and that the best idea was to abandon it. Late in 1856, Young said that the settlers should try to extract all the lead they could before leaving the mine for good. They abandoned the mine in January 1857.

The problems at the settlement in Las Vegas extended beyond the failing mine or the friction between the followers of Jones and Binghurst. For some time Young had been receiving reports of less than favorable conditions. While many of the Paiutes had converted and worked along side the missionaries, there were still Indian raids on property and crops. The summer heat turned the settlement into a blast furnace and despite some success at agriculture, the settlers found the soil woefully inadequate.

A month after they had abandoned the mine, Brigham Young gave the Mormon brethren permission to leave the fort, and the mission was officially closed. Only a small number of settlers remained for a few months to harvest the crops. Whether hardened by the need to abandon their mission or just not mindful of Bringhurst's admonitions to honor the Indians, their attitude toward the native population became far less generous and kind.

The Paiutes, disillusioned by the treatment they were now receiving at the hands of the remaining settlers, wrought their revenge. As soon as harvest time came, the Paiutes swooped in and absconded with the entire crop. The discouraged settlers packed and departed the Las Vegas Valley in 1858.

The Ranchers: Cowboys and Killers

It had been six years since Hosea Stout had first set foot in Las Vegas and only three short years since the establishment of the Mormon settlement, and they were gone. The next significant attempt by those other than Native Americans to locate in the area came seven years later. In 1865 Octavius Decatur Gass began what would be the first lasting settlement in the Las Vegas Valley.

Octavius Decatur Gass, a native of Ohio and an educated man with a sense of adventure, had followed the Gold Rush to San Francisco. Unable to find his fortune in the gold fields, he headed for Los Angeles where he became an irrigation inspector. Still suffering from a touch of gold fever and hoping for a bonanza, he filed a few mining claims in Eldorado Canyon, about 40 miles southeast of Las Vegas on the Colorado River during the early 1860s. Gass never struck paydirt, but by the mid-1860s there were between 300 to 500 people working claims in the Eldorado Canyon area.

Gass' friend, William Knapp, owned a small property near the old Las Vegas Fort where he planned to run a small store for travelers on the Mormon Trail. Mining hadn't panned out for Gass, and when he saw the area around Las Vegas, it seemed to offer him hope for a new direction in life.

He decided to give ranching a try and invited two prospector friends to join him as partners. The men took over the abandoned Mormon fort in 1865, rebuilding and restoring the adobe buildings. They cleared weed-infested, rock-strewn fields for cultivation. The former irrigation inspector constructed irrigation works on the land and soon the partners' property, which they'd christened the "Los Vegas Rancho," comprised 400 acres of irrigated land.

They grew wheat, oats and barley and hired Paiute workers to help with the harvest. Next, they planted cabbages, onions, potatoes, beets and melons. As the years passed their fruit trees blossomed, bearing figs, apricots, apples and peaches, which they sold to passing travelers.

The rancho's vineyards produced plump grapes, which the partners pressed into wine. Travelers, sampling the wine, came to know the ranch as an oasis of refreshment. Word spread and wagon trains wheeled up to the rancho to rest and take on supplies.

Octavius Decatur Gass, who had bought out his partners and expanded his ranch to 640 acres, spoke Spanish and several Paiute dialects. Particularly adept at dealing with Mexican and Indian leaders, he served four

After Gass married Mary Virginia Simpson in 1872, the ranch became decidedly more luxurious.

consecutive terms as a legislator in the new Arizona Territory, which Las Vegas had become part of in 1863. The new state of Nevada was created that same year. As a legislator Gass had lobbied for the Las Vegas area to be broken off from Arizona's Mojave County and to be named Pah-Ute Country.

That didn't happen, and when federal mapmakers gave Nevada a portion of Arizona west of the Colorado River, Gass' ranch remained in disputed territory. That's where it stayed until about 1872 when Las Vegas became part of Lincoln County, Nevada.

Many prospectors sought their fortunes in the El Dorado Canyon area. *UNLV Special Collections*

Octavius Decatur Gass founded the "Los Vegas Rancho," which would spearhead the first lasting settlement in the Las Vegas Valley.

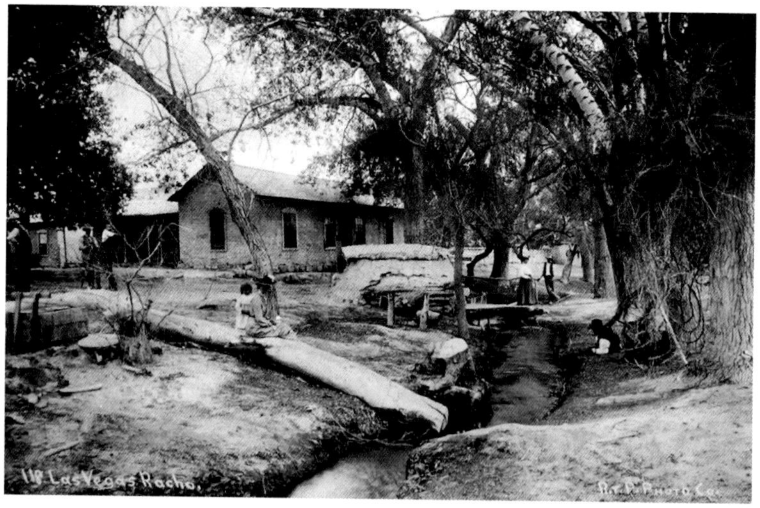

The year of 1872 was a turning point for Gass. He married Mary Virginia Simpson, the daughter of a wealthy Missouri farmer, and the desert rancho began to acquire the characteristics of a grand villa. Gass added new buildings, including a spacious ranch house. Mary Gass hired Chinese and Bavarian cooks for her kitchen and Paiute servants to clean the house and do the laundry.

While much on the ranch was good, there were some problems in paradise. When the area had become part of Nevada, the state had sought back taxes. Perhaps Gass' management skills weren't up to supporting the new extravagances, or maybe he just hit a run of hard luck, but by 1879 he was deeply in debt. Threatened with loosing his property, Gass borrowed $5,000 in gold from Archibald Stewart, a prosperous rancher and businessman who lived in Pioche.

Octavius Decatur Gass, who spoke Spanish and several Paiute dialects, lobbied for the Las Vegas area to be broken off from Arizona's Mojave County and to be named Pah-Ute Country.

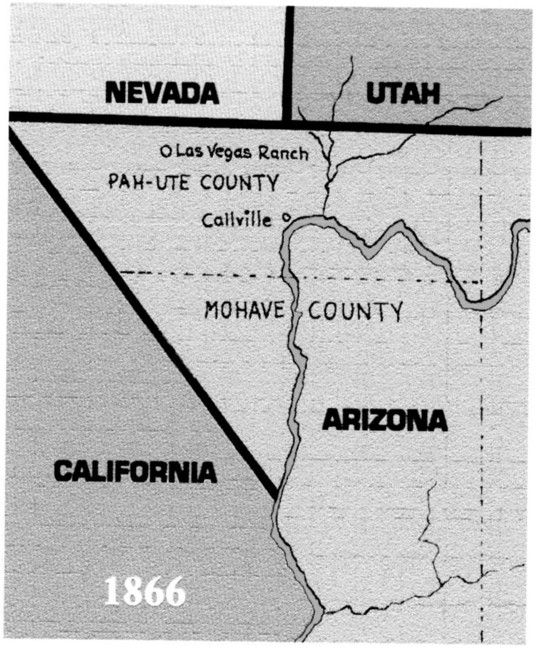

Gass wasn't able to get back on his feet, and when the note became due a year later, he had to be granted a nine-month extension. The extension ended, and Gass was still unable to pay. Stewart foreclosed on the property on May 2, 1881.

Stewart remained in Pioche and handled the ranch from a distance. Despite his absentee management, the ranch thrived under his direction. The following year, however, when Stewart and his partners ran afoul of each other, the successful Pioche businessman took his beautiful wife, Helen, and their three children and moved to the Las Vegas ranch.

It was 1884, a little more than two years since Stewart and his family had come to live on the ranch. Helen Stewart was home with her four children. Pregnant again, she was doing her best to rest and keep cool in the sweltering July heat. It was mid-afternoon, and the sun's quiet rays baked the ground hard. The sound of a rider approaching broke the languorous spell. Helen went out on the porch to greet him.

The man had brought a note from a neighbor, Conrad Kiel (sometimes spelled Kyle), who owned a ranch two miles form the Stewart property. Helen took the note and unfolded the paper, staring in disbelief at its blunt message: "Your husband is here dead. Come take him away."

Stiff with anger and pain, Mrs. Stewart saddled her horse and rode hard to the Kiel ranch. She found Archibald's body lying on the ground covered by a blanket. Her hired farm hands loaded her husband's lifeless form onto a wagon and carried it home. Watching them dig a grave and bury her husband, Helen Stewart read aloud from the burial service in the Book of Common Prayer.

It took 13 days for the sheriff to arrive. Conrad Kiel's story was that he'd been away from home when the killing had occurred. Schuyler Henry, a ranch hand once employed by Stewart, claimed he'd shot his former boss in self defense. Helen Stewart didn't believe him. She told the sheriff that she thought Conrad Kiel had conspired with Henry and notorious gunfighter Hank Parrish to slay her husband. A jury listened to testimony from the widow, Kiel and Henry; Parrish couldn't be found. The jury voted 16 to 1 to dismiss charges against Kiel and Henry.

Most people in the area thought that Stewart was an overbearing boss, and they sided with the jury. The consensus seemed to be that Stewart and Henry had been at odds for some time. When Stewart found out that Henry had walked off the job, he grabbed a rifle and headed out to the Kiel ranch to find him. The story goes that as Stewart, rifle in hand, approached, Henry saw him aiming at him, jumped up, grabbed a gun and fired.

Time passed, and life on the two ranches went on. Then, on October 11, 1900, 16 years after Archibald Stewart's death, his widow, Helen, who had continued to run the Stewart spread, her son Will and her foreman, Frank Stewart (although no relation to Archibald Stewart, he did later marry Helen), went to the Kiel Ranch to visit and replenish their supply of tobacco.

Conrad Kiel had died in 1894, and his sons, Edwin and William Kiel, were running the ranch. Now, when the Stewart party arrived they found the front and back doors ajar. Looking inside, they saw Edwin Kiel's body lying on the kitchen floor, a pistol near his right hand. They discovered the body of William Kiel lying in an irrigation ditch about 30 feet from the house. A double-barreled shotgun lay at his feet. With no witnesses, the coroner's jury ruled it a murder suicide, finding that Edwin had killed William and then in remorse had shot himself.

Two University of Nevada, Las Vegas (UNLV) anthropologists, Richard and Sheilagh Brooks, had Archibald Stewart's body exhumed in the 1970s, hoping to find a clue as to who killed him. They determined that a bullet had entered through his right cheek, passed through his skull and exited from the back of his head. The truth about who fired the shot remained buried in history.

UNLV researchers also had the Kiel brothers' bodies exhumed in the 1970s, and this time the investigation cast doubt on the jury's findings. Forensic evidence indicated a double murder, rather than a murder suicide. Edwin Kiel had died from a bullet wound to the back of the head, rather than to the front of the face. Although there were many theories, including revenge by Helen Stewart, just who pulled the trigger remains a mystery.

Helen Stewart held on to her ranch until 1902 when she sold it to Montana Senator and copper king William Clark for his San Pedro, Los Angeles & Salt Lake Railroad. Las Vegas' brief ranching episode was ending. Smaller ranches still dotted the region, but the sale of the Stewart property signaled a change in direction.

Geography and resources had made Las Vegas a wayfarer's delight. Traveling bands of Indians, traders, missionaries and highwaymen had all enjoyed the desert oasis. Now a new age was steaming into view. America's Manifest Destiny was on the fast track, and Las Vegas was beginning to look like a pretty good place to stop.

Archibald Stewart foreclosed on Gass' Las Vegas Ranch on May 2, 1881.
UNLV Special Collections

Archibald Stewart's wife, Helen, a pregnant mother of four, received a note from neighbor Conrad Kiel. It read, "Your husband is here dead. Come take him away."
UNLV Special Collections

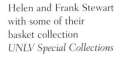

Helen and Frank Stewart with some of their basket collection
UNLV Special Collections

Helen Stewart kept her ranch until 1902 when she sold it to Montana Senator William Clark for his San Pedro, Los Angeles & Salt Lake Railroad.
UNLV Special Collections

Edwin Kiel (left) and Conrad Kiel at the Kiel Sawmill
UNLV Special Collections

CHAPTER TWO

PICKING UP STEAM

Las Vegas had become a regular stop on the mail route between Salt Lake City and Los Angeles in 1854. At the beginning of the 20th century with Salt Lake City, the largest town between the Rocky Mountains and Los Angeles, linked by rail to New York, Chicago and San Francisco, the time seemed right for a railroad connection to Southern California and Los Angeles.

Rumors had spread that the railroad was coming to Las Vegas. It seemed a natural. The area had served as the rest stop on the Mormon Trail between Salt Lake and Los Angeles, and the hospitable valley had abundant water supplies. There had been mysterious strangers casing the area, including surveyors hauling chain and tripods. Yet, they all seemed to disappear and the wind, rather than locomotives, remained the only thing whistling through the valley.

When the money tree finally got ready to bear fruit, two titans squared off over the pickings. The fight between Montana Sen. William Clark and Edward H. Harriman's Union Pacific Railroad for the right to construct the link between the Rockies and the Pacific Coast began when the Union Pacific put together a string of short-line railroads in Utah, which terminated at Cedar City, close to the Nevada-Utah border.

A year later, in 1900, copper king William Clark made his bid. He purchased the Los Angeles Terminal Railroad and began to construct his own line, the San Pedro, Los Angeles & Salt Lake Railroad. In 1902 he bought Helen Stewart's ranch for $55,000. He got 1,800 acres, the ranch house and other buildings and all the water from the Las Vegas Spring. To strengthen his hold on the Las Vegas Valley, Clark also bought the Kiel ranch, including its springs.

The showdown between Harriman and Clark came at Meadow Valley Wash, north of Las Vegas. The two faced off over the right-of-way to lay track through the valley. They finally settled the dispute, known as The Clark-Harriman War, with a compromise allowing the

Union Pacific to acquire a 50 percent share in the San Pedro, Los Angeles & Salt Lake Railroad. Clark maintained control of the operations.

The railroad had blazed a trail of prosperity all across America. Land values increased and towns sprang up as new areas opened to development. The lure of fast cash would draw speculators, investors, businessmen and gamblers. J.T. McWilliams was a surveyor. But when he came to Las Vegas, he made a wager. He bet on the town of Las Vegas.

Helen Stewart had hired McWilliams to survey her land in 1902 for its sale to Sen. Clark. While he was conducting that survey, McWilliams noticed an 80-acre tract of land just west of the ranch, which was owned by

The Stewart Ranch house
UNLV Special Collections

Water had put Las Vegas on the map. The railroad powered the city's early development.
UNLV Special Collections

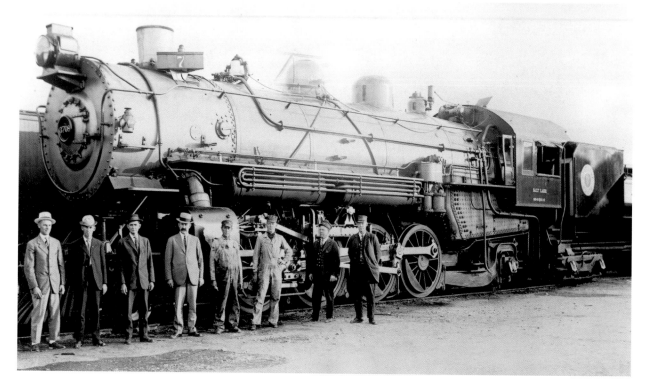

the government. McWilliams knew that the railroad intended to run its tracks along the corner of the land, and he immediately filed a claim.

Las Vegas, with its artesian springs, had been a safe bet for nomads and travelers for millennia. Now McWilliams was betting that with the railroad passing through the area, its water supply and midway location between Salt Lake City and Los Angeles would make it a natural place to put a town. The population of the Las Vegas Valley in 1900 was 19. By early 1904 it had only climbed to about 30 people. Still, to McWilliams the signs of a boom were obvious.

In 1904 he laid out what he dubbed the, "Original Townsite of Las Vegas." By the summer of that year, grading for the railway line had reached the valley and as the tracks were laid, a tent city sprang up just ahead of the construction. In early 1905 McWilliams began selling lots. He planned to cash in quickly, selling cheap and offering favorable terms.

McWilliams must have had a gambler's winning smile as he began to rake in the cash. His first customers included not just investors. Miners, railroad workers, cowboys and thieves all snapped up the lots that were going for as little as $100 each. A tent city, known as "Ragtown," sprang up. Within a few weeks there were a hotel, meat market, store, four restaurants, a dozen bars and gambling halls, all canvas-covered.

It was a boomtown, rough and crude. In winter, cold winds blew straight through the fabric covering the unheated tents. Drivers and hustlers of the freight teams were the town's main support. With the railroad under construction, the freighting business was very active and Ragtown had several large corrals housing the many horses

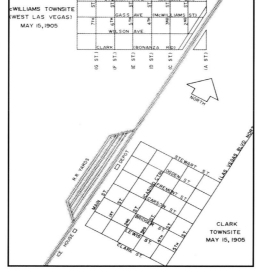

and mules used by the freighters. Flies buzzed incessantly, and the smell of fresh manure wafted across Original Townsite of Las Vegas.

But McWilliams had competition, and it was cutthroat. Las Vegas was shaping up to be a railroad town. The railroad created a townsite on the old Stewart Ranch. It formed a wholly owned subsidiary, the Las Vegas Land and Water Company, to oversee the sale of lots. Just as important as the sale of lots, however, was the protection of railroad interests. Clark's people were determined from the outset that McWilliams wouldn't profit from their investment.

The copper king, William Clark, senator from Montana and neophyte railroad tycoon, was a man used to getting what he wanted. When it came to Las Vegas, he wanted it all. Once charged with bribery, Clark quipped in his defense, "I never bought a man who wasn't for sale." He was famous for having bought himself a senate seat from Montana at a time when senators were picked by state legislatures rather than by popular vote, by paying off politicians with thousand-dollar bills.

During the election a state senator held up four envelopes containing $30,000, which he said were bribes intended to buy votes for Clark. A Montana newspaper lampooned Clark, accusing him of "buying votes like eggs." But after 18 ballots the state senate had elected William Clark, a Democrat, who had managed to persuade 11 Republicans to vote for him.

Clark's railroad interests laid out plans for a town on the east side of the railroad tracks and advertised lots for sale for between $100 and $300 per acre. More than 3,000 offers poured in as if a dam had burst open.

J.T. McWilliams took a gamble on Las Vegas. *UNLV Special Collections*

The McWilliams and Clark townsites

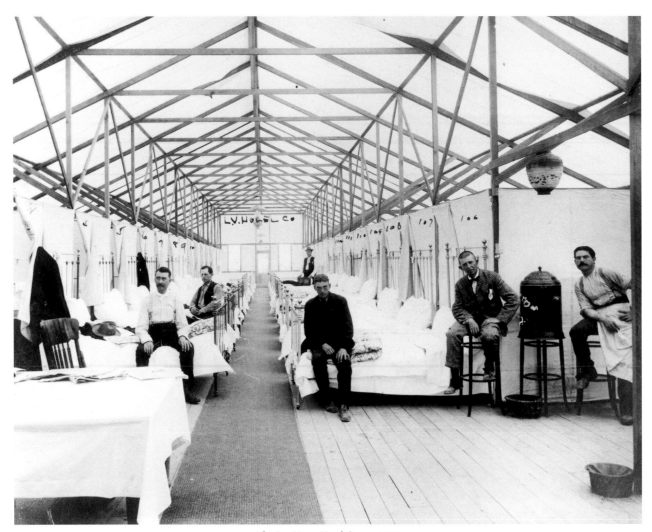

The Las Vegas Hotel Co., c. 1905
UNLV Special Collections

Realizing the incredible demand, the Clark interests cancelled their offer and instead said they would hold a public auction on May 15, 1905.

McWilliams tried to fight back, but he should have realized that his Original Las Vegas Townsite on the west side of the tracks had its days numbered. He advertised in the newspaper, telling prospective buyers, "Get in line early, buy now, double your money in 60 days." He lectured them about the dangers of buying in the midst of the excitement at an auction; he criticized

Clark's townsite's lack of public improvements. It was a desperate effort, and it didn't work.

Clark's auction opened to 3,000 bidders and spectators. Many had come in on special excursion trains from Los Angeles and Salt Lake City. Bids on a few prized pieces reached as high as $1,750. Lots on Fremont Street between Main and First streets sold for $750, $800 and $850. By 3 p.m. that first day, the auction sold 176 choice lots to the tune of $79,566. Each parcel came with a guarantee of water delivery and graded

Wilson Street in McWilliams' Original Las Vegas Townsite, 1905
UNLV Special Collections

Montana copper king and Las Vegas railroad baron Sen. William Clark in his private car

and oiled streets. Buyers were also guaranteed access to a railroad depot, complete with maintenance and repair shops that would ensure the employment of several hundred men.

This town was literally booming. The pounding of hammers and the sound of saws rose into the air along with tall plumes of dust as building got under way and continued through the night. Those who hadn't bought could see a town rising right before their eyes. When morning dawned, new establishments were opening for business. Bidding opened on the second day to pandemonium. By the close of bidding that afternoon, the railroad had hauled in nearly $265,000, and only half of the available lots had been sold.

Many who bought lots in the Clark townsite were former residents of the McWilliams townsite, and they were now dragging the wooden frames and canvas coverings of their structures over to the new town. The freight business hauled itself across the tracks to the Clark townsite, too. To add insult to injury, the railroad built the tracks so high that it was extremely difficult for wagons to cross from the townsite on the west to Clark's

on the east. The McWilliams site began to deflate like a punctured balloon. The final blow came when a devastating fire raged through what was left of McWilliams' town on September 5, 1905.

Profit was only part of Clark's mission, control played an important role, too. The contract for every lot sold contained a "no liquor" clause. Hotels, drug stores, establishments serving liquor with meals, doctors' prescriptions and Blocks 16 and 17 between First and Third streets on Ogden and Stewart streets were exempted.

With unrestricted liquor sales, gambling and prostitution, Block 16 was famous as a red-light district. It was bawdy and rough. Riots, shootings and fights were common, and the entire block was filled with saloons and gambling halls. There was the Gem, the Red Onion, the Double-O, and the most famous of them all, the Arizona Club. Relatively high class, the Arizona Club was certainly luxurious by turn-of-the-century Las Vegas standards with its beveled glass, mahogany bar and marble baseboards.

John Wisner, one of the first residents of the Clark townsite, had purchased lots on Main and Fremont streets outside Block 16. When he built the Overland Hotel and opened a saloon, the railroad decided to enforce its restrictions. The trial was held at the county seat, Pioche, and the railroad sent an employee named Charles "Pop" Squires to testify against Wisner. Decades later Squires' daughter told the story:

"Pop took the train to Caliente — the branch line was built to Pioche — and he was there five days in the middle of the winter. The company, I believe, won the suit on five counts and Wisner was given the decision on three counts, which never decided anything. Since then there's been no suit or attempt to enforce the "no liquor" provision." The daughter added, "When my father got home, he sent in his expense accounts, which he said he arrived at by deducting the $3 he had in his pocket when he got home from the $75 he had when he started out. In a few days he got a letter back from railroad official C.O. Whittemore, which said, 'Squires, the company does not expect to pay for your poker losses in Pioche.'

My father wrote in reply, 'Whittemore, when spending five days in Pioche, poker losses are legitimate expenses. Please send check.' And they sent the check."

Interestingly, Charles "Pop" Squires had opened his own hotel, the Hotel Las Vegas, in the McWilliams town on May 14, 1905, the day before the Clark land auction. Although it was a tent, the Hotel Las Vegas had a plank floor and a front porch. Canvas partitions divided the main part of the hotel into a front lobby, 30 rooms and a dormitory. A separate tent held the dining room, and another housed the kitchen. An iron and copper bedstead, chair, washbowl, chamber pot and pitcher served as the furnishings for each room. There was no indoor plumbing.

Vegas Home Bakery and Delicatessen, 1905
UNLV Special Collections

The Hotel Las Vegas was a considerable improvement over Ladd's Hotel, the first in the community, which had opened three months earlier. Ladd's Hotel had only four double beds, each of which accommodated two persons for an eight-hour shift. Captain James H. Ladd, the hotel's proprietor had one hard and fast rule: "If you scratch you get no bed in this hotel." Potential customers had to wait while Ladd watched to see if they started scratching.

The Clark townsite had totally overtaken the McWilliams site as the location for the town of Las Vegas. Tents were gradually replaced by frame and concrete block homes and stores. The Las Vegas of 1908 had many permanent buildings, graded and oiled streets, wooden and concrete curbs and a volunteer fire department. A subsidiary of the railroad provided electricity, which was available only after nightfall. The first 24-hour service wasn't available until 1915.

The first two Las Vegas townsites sprang up with the clamor and bustle of boomtowns, but the early rise soon leveled off. Las Vegas was a railroad town. The only

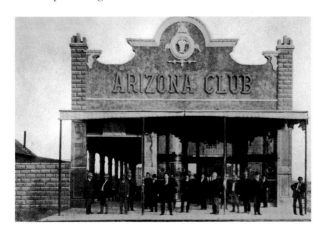

(Left & Right)
The Arizona Club was one of early Las Vegas' most luxurious.

(Left)
The Depot, Clark's
Las Vegas Townsite
UNLV Special Collections

(Right)
Nevada's mining industry
offered the railroad new
freight markets.

Las Vegas Hospital,
c. 1909
UNLV Special Collections

Soon another railroad began competing with Clark's lines for the mining business. The Bullfrog and Goldfield Railroad was incorporated as part of the Goldfield and Tidewater line owned by F.M. "Borax" Smith. Clark had previously run Smith out of Las Vegas in his efforts to dominate rail traffic to and from the mines. But now "Borax" Smith was back. His railroad connected Goldfield with Beatty and he was successfully challenging Clark's dominion over the freight business.

expansion came as a result of railroad activity, which was conservative. Mining was the only other industry and the railroad's efforts to service that sector provided the city's only growth.

Nevada's mining frontier offered new freight markets, and Clark was eager to capture them. Once again, geographical location and water played an important role in the city's fate. Las Vegas was well situated to serve the mining centers of Tonopah, Goldfield, Bulfrog and Rhyolite. Plus, steam locomotives needed water, and Las Vegas had plenty of that.

Clark began adding lines running out of Las Vegas to the various mining communities. He enlarged the railyards and expanded the repair shops in 1909. The railroad provided its nearly 400 employees and their families with company housing in cement block structures on Second through Fourth streets.

Originally part of Lincoln County, which covered all of southeastern Nevada, Las Vegas had effectively lobbied for county division. In 1909 the Nevada Legislature passed a bill creating Clark County with Las Vegas as its county seat. Las Vegas was incorporated on March 16, 1911. The bill, signed by Governor Tasker Oddie, provided for government by a mayor and four commissioners. That same year, Las Vegas' population stood at about 1,500 with two railroads providing about 450 jobs.

By 1913 the city's population had doubled. But by then mining was beginning a severe downturn. When mining slowed, the railroads suffered and Las Vegas felt the pinch. Some politicians and investors made attempts to lure other businesses to the area. Las Vegas Mayor Peter Buol, in 1913, recruited Scottish investors to develop farms in the valley. Community leaders had visions of pastoral delight with bucolic farms filling the well-watered valley. The hard alkaline soil, however, proved too tough a row to hoe, and the investors soon abandoned their agricultural ventures. The railroad remained the only game in town.

Mining, the railroads and Las Vegas had all seemed to run out of luck by 1914. Both railway lines were literally ripping up their tracks to be used elsewhere. The Las Vegas & Tonopah Railroad discontinued some service in 1917, and at least 150 people lost their jobs. The line completely suspended operations in 1918 and the following year tore up all of its track to sell as salvage. Clark sold Las Vegas' other line, the San Pedro, Los Angeles & Salt Lake to the Union Pacific Railroad four years later.

Tom Williams came to Las Vegas from Utah in 1917. Williams purchased about 140 acres of the old Kiel ranch site, located about a mile north of Clark's town. Keeping 40 acres for himself, he subdivided the rest with the idea of creating a town with the least amount of government restriction possible. He envisioned a community made up of "strong minded people," which would not impose the need for business licenses or almost any other kind of law or restriction on its residents.

What he got was bootleggers. Prohibition, brought in by passage of the Volstead Act in 1919, was a boon for what came to be called North Las Vegas. Although Las Vegas was not the most stringent enforcer of prohibition, it did sometimes prosecute violators. Many moved north. Of the first 80 lots sold by Williams, 31 were

purchased by bootleggers, and speakeasies proliferated like desert rabbits.

Clark had exercised tight control and run Las Vegas like a company store. Still, his self-interest had helped the city prosper. Union Pacific's headquarters were in New York. Las Vegas barely seemed to exist to the new management. Local employees felt deserted and dissatisfied. They joined a nationwide strike of 400,000 railroad workers in 1922. Once they settled the strike, Union Pacific punished the town by closing the Las Vegas repair shops, putting hundreds out of work. Union Pacific then replaced the shops with smelly stockyards.

Although not booming as it did at its beginning, Las Vegas did continue to grow. Despite the punitive job cuts and the absentee management, the railroad continued to be a reliable employer. By the mid-1920s the city had two banks, five churches and two newspapers. Mining

Interior of the San Pedro, Los Angeles and Salt Lake Railroad's machine shop in Las Vegas
UNLV Special Collections

Railroad cottages, 1909-1911
UNLV Special Collections

Peter Buol,
Las Vegas' first mayor

Western Air Express
initiated passenger
service in 1926.

had gone bust, agriculture was a nonstarter, railroad jobs were declining and there was no other industry to speak of. What Las Vegas did have was water and its geographical location.

The city was successful in its efforts to have a highway connecting Salt Lake City and Los Angeles routed through the town. More than 450 cars were passing through Las Vegas every day by 1927.

Las Vegas' first recorded flight was by a native of Blythe, California, who flew a DeHavilland Jenny into the area in 1920. The city's first airport was completed in 1921. Rockwell Field was located about three miles south of town, and in 1926 it became a refueling point for the mail flight between Salt Lake City and Los Angeles. In May 1926 Western Air Express initiated passenger service, flying M-2 biplanes covered with red canvas. The roundtrip fare between Las Vegas and Los Angeles was $80.

Once an oasis of promise and a boomtown, Las Vegas had struggled to survive. Newspaperman John Cahlan, who arrived in 1929, commented on the city's bleak prospects: "People in the city of Reno or northern Nevada would have been very happy if Las Vegas had seceded from the state. It was just so isolated that there didn't seem to be any possibility that it would grow. When I came here first, I thought this was the least likely to succeed of any (in) the United States."

The Las Vegas Grammar School, c. 1920s
UNLV Special Collections

CHAPTER THREE
THE DAM, DOLLARS AND DIVORCE

Had it not been for good luck, Las Vegas may have been one of the places least likely to succeed of any in the United States. But Las Vegas was lucky. Its artesian wells and fortuitously strategic location had established it as an oasis, settlement and city. Las Vegas' abundant water supply had been key to its early development. The verdant valley with its bubbling springs had attracted ancient nomads, frontier traders and ranchers. Water had been a significant factor in the railroad's decision to invest in the area.

The railroad had created the Las Vegas Land and Water Company on May 2, 1905, to guarantee its control over this vital resource. This control allowed the railroad to satisfy its own requirements and regulate distribution to the remainder of the town. The water company's franchise extended only to the Clark townsite. It had no responsibility to provide water beyond the town's original boundaries.

The effect of the railroad's control was disastrous, partially because it impeded growth but mostly because it resulted in the wasteful squandering of Las Vegas' most precious resource. The railroad's agent, and later vice president

(Left)
Boulder Dam, one more jackpot in Las Vegas' string of luck
UNLV Special Collections

(Right)
Wasteful practices threatened Las Vegas' underground artesian water supply.

Walter R. Bracken, functioned as a water czar, enforcing the company line of restricted growth and development. But there was water underground, and private wells and independent water companies proliferated. Builders of new homes, unable to get water beyond the town limit, would drill for their own.

Over the years these wildcat water wells seriously depleted the underground artesian water supply. The problem wasn't only the number of wells, but also the fact that they were wasteful; some were free flowing and spewed fresh water onto the dry desert floor only to stagnate and evaporate.

With the railroad's dictatorial control over the water supply, its seeming concern only for the welfare of its lines, its blatant antigrowth policies and ensuing depletion of the water table, Las Vegas' development may not have gotten out of the gate. But luck was on her side.

The city's next stroke of good fortune came in the colossal form of a concrete superhero. Hoover Dam, weighing in at six million tons of concrete, standing 727 feet high, 45 feet thick (660 feet at its base) and 1,244 feet long, rescued Las Vegas.

The idea of a dam in the area was not new. Government engineers had been talking about damming the Colorado since 1905. Henry C. Schmidt, a Tonopah businessman, had surveyed a dam site and filed an application with the U.S. Department of the Interior and the states of Nevada and Arizona in 1910 to build a dam and power plant at Boulder Canyon. Although Schmidt's plans progressed, they were abandoned with the outbreak of World War I. Efforts to keep the project alive fizzled when the permit was canceled in 1922.

It was in the early 1920s, however, when the seven states of the Colorado River Basin signed the Colorado River Compact and the seeds for Hoover Dam were sown. President Calvin Coolidge signed the Boulder Canyon Project Act, which included a $165 million appropriation, in 1928. Like an earthquake beneath the sea touching off a tidal wave, real estate speculation flowed from this act and washed across the entire Southwest.

The lure of jobs drew legions of the Great Depression's unemployed to the area. Poverty-stricken hopefuls filled shantytowns, called Hoovervilles, which sprang up near Las Vegas' business district, in North Las Vegas and along the Colorado River. Makeshift shacks and old, dented cars served as homes for the desperate jobseekers. The Las Vegas population grew from 5,200 to 7,500 in 1930 alone.

Hoover Dam, called Boulder Dam for many years, at nearly $48 million, was then the largest project ever undertaken in the United States. City leaders and businesspeople in Las Vegas lobbied hard for the chance to provide housing for the thousands of workers anticipated for the project. Secretary of the Interior Ray

Lyman Wilbur wasn't swayed. The government wanted to keep Las Vegas with its rowdy frontier image at arm's length.

The U.S. government built "wholesome" Boulder City close to the dam site. Former residents of the Hoovervilles who got jobs on the dam moved into the new city. Six Companies, the dam's primary contractor, built eight two-story dormitories for single men, 250 one-room cottages, 260 two-room houses, 123 three-room houses and additional buildings, including some surplus cottages from the 1932 Olympic games that were trucked in from Los Angeles. In early 1933 the new Boulder City Golf Course southeast of town was ready for play.

Las Vegas was the building site's main supply point. Union Pacific built a special 23-mile line of track connecting Las Vegas and Boulder City. Materials rolled into Boulder, and a good portion of the huge worker

The prospect of employment in Depression-era America lured thousands of jobless souls to the Las Vegas desert.

payroll flowed back to Las Vegas, that rowdy frontier town. That cash was just the tip of the iceberg of benefits.

The water contained behind the massive concrete wall sealing off Black Canyon created Lake Mead, which became a major tourist attraction just 30 miles east of Las Vegas. The water and power produced by the Hoover Dam project transformed the entire American Southwest. From it flowed Lake Mohave, created by Davis Dam down river from Hoover; Lake Havasu resulted from Parker Dam. A vital supply of water poured into Phoenix from the Granite Reef Aqueduct, and the Colorado River Aqueduct connected to the San Diego Aqueduct to carry Colorado River water to that thirsty city.

Congressional delegation along the Colorado River, c. 1920

Las Vegas began billing itself as the "Gateway to Hoover Dam." The dam and its fountain of federal funds poured $23 million into Las Vegas' economy between 1930 and 1939, helping the city sidestep most of the Depression's devastation.

Construction of Hoover Dam began in 1931. That same year, the Nevada State Legislature legalized gambling and quickie divorces. From Las Vegas' very beginning in 1905, games of chance had flourished in the town's canvas-covered hotels, bars and gambling houses. Although attempts were sometimes made to clean it up, such as when the state outlawed gambling in 1910, whether by going underground or through lax enforcement of laws, gambling had always thrived in the city.

Hoover Dam under construction

At nearly $48 million, Hoover Dam was then the largest project ever undertaken in the United States.
UNLV Special Collections

The dam attracted nearly 100,000 tourists in 1932 while it was still under construction, and 265,000 came to gawk and marvel at the giant structure in 1934. Most of the visitors also stopped in Las Vegas and many of them found the rowdy frontier town quite to their liking. Its games of chance and busy brothels on First Street between Ogden and Stewart streets were licensed and regulated, not to mention patronized, by city officials.

Boulder city was different. Secretary Lyman Wilbur appointed Sims Ely to manage the town, and Ely wasn't about to allow any of the carousing so prevalent in Las Vegas to mar Boulder City. Ely has been characterized as an unsmiling, unforgiving purity czar of Boulder. His mission was to keep the town clean, and that included exiling workers who showed up drunk. Alcohol and gambling were among the many activities banned in Boulder, much to the pleasure it must be said of the many families who were made to feel safe in the strictly regulated community. Single workers who lived in the

dormitories, however, often couldn't wait for the work week to end so they could "cut loose" in nearby Las Vegas.

Between the workers from Boulder City and the tourists passing through town, Las Vegas began to gain a reputation as a place where fun and victimless vice were freely available. More than a conventional getaway, Las Vegas was a vacation not just from the normal routine, but an escape from many of the regularly accepted moral prohibitions as well. It was legal and it was fun.

The 1930s had been good to Las Vegas. The New Deal channeled large amounts of money into local projects. Federal funds helped expand sewer lines, repave roads, build parks, construct schools and erect the city's first venue for conventions, the War Memorial Building, which opened in 1936. Additional projects included a public golf course and fish hatchery for the newly created Lake Mead (then Boulder Lake).

Hoover Dam's completion in 1935 signaled a great engineering and construction feat. It had infused much cash into the city's coffers. But with construction finished, the workers' salaries gone and the ensuing slowing of New Deal spending, Las Vegas needed to increase its income. Efforts to make Las Vegas more attractive to industry by restructuring the power company, replacing it with a public company and putting in a new line to tap power from the dam, stalled.

Tourism seemed to be the city's only ace in the hole. As the Gateway to Hoover Dam, Las Vegas was attracting 300,000 tourists annually, but it needed to attract more if it were going to survive, let alone grow.

Las Vegans had made earlier attempts to lure tourists by capitalizing on the city's sun-drenched western atmosphere. Previous efforts to promote spas and tourism included eastern capitalist Edward Taylor's 1924 purchase of the old Kiel Ranch, which he planned to turn into a dude ranch. Slightly before Taylor, David Lorenzi had begun construction on a resort that included twin lakes for boating and swimming, a dance hall and tavern. Las Vegas' first golf course was begun in 1927. But promoters' dreams of rivaling Tucson and Palm Springs as desert playgrounds never materialized.

The local Elks Club, in an effort to exploit and promote the town's wide-open western image, started the Helldorado rodeo in 1935. The local populace embraced the plan. The following year they constructed a Helldorado Village, boasting wooden sidewalks, hitching posts, watering troughs and town pumps.

While Helldorado was popular, it seemed to be the wide open, rather than the western part, that brought in the dollars. The city's main draw was no longer its artesian springs, or railroad, nor Hoover Dam's job bonanza or bucking broncos. It was sin, not the fang-bearing, cloven-hoofed variety, but a more sanitized version. The city offered a legal flirtation with usually forbidden fruits.

Las Vegas had been bawdy from birth. It began as a tent city with free-flowing booze, ladies of easy virtue and gambling galore. When in an effort to curb venereal disease, neighboring states passed laws requiring couples to wait for blood tests, Nevada kept its unrestricted marriage laws. The legislature passed quick-divorce laws along with legalized gambling in 1931. A person needed only to establish six weeks residence to obtain a divorce. Easy was the city's promise: easy money, easy love, easy marriage and easy divorce.

By virtue of the 1931 gambling legalization, Nevada cities and counties gained the power to issue gambling licenses and collect taxes. Clark County at first only issued licenses for slot machines. With the intent of

Fremont Street in the 1930s

Inside the Apache Casino, 1931

The Las Vegas Club, c. 1930s

California gambler Tony Cornero, seated at left, front, built Las Vegas' first real nightclub, the Meadows Club.

Las Vegas' first real nightclub was the Meadows Club. California gambler Tony Cornero built it with his brothers near what is now the intersection of Fremont and Charleston. The Meadows Club was relatively luxurious and featured faro, twenty-one, roulette, craps, poker and a cabaret. Among the performers to appear there were The Gumm Sisters, one of whom, Frances Gumm, was later famous as Judy Garland. Several other small clubs opened during the early 1930s on the Los Angeles highway south of town.

Throughout the 1930s, Nevada's easy divorce laws were a constant revenue source. It was Reno, rather than Las Vegas, first identified with easy divorce, much-publicized by Mary Pickford's famous split. Las Vegas-style quickie divorce hit the headlines in 1939. Clark Gable's wife, Ria Langham Gable, came to the city to dissolve her marriage to the famous movie star. While her husband carried on his affair with Carole Lombard in Los Angeles, Ria Gable played the glamorous, gay divorcee in Las Vegas, shooting craps and playing roulette and blackjack at the Apache Club on Fremont Street.

keeping gambling establishments from spilling over into residential areas, the town of Las Vegas passed an ordinance confining gambling to Fremont between First and Third streets. They eventually extended the boundary, and Clark County allowed table games.

The first gaming license issued by Clark County after the 1931 legalization went to the Northern Club on Fremont Street. Soon there were others, such as the Golden Camel, the Vegas Club, the Apache Club and the Boulder Club. The latter three plus the Northern, were famous as the big four on Fremont Street.

The Gable divorce did much to popularize the city for those seeking quick dissolutions of unhappy unions. Dude ranches sprang up for the purpose of housing prospective divorce filers while they gained the required six weeks residency. The first such establishment appeared in 1939 when investors remodeled the old Kiel (Kyle) Ranch and renamed it the Boulderado Dude Ranch.

Las Vegas continued to project the image of a frontier town. Albeit, with gambling, drinking, quickie marriages, divorces and prostitution, a rather wild one. While

(Top) Las Vegas continued to try to capitalize on its frontier theme.
(Bottom) Las Vegas in the 1930s was not yet one of the world's more sophisticated gambling venues.

Guy McAfee (far right), a former Los Angeles police caption and vice squad commander, was one of the first West Coast gamblers to set up operations in Las Vegas after the 1938 crackdown in L.A.

movie stars may have made a splash with their marriage breakups, gambling in Las Vegas still resembled the ramshackle gaming rooms of the Wild West. It was no rival for Monte Carlo. The city offered gambling and all the attendant vices, but it remained rather small-time. With gamblers in nearby Los Angeles forced to play underground, since that city's 1938 crackdown on its casinos, modernization and advertising may have lured thousands of California's gamblers and swingers to the city. Some, such as Guy McAfee, did come.

McAfee, a former Los Angles police captain and vice squad commander, was one of the first L.A. gamblers to migrate to Las Vegas. A longtime operator in L.A. before the 1938 crackdown, McAfee purchased the Pair-O-Dice club on the Los Angeles highway and renamed it the 91-Club. McAfee, who is generally credited as being the first to call that 4-mile stretch of Highway 91 the Strip, would go on to own other Las

Vegas night spots, including the Pioneer Club and later the Golden Nugget. The influx of gamblers from L.A. and Texas began to transform the Las Vegas gambling scene, but it still paled compared to what McAfee was used to in Los Angeles.

It was in the middle of the desert and difficult to get to. Before air-conditioning its scalding summer temperatures were unbearable for almost all but desert rats. There were no fine shops or restaurants and the interior of many of the gambling halls left the impression that there were still horses hitched up out front.

Although the divorce business in Las Vegas was relatively robust, it still wasn't enough to carry the city. The town's small-time gambling halls weren't either, and the local economy had sputtered through the late 30s.

Wartime Investment

As the 1940s got under way, gamblers, drinkers and those playing fast and loose with the holy bonds of matrimony weren't the only ones attracted to Las Vegas. The U.S. government seemed to like it, too.

War had broken out in Europe. The Nazis were blasting their way through the continent, brutally attacking America's allies. Although many in the United States advocated avoidance of what they deemed a foreign war, many in the military realized that the fighting was getting too big to ignore.

The United States wasn't really ready to go to war. Germany had it woefully outgunned. America in 1940 was not a great military power. Hitler's air force was the

(Left)
An aerial view of the Basic Magnesium, Inc. plant

(Right)
Western Air Express Douglass M-2 at Rockwell Airport, 3 miles outside Las Vegas, in 1926

most powerful in the world, while all the United States could muster were World War I vintage aircraft. The United States military had to gear up. The new cities in the Sun Belt, including Las Vegas, were seen as ideal training and manufacturing sites. The good flying weather was one plus. Their inland location made them less vulnerable to the new fleets of modern long-range bombers that could threaten coastal cities.

Las Vegas' enthusiastic support of Hoover Dam had won the favor of President Franklin Roosevelt and the War Department, which in 1940 began construction of a small marine auxiliary base at Boulder City's airport. The facility comprised only a hangar, storage tanks and a dormitory for crews that could service Navy planes.

With New Deal funding the city had tried for years to acquire the airfield used by the small commercial carrier, Western Air Express, for use as a municipal airport. Western Air Express had successfully blocked those efforts. The wartime buildup, however, changed everything. With Hitler storming through Europe, federal officials turned a blind eye to the private company's interests. The Civil Aeronautics Authority pledged $340,000 to acquire the property, the site of present-day Nellis Air Force Base, for joint civilian and military use.

The city, with the support of many civic organizations, purchased the site. It granted Western Air Express the right to use the field rent-free for 30 years and leased the military portion to the Army Air Corps for $1 per year. The U.S. government invested more than $25 million in the facility, constructing hangars, storage facilities, barracks, fuel tanks and three runways. This provided the city with its first decent airport for both military and civilian airline use.

The War Department unveiled its plans to use the field as an air-training school, replete with a million-acre shooting range, to prepare pilots and gunners for aerial combat. Pearl Harbor steeled America's determination to gear up for the fight. Air training began on January 13, 1942. By May of that year the Las Vegas Air Gunnery School was training 4,000 students every six weeks.

Government largesse continued with the announced plans to build a giant magnesium plant near town. In 1941 the U.S. Defense Plant Corporation signed a contract with Howard Eells' Basic Magnesium, Inc. to produce 33.6 million pounds of magnesium a year. The

factory was to be built on a barren hillside 15 miles southeast of Las Vegas. The federal government would own all land, buildings, equipment and magnesium, and BMI would manage the operation.

No plans had been made to construct a special town to house the thousands of workers. Las Vegas, especially having lost out on the Hoover work force, hoped to land this new population boost. But the city's reputation for fast living wasn't helping its cause. Howard Eells had his eye on Boulder City; a location he thought would help maintain a more disciplined work force. The Bureau of Reclamation, however, had reservations, stating that Boulder City was ill equipped to accommodate an additional 10,000 workers and their families.

Las Vegas lobbied hard to prevent the construction of another new town near the construction site. Hoping to avoid the cost of such an operation, federal officials were less critical of Las Vegas' rowdiness than Ray Lyman Wilbur had been. Surveys, however, soon showed that the city's sewer, water and utilities were not sufficient to handle an immediate influx of so many workers.

Water tower construction at the site of the Las Vegas Army Airfield
UNLV Special Collections

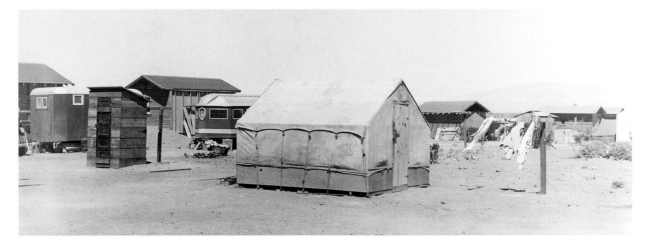

Housing at Basic, later
Henderson, Nevada
UNLV Special Collection

Eells opposed building an entire town but did agree to construct some housing near the site. The Defense Plant Corporation and other federal agencies, however, insisted that any employee housing Eells build meet U.S. Public Health Service standards before they would approve any funding. That meant the housing development would require not only water, power and gas supplies but also streets, sewers, stores and recreational facilities. Eells had no choice; he had to build a company town.

Construction of the plant and the Basic Townsite — later renamed Henderson in honor of Reconstruction Finance Corporation Chairman and former Nevada Senator Charles B. Henderson — began in September 1941. The government greatly enlarged the plant's capacity during construction due to federal concerns over dwindling magnesium supplies. More than 13,000 workers were laboring on the plant by the spring of 1942. While the town was being built, they lived in a tent city with no power, flush toilets or running water.

Basic Townsite school

The town of Basic eventually comprised four housing developments: Basic Village and Victory Village, begun in 1942 for white workers and their families, Carver Park, built in 1943 for single African-American workers and those with families, and Anderson Camp. The latter, near Carver Park, was at first just a tent city with dormitories for single white and a few single black workers.

TOWNSITE SCHOOL

Basic, (not named Henderson until the post office opened on January 10, 1944) had two segregated elementary schools. The plant's restrooms, commissary and water fountains were also segregated. The high school admitted both white and black students. This was at a time in America's history when division of the races was not uncommon. Even the U.S. military had not yet integrated its forces.

Despite these divisions, residents of Basic began to establish a sense of community quite quickly. The town's first Boy Scout Troop, sponsored by a local American Legion post, was created in the BMI school in October 1942. The Railroad Pass School got a P.T.A. chapter that same year. By the following year the town was Nevada's third largest and boasted a full roster of social events, including clubs, arts and crafts and sewing classes and orchestra rehearsals.

North Las Vegas, which was also segregated, was growing too. Stimulated by the air gunnery school, its population, which had grown at a slow pace throughout the 1930s, was beginning to increase rapidly.

Las Vegas benefited from its proximity to BMI and the gunnery school, just as it had from the workers living in Boulder City. While the majority of workers resided in Basic, a substantial number as high as 35 percent lived in Las Vegas. And the city's many avenues of entertainment attracted all the workers in droves.

Government projects, such as Hoover Dam, BMI and the gunnery school had helped pump money into Las Vegas' economy, and that economy was based on entertainment. The city's casinos, clubs and bordellos had been prospering. Las Vegas wasn't just attracting the workers from nearby projects. Servicemen stationed on the West Coast were making the trek across the desert by the thousands. And since Southern California's once bountiful gambling scene had dried up, other prospective casino operators and players were doing as Guy McAfee had done. They

Judge Henderson swearing in the newly elected Basic/Henderson City Council: from left to right are Paul Dickover, Lou LaPorta, John Ivary, Bill Engle and N.D. Van Wagener.
UNLV Special Collections

were coming to Las Vegas. Once known for its bubbling springs in the middle of the desert, the city's legalized gaming had turned it into a gamblers' oasis.

First boy to attend segregated Carver School
UNLV Special Collections

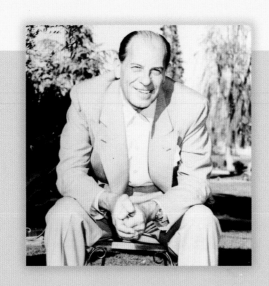

CHAPTER FOUR

BILLY, BUGSY AND THE BOYS

Las Vegas' gambling scene had been evolving. The flood of federal funds and the steady stream of soldiers and government workers during the war years and the immigration of some out-of-state players, movers and shakers had begun to transform the city. One was California hotel owner, Tom Hull.

A popular story recounts Hull having a flat tire on the Los Angeles highway outside Las Vegas one afternoon in 1941. While sitting in his car beside the narrow desert road, he was amazed at how many out-of-state cars passed by the site, and he decided to build a hotel there. Another version has a couple of Las Vegas businessmen inviting Hull out to see the city's potential and convincing him that he should build his next hotel in the city. This account has it that persuaded by lower taxes and land costs, he decided not to build downtown but out on the highway. Hull paid $150 an acre for 33 acres, which the woman who sold it to him thought was "worthless."

Either way, Hull broke ground for more than just a casino when he built on that stretch of desert land about three miles from the center of Las Vegas. His hotel, the El Rancho, marks the beginning of the Las Vegas Strip.

The El Rancho, the construction of which marked the beginning of the Las Vegas Strip.

Differing from the downtown gambling halls, the El Rancho offered more than gambling.

(Far right) Fremont Street's sea of neon had turned it into Glitter Gulch, but Las Vegas still hadn't shed its frontier image.

It was a gamble. Many if not most observers thought the location was too far out of town and doomed to failure. There was nothing but vacant ground between the city limits, which ended at Fifth Street and Hull's property.

But the El Rancho, which opened on April 3, 1941, surprised its doubters. It succeeded and set the pace for the future of Las Vegas gaming. The downtown gambling halls concentrated on one activity — gambling. The El Rancho offered a plethora of services in addition to gaming. These included lodging, parking, restaurants, shops, a travel agency, horseback riding and swimming. There was also entertainment. The scantily clad chorus girls were brought in from Hollywood, as were the headliners who eventually played there. Milton Berle, Jackie Gleason, Jimmy Durante and Nat King Cole helped draw in the crowds. The El Rancho was a step up for Las Vegas gambling clubs, but built in the Spanish mission motif with a rustic interior, it still maintained the city's western atmosphere.

The Strip's second property continued in the cowboy vein. The Last Frontier was the brainchild of California

theater mogul, R.E. Griffith, who owned 475 movie theaters throughout the Southwest. Griffith and his nephew, William J. Moore, had stopped while on a business trip to spend the night at the El Rancho. The savvy businessman was searching out locations for his plan to develop a chain of motels, and he could see Las Vegas' potential. The El Rancho was raking it in. Plus, the government's wartime investments in Nevada were providing an enormous captive audience. Griffith purchased the old Pair-O-Dice club, which had been renamed the 91-Club, from Guy McAfee. He paid $1,000 an acre for the 35-acre parcel.

The Last Frontier, which opened on October 30, 1942, looked like it could have been the set for a Western movie. Navajo art was used in the main showroom and

The Last Frontier sported a decidedly western motif.

(Left)
The swimming pool at the Last Frontier, 1945

(Right)
The development of "The Strip," transformed Las Vegas.

(Left)
The El Cortez was Fremont Street's first major resort.

Horn Room and Gay 90s bar. Headboards in the 107 rooms were fashioned to look like large oxen yokes and adorned with cow horns. A stagecoach transported VIPs to and from the resort. All development wasn't on the Strip. Within weeks of the El Rancho's opening in 1941, California investors, Marion Hicks and John Grayson, announced plans to build a $240,000 hotel downtown. The El Cortez became Fremont Street's first major resort. With neon signs pulsing to the beat of the Las Vegas night, the Monte Carlo, Boulder, Pioneer and Las Vegas Clubs, Guy McAfee's Golden Nugget, plus several smaller establishments, turned Fremont Street into Glitter Gulch by 1945. Yet, the ambiance of 19th century saloons and gambling halls still dominated the downtown area. Although the El Rancho and the Last Frontier were much more sumptuous, they lacked sophistication and were not much more than extravagant dude ranches. To hit the big time, Las Vegas had to trade cowboy boots for alligator shoes.

dining room and the mahogany-backed bar came from the old Arizona Club. Large, stuffed animals lined the Trophy Room. The Ramona Room, a banquet facility to seat 600 guests, featured expensive flagstones and large wooden beams. Lighting fixtures shaped as wagon wheels hung from the ceiling on chains to illuminate the

The Flamingo Takes Flight

The resort that had the most dramatic effect in elevating Las Vegas' status was the Flamingo. It replaced rustic and ribald with rarified and risqué. More than that, the Flamingo marked a pivotal turning point in the city's history, shifting its axis from regional entertainment attraction to a universal center for the creation of wealth.

The man usually recognized for creating the Flamingo and bringing worldly atmosphere and accoutrements to the city is Bugsy Siegel. Popular history seems to have cast Siegel in the central role. He may have gotten the credit and the blame but he didn't reap the profits, other than the wages of sin, which of course are death.

Benjamin Siegel and Meyer Lansky had known each other since their childhood days on New York's Lower East Side. Both were the children of immigrant Jewish parents who had fled the anti-Semitism in Eastern Europe for the hope of a peaceful life and opportunity in America. Unlike most immigrant children of the time who fought their way out of poverty through education or moxie, as valedictorian or vaudevillian, Benny and Meyer became hardened thugs. They clawed their way to the top through any means necessary, including cold-blooded murder.

Drawn to the streets and back alleys of New York and sucked into a world of pimps, prostitutes, gambling, drugs, extortion and violence with its links to the rich and powerful in politics and business, they became brutalized. They came to see America not through eyes of

Flashy and crass, Bugsy Siegel wanted to be suave and sophisticated. *UNLV Special Collections*

gratitude and hope but a jaded viewpoint that saw crime and corruption as an essential part of its foundation.

Meyer Lansky was a gifted mathematician with a sound and calculating head for business. He was slight in stature with a rather unremarkable countenance. Yet beneath the surface ran a river of ferocity.

As a child, the meek-looking boy had gained a reputation for bravery. His New York neighborhood was a patchwork of rival gangs and ethnicities where prejudice and bigotry were often expressed in acts of violence. One day, Lansky was walking home carrying a plate of food when an Irish gang stopped him. The leader, holding a knife to Meyer's throat, demanded that he lower his trousers and show them if he were circumcised.

Before the knife-wielding thug could say another word, Lansky smashed the plate he was holding and slashed at his attacker with the sharp edges of the broken china, nearly killing him. The rest of the gang pulled Meyer off and began to beat him mercilessly. Someone stopped the fight before the mob killed Lansky. Although the little boy would become known for his brains rather than his brawn, Meyer Lansky was forever regarded as a loaded pistol.

When Lansky was just 16, he and Siegel ran what was eventually known as the Bugs and Meyer Mob. The gang was renowned for its efficiency. Murder and kidnapping specialists, they served the interests of crime bosses, companies and unions, such as the Teamsters and Longshoremen.

Lansky established himself as a power in the crime world. He became the mob's top investment

The club that told the world Vegas was ready to fly high was the Flamingo.
Photo by Rex M. Oppenheimer

banker and broker. His managerial skills helped forge the loose confederation of multiethnic underworld concerns, which lay beneath a nationwide network of legal and illegal activities, including bootlegging, gambling, prostitution, drug sales, and extortion, into a syndicate run along corporate lines. He put the organized in organized crime.

Meyer Lansky sent Bugsy Siegel to Los Angeles after the repeal of Prohibition to extort money from the film industry and handle other mob activity on the West Coast. Siegel was soon living the high life in Hollywood. Charming, with money to burn and wearing the most expensive suits, silk shirts and alligator shoes, he hung out in posh places with famous people and became a celebrity in his own right. A well-known womanizer, he dated and bedded Hollywood stars and even had pretensions of becoming a movie star himself.

But Bugsy, a nickname earned for being crazy as a bedbug, which no one dared utter to his face, had a legendary flash temper. The smiling charmer could instantly explode in a white-hot, murderous rage. Beyond a tantrum, he became a bug-eyed monster seemingly possessed by the Devil. He was a conscienceless killer.

In the early 1940s Nevada legalized betting on horse races by wire, and Meyer Lansky sent Siegel and Moe Sedway to Las Vegas to get a piece of the action for the mob. Some accounts say that Siegel was impressed with the El Rancho and the Last Frontier and began to imagine what would one day become the Flamingo Hotel.

Bugsy's ostentatious taste and vision of himself as a worldly gentleman certainly played a part in the making of the Flamingo. But Sally Denton & Roger Morris, in *The Money and The Power, The Making of Las Vegas and its Hold on America*, quote Meyer Lansky as saying, "What I had in mind was to build the greatest, most luxurious hotel casino in the world and invite people from all over America — maybe the high rollers from all over the world — to come and spend their money there."

Lansky had been keeping his eye on Las Vegas for a long time. Meyer had once said, "There's no such thing as a lucky gambler, there are just the winners and the losers. The winners are those who control the game…all the rest are suckers." He had acquired hidden interests in the Golden Casino and the Bank Club, both in Reno, shortly after Nevada had legalized gambling. No doubt Lansky had plans for Las Vegas, and the Flamingo was eventually taken over by Siegel with Lansky in the shadows, but neither man originally conceived of the hotel.

W.R. "Billy" Wilkerson was a legendary compulsive gambler, able to win or lose a fortune on the turn of a card. Suave and debonair, the fastidiously dressed Wilkerson was a true sophisticate with impeccable taste. The founder, owner and publisher of the *Hollywood Reporter*, a bon vivant and businessman extraordinaire, Wilkerson reigned over Hollywood's Golden Era as creator and owner of some of its most dazzling restaurants and nightclubs, the Vendome, Café Trocadero, Sunset House, Ciro's, LaRue and L'Aiglon.

Wilkerson's gambling went beyond enjoyment, it was an obsession and an addiction. After Los Angeles outlawed gaming in 1938, Wilkerson had to find other venues. He frequented private games, often at the homes of movie moguls, and along with many other members of the Hollywood elite, gambled at Agua Caliente on the Mexican border. Billy Wilkerson also began to haunt Las Vegas. Although the town didn't sport the ambiance or finery he appreciated, there was plenty of gaming to indulge in. He'd often charter a plane in the morning, fly to Las Vegas, win or lose $10,000 to $20,000, and be home in Beverly Hills by evening.

tennis, badminton, handball and squash courts and a nine-hole golf course. Plus, there would be a trap-shooting range and stables for 45 horses. It would be Las Vegas' biggest hotel and the first in the country to employ the latest innovation in indoor comfort, air conditioning.

Billy Wilkerson's restaurants and clubs had helped transform Hollywood from a hotdogs and beans town into a chic entertainment capital. Now, he was using those same talents and tastes to change Las Vegas' image from Main Street in a Western to the Champs Elysees in a Parisian fantasy. It would be an incredible entertainment paradise capable of attracting the high rollers of the world.

Other Las Vegas establishments combined hotel, casino, restaurant and showroom, but none affected such size, grandeur and elegance. Gambling had been outlawed in Southern California. Maybe Las Vegas was a dinky desert town in the Nevada boondocks, but it was closer than Monte Carlo. Wilkerson knew that the key to his success in Las Vegas was being able to attract the Beverly Hills high rollers. His audience was strictly the wealthy and powerful, and the Flamingo would provide the style and service that would bring them to the middle of nowhere.

Billy Wilkerson projected an aura of success. He always surrounded himself with the best. That was true in food, clothes and cars, and it applied to the people he hired. They were at the top of their craft, such as the master chefs who made his West Coast eateries world famous.

Wilkerson had great business and restaurant experience, and he certainly knew gambling from the player's side of the table. Yet, he knew he needed help to learn about things from the house side. He wanted to run the best casino possible, and so he went to the best.

Moe Sedway and Gus Greenbaum were among the top casino operators in the business. They had made a great success of the gaming tables at the El Cortez Hotel, which they were running in 1945. At first skeptical about the Flamingo's prospects, the "boys," as Wilkerson called them, were soon convinced of its potential. For a share of the profits and a silent partnership, they agreed to operate and manage the casino and all aspects of

Unfortunately, the losses usually outstripped the winnings. In 1944 Wilkerson was facing more than a million dollars in gambling losses long before the year was through. But he couldn't stop. Many of his wealthy and influential friends loaned him considerable amounts and his close pal, movie mogul Joe Schenck, forgave him enormous debts. Schenck also gave Wilkerson some advice, "Be on the other side of the table if you're going to suffer those kind of losses. Build a casino. Own the house."

With his management experience and flair for creating fabulous properties, Wilkerson took his buddy's advice. After one illegal venture at Arrowhead Springs, W.R. Wilkerson's vision turned toward a place in America where gambling was legal — Las Vegas.

Wilkerson had his attorney, Greg Bautzer, purchase a 33-acre piece of land outside of town. Afraid that his reputation as a high roller would inflate the price, he had Bautzer purchase the property in his own name. Billy Wilkerson brought in renowned architect George Vernon Russell and designer/decorator Tom Douglas from Hollywood. Both men had worked on Wilkerson's prestigious California properties and had built and designed homes for many famous stars.

The sophisticate outlined his plans for a huge, stylish complex, including a casino, showroom, nightclub, bar-lounge, Parisian style restaurant with top European chefs, café, hotel, shops bearing the names of the finest international designers, such as Cartier and Chanel, and a health club with steam rooms and a gym. Outdoors, there would be private bungalows, a swimming pool,

Gus Greenbaum,
Moe Sedway and
Moe Dalitz —
"the boys"
UNLV Special Collections

gaming at the property. Greenbaum, an Arizona book-maker with a long police record, was a magician when it came to casino management. Moe Sedway was Meyer Lansky's faithful lieutenant.

What Wilkerson knew of their involvement with the mob at that time isn't clear. He wasn't involved directly in organized crime, but gangsters were not strangers to him. He dealt with them when he ran speakeasies, first in New York for Mayor Jimmie Walker and later on his own. He'd hobnobbed with mob figures when they'd dined in his clubs, gambled with them, and met them when he shopped at the finest boutiques, tailors and barbershops in Hollywood. Billy probably first made Siegel's acquaintance in Hollywood back in 1936 when Bugsy had dined in one of the restaurateur's properties. Ciro's was a particular Siegel favorite.

Financing Woes

Wilkerson's architect and designer were outdoing themselves, and the elaborate resort was outgrowing its budget. Financing began to become a problem. Bank of America, which had always extended Wilkerson a generous line of credit, balked at totally covering the cost of the property. The previous year, Billy Wilkerson had gambled away a $200,000 Bank of America loan, and the establishment was leery. The bank had confidence in his business acumen but considered that his gambling obsession could cancel out any success he may enjoy. They did agree, however, to partial financing.

Howard Hughes, a friend of Wilkerson's, came through with an additional $200,000, which he extended under the pretext of prepaid advertising in the *Hollywood Reporter*. Hughes thought his friend was foolish to venture such a gamble on a desert hellhole. Ironically, two decades later he too would plunge into that fire.

Still short of money, the hapless gambler sought to solve his problems at the gaming tables. In less than a month he'd lost $200,000. Fearful of his ability to pay for his dream, falling deeper into debt and weary of the struggle for whatever the reason, Wilkerson suddenly soured on the whole plan.

He wrote a letter to Moe Sedway, officially turning the project over to him and Greenbaum. His letter began, "I am convinced that Las Vegas is too dangerous for me." He went on to elaborate that he meant his addiction to gambling was too strong, and being in Las Vegas was a constant temptation he could not withstand. He further suggested that the whole thing was a harebrained scheme from the beginning.

Yet, several months later Wilkerson was back in the picture. With a new head full of optimism, help from friends and some gambling wins amidst staggering losses, he repurchased the land from Sedway and launched anew into the project. Almost a year after he'd first acquired the 33 acres, Wilkerson began construction of the Flamingo, breaking ground in November 1945.

The project had been scaled down with the hotel eliminated, but it still ran into more financial difficulties. Immediately after World War II, building materials were scarce and expensive. The costs kept rising. Wilkerson searched high and low, exhausting his Hollywood and studio contacts, but he was still sinking.

One day while Billy Wilkerson was walking the construction site with his builder, Bud Raulston, an expensive car pulled onto the lot. A well-dressed man stepped out and introduced himself. He was G. Harry Rothberg, an East Coast businessman. He said he represented a New York firm that wanted to invest in the Flamingo. Rothberg said that his associates knew of Wilkerson's financial problems and wanted to help him complete his project.

Rothberg laid it all out. His people would fund the Flamingo; Wilkerson would retain a one-third share and continue to call all the creative shots. He would be the club's sole operator and manager; the others would be silent partners. Smiling, Rothberg praised Wilkerson as the only man who could pull off a project as grand as the Flamingo, and he assured him that there would be no outside interference.

After thinking it over, Wilkerson could find little to object to. Besides, he didn't have much choice. Wilkerson and Rothberg signed a contract in February 1946. By the beginning of March, Wilkerson received all the funds he needed to complete the Flamingo. Happy and with a head full of steam, W.R. Wilkerson resumed construction of his prize property. A little more than a month later, Moe Sedway and Gus Greenbaum visited the construction site.

The boys brought with them a gaudily dressed dandy. It was Ben Siegel. He stuck out his hand and introduced himself to Wilkerson as his new partner.

Siegel was in Las Vegas under Meyer Lansky's orders. He didn't like the desert and wasn't that much interested in the city's future. He would much rather be back among his swank surroundings in Beverly Hills. Once when the two men were standing at the Flamingo's construction site, Wilkerson pointed off into the distance, "One day," he said, waving his arm, "there will be hotels lined up and down this road as far as the eye can see."

"Why?" asked an astounded Siegel, "Why would anyone want to come here?"

Bugsy was there because he was working for Meyer. He might not have been able to see the potential in Las Vegas, but he admired Wilkerson. Billy Wilkerson represented the classy lifestyle and superb taste Siegel aspired to. He was suave where Siegel was crude, knowledgeable where the gangster was ignorant. At first Bugsy was the avid student, willing to let Wilkerson do things his way. It didn't take long, however, before respect turned to envy, jealousy and resentment.

Bugsy had to be the big shot. He started giving orders, often demanding changes that conflicted with the blueprints. He began to reverse Wilkerson's orders. Soon, Bugsy Siegel was boasting to everyone that the Flamingo had been his idea. The conflict between Siegel and Wilkerson escalated.

Siegel had been a sedate enthusiast at first, but now, almost anytime he'd hear Wilkerson's name he'd fly into one of his famous rages. He once shouted to an inquiring reporter, "This is my fucking hotel! My idea! Wilkerson has nothing to do with it! Do you understand? Nothing to do with it!"

Eventually they split the project in two. Siegel supervised the hotel portion and Wilkerson ran everything else. There were two crews and almost no communication between the two sections. It didn't take long for the project to fall into disarray.

Wilkerson hoped that seeing the mess Siegel's ego was causing, his higher ups would take him off the project. But instead, Lansky turned the Las Vegas venture over to his friend Ben.

The Flamingo Hotel, late 1940s
UNLV Special Collections

Bugsy's greed and grandiosity grew wildly. He persuaded the syndicate to give him complete control, assuring them that Wilkerson would not be eliminated from the creative process. Yet, with pressure and intimidation, plus the toll his irrational behavior was taking on Wilkerson's nerves and the project, Siegel made the publisher an offer he couldn't refuse. He bought out Wilkerson's creative participation for an additional five percent ownership in the operation.

Then Bugsy formed the Nevada Project Corporation of California, with himself as president. He was the largest principal stockholder. The Flamingo had become a syndicate-run operation, with Siegel firmly in charge. Siegel fired all of Wilkerson's staff, including the architect and decorator. Bugsy was the expert and insisted on making every decision himself.

Bugsy's pomposity knew no limits; he was building himself a palace, and it was costing a king's ransom. Everything had to be the best, the rarest, the finest, no matter what the expense. If his plan called for marble, it had to be the most costly Italian marble in existence. Extravagances were extreme. Siegel ordered that each bathroom in every one of the hotel's guestrooms should have its own private plumbing and sewer system.

The costs were astronomical, and soon Siegel's checks started bouncing. The Syndicate was not happy. Other ventures in Nevada, such as the El Cortez, were showing a safe, steady return. The Flamingo was siphoning millions. It was beginning to look like those wildcat wells that poured out valuable water to waste away on the hot, unforgiving desert floor.

Siegel had bought out Wilkerson's participation, but the publisher still owned the land. A subsequent agreement gave Siegel half the property and still another netted the mobster all of the land. Wilkerson, who had chosen to take stock rather than cash in payment was the majority single stockholder in the project with a 48 percent share.

Bugsy was trying to raise cash anywhere he could. Finally, he had a showdown with Wilkerson. He told him that unless he personally signed for a $600,000 loan the whole project would go down the tubes and they would lose all. It was a tough call for the gambler. Was the gangster bluffing just to get his hands on the cash? In the end the publisher had to go along. But the $600,000 wasn't enough to plug the hole in the dyke. Siegel tried to stanch the flow any way he could, even selling nonexistent stock. He was in a tailspin.

Desperate to raise money, having dried up all his sources of borrowed or purloined funds, Siegel decided to open the Flamingo early. He'd change the date from the original March 1, 1947, to the day after Christmas, December 26, 1946, attract customers and start pulling in cash. Wilkerson was furious. The hotel wouldn't be finished. Plus, the Hollywood crowd always stayed home the last two weeks of the year. The holiday opening was mistimed even if the property would be ready, and it wasn't. Wilkerson predicted a disaster.

Siegel tried everything. He'd admitted to selling 150 percent of the Flamingo. In actuality it was closer to 400 percent. He met with Wilkerson and his attorney and asked the publisher to give up his interest. "How much are you offering me?" asked Wilkerson. "Nothing," replied the gangster. Bugsy said his life was on the line and before he'd go down he'd kill Wilkerson. The publisher's lawyer countered saying that he was filing affidavits with the district attorneys of Las Vegas and Los Angeles and with the FBI. "You better hope that Mr. Wilkerson doesn't sprain an ankle walking off a curb," he told the gangster.

Bugsy tried to make Wilkerson another offer, but the publisher had fled to Paris. He thought he'd hide out in France. Once the syndicate learned about how Siegel had botched the job they'd fire him. Just to help things along, Wilkerson ran full-page ads in the Hollywood Reporter boasting about the Flamingo's true cost.

Bugsy was going bananas. Frantic, he changed the opening date to December 28, thinking that a weekend would bring in more people. Then, in a panic, he changed it back.

When the Flamingo opened on December 26, 1946, it was a worse disaster than even Wilkerson had predicted. Locals came out in numbers, but the big spenders and celebrities mostly stayed home. A handful of movie folk did show up, including June Haver, Vivian Blaine, George Raft, Sonny Tufts, Brian Donlevy and Charles Coburn.

They walked into a lobby covered by drop cloths and filled with the din of hammers and saws. There were no hotel rooms finished. Guests had to be housed in other Las Vegas hotels. The air-conditioning system broke down. The kitchen and service staff were untrained and unready. The only thing that came off was the entertainment, which Wilkerson had prearranged months earlier. Jimmy Durante, George Jessel, Xavier Cugat and his band, Rosemarie, Tommy Wonder and the Tunetoppers, all among the hottest stars of the time, gave it their best. But they might as well have played Taps.

The Flamingo was a flop. It was $275,000 in the red after being open two weeks. Siegel, disgraced, dumbfounded and disillusioned, shut the property down in late January and blamed everything on Wilkerson. Lawyers representing the publisher and the gangster eventually worked out a deal that relinquished Wilkerson's interest in the Flamingo.

After another death threat, Wilkerson high-tailed it back to Paris. He was in that European city when he sat down to coffee one morning, unfolded the newspaper and saw an article reporting the assassination of American mobster Bugsy Siegel. The gangster's bullet-riddled, blood-splattered body was found sprawled on the couch in longtime girlfriend Virginia Hill's rented Beverly Hills home. Ironically, Hill was also in Paris at the time.

Although theories ran rampant, Siegel's killers were never caught. The boys, Moe Sedway and Gus Greenbaum, took over the Flamingo. Siegel's excesses and preposterous notions had turned the project into a debacle, but perhaps Wilkerson's super sophisticated ideas weren't the way to go either.

Sedway and Greenbaum made the Flamingo much more egalitarian. They abandoned Wilkerson's vision of a formal dress code and made temptation more affordable. They were doing something right. Within the first year, the boys turned a $4 million profit. It was a Las Vegas formula for success. As Benny Binion would say, "If you wanna get rich — make little people feel big."

In the end it wasn't Siegel's flamboyance or Wilkerson's savoir faire, but Moe Sedway and Gus Greenbaum following Benny Binion's Vegas credo of making little people feel big that gave the Flamingo wings. *UNLV Special Collections*

CHAPTER FIVE

SKIM CITY —
WISE GUYS GET SMART

Lester "Benny" Binion was an ex-cowboy and gun-toting bootlegger. In 1926 at the age of 22, he challenged his former boss, Dallas' leading racketeer Warren Diamond, and emerged as Texas' El Supremo gangster. His operation included gambling, loan-sharking and the numbers rackets. Known by some as an honest game boss who might even return money to a hapless loser, he was also famous for once poking a pencil through the eye of a numbers runner he thought had double-crossed him. Binion's motto was "do your enemies before they do you," and he left a trail of bullet-riddled bodies in his wake.

In the early 1940s, with 27 illegal casinos operating in the city, Dallas was a gambler's town. And until he was pushed out of town by a gang war that swept the nation in 1946, Binion was its king of vice. When Chicago mobsters took over the underworld operations in Dallas, Binion called Meyer Lansky to help him get a new start.

A month later Binion, his wife, five children and several cash-stuffed suitcases comfortably ensconced in a chauffeur-driven Cadillac, pulled into

(Left)
Fremont Street, 1940s

(Right)
Benny Binion, responsible for much murder, mayhem and malevolence, was also the inventor of some of Las Vegas' most profitable money-making innovations.

Senator Pat McCarran, seen here at the BMI plant in Basic, was a regular at the Thunderbird Casino, along with many other members of Nevada's political elite. *UNLV Special Collections*

he opened the Horseshoe Club. Benny was the first of the downtown impresarios to sweep the sawdust off the floors and put in carpet.

Although some people claimed Binion had a soft spot and even credited him with acts of kindness, he was an inveterate tough guy and criminal. Within a few years of opening the Horseshoe, Benny's new life was put on hold. Federal authorities convicted Binion of income tax evasion and shipped him off to Leavenworth Penitentiary for a five-year sentence. He served three and one-half years. After his release Binion was never licensed again in Nevada. But he continued to run the casino, as he had in fact done all the time he was incarcerated.

He ran the Horseshoe his way, and it was the antithesis of the Flamingo. He offered the best odds in town. Regular people in everyday work clothes crowded the casino. There was no glamour or luxury. Not even flowers or buffets. The menu consisted of greasy Texas chili made from a Dallas jailhouse recipe. When people walked past the seven-foot gold-painted horseshoe that encased 100 $10,000 bills, they knew they were in for "a good gamble," as Binion said, "that's all there is to it, son."

The Mafia had declared Las Vegas an open city shortly after Nevada's 1931 legalization of gambling. The Flamingo wasn't the first casino with mob backing.

Las Vegas. On New Year's Day 1947, one day after his Texas casinos had ceased to operate, the 42-year-old Binion took his place as a partner in the Las Vegas Club.

Benny Binion, who had served time for murder and fled gang wars and government prosecution, would still find his brightest and most profitable days ahead. He was a Las Vegas natural. Binion blended underworld know how, cutthroat violence, gambling savvy, a good-old-boy smile and western grit.

Wearing a cowboy hat and western-cut suits with buttons made from solid gold coins, he instituted some important Las Vegas innovations. He created the World Series of Poker, raised house limits and offered free drinks, good food at low prices and high-quality but inexpensive whisky to players. After the Las Vegas Club,

At least 24 Mafia families had divided up various gambling interests in the city. To circumvent Nevada's gaming laws most of the mob's participation was as hidden owners or partners, but Las Vegas was their city. Las Vegas has been called "America's Playground," but in the 1950s it was the Mafia's.

Whether the casino was successful in the conventional sense wasn't even that important. The mobsters were buying and building the properties with somebody else's money. They were borrowing the funds from legal entities, such as the Teamsters pension fund, that were in fact illicit partners in crime. If the project failed, the mob would back another with borrowed or extorted money. In the meantime, they were skimming off pure profits.

If the casinos would have been farms, the mobsters may have been taking home some butter and beef. But the town's main product was money. Cash was flowing across the tables and the boys were skimming it off like fresh cream. It was plentiful and it was tax free. Gangster

David Berman's daughter, Susan, recalls sitting in the counting room with her father, "I saw them go — three for us, one for the government, two for Meyer (Lansky)."

Bills were skimmed and so were coins. Casino owners set up fake weighing machines to conceal the illegal siphoning of coins from the slots. It all amounted to millions. One expert estimated that coin-skimming scams at the Fremont and Stardust netted more than $12 million a year in untaxed income.

Mob involvement in the casinos would sometimes surface and licenses would be lost. Such was the case with the Thunderbird, the Strip's fourth major resort. The Thunderbird, which opened in 1948, sported a Native American theme. Built by Marion Hicks, builder of the El Cortez, and Cliff Jones, Nevada's lieutenant governor, known as "The Big Juice," the Thunderbird was frequented by Nevada's political power elite. The state's political boss, Senator Pat McCarran, was a regular.

Moe Dalitz, seen here with Elvis Presley

The Golden Nugget was billed as the "brightest spot in the world."

The Thunderbird's success led to expansion plans. As was his wont, The Big Juice made the deal, putting together the people who had the ideas with those who held the purse strings. Authorities eventually linked the funds Jones procured to gangland interests. The Thunderbird lost its license in 1955. Although the property was later sold and reopened, it never regained its former status.

While the Thunderbird's and Cliff Jones' reputations were dimming, others, such as Guy McAfee's Golden Nugget, were growing brighter. The Barbary Coast style Golden Nugget's Million Dollar Casino was the city's largest when it opened in 1945. A few years later McAfee erected a 100-foot neon sign and billed his property as "the brightest spot in the world."

While Las Vegas had largely outgrown its former frontier image, it still wasn't ready to spotlight gambling as its finest feature. In the late 1940s the chamber of commerce invited proposals from eight advertising agencies on ways to promote the city. The winner was the J. Walter Thompson Company, one of the world's top agencies. The campaign promoted the city's climate, location and scenic sites. Ads focused on the luxury hotels and quality entertainment.

Las Vegas had previously tried to promote itself as a desert resort, ala Palm Springs, but had failed. A lot had changed since then. No matter how the city was promoted the truth that it offered regular, law-abiding

citizens a fling on the wild side was well known. The Japanese have a saying that, "When away from home abandon shame," and Las Vegas was a place where ordinary people could do things that they would never do at home; it was legal, and people said it was 'just in fun.'

W.R. Wilkerson had thought that he had to lay on the splendor to attract the high rollers. He had to make the Flamingo so attractive a magnet that it could pull the rich and famous away from their regular haunts and lure them to the middle of nowhere. But he'd underestimated the attraction that gambling can have on people. Ironic, since he was addicted to gambling himself.

When the Flamingo debuted, it was a high-stepping bird but it still laid an egg. It was after Gus Greenbaum and Moe Sedway made it more accessible to regular folk that those eggs turned gold. Benny Binion, who said that the way to get rich was to make little people feel big, also told casino owner Steve Wynn to, "Give gamblers a good excuse, they'll thank you for it."

Making little people feel big and giving them an excuse to indulge in vice was Las Vegas' winning combination. It took it from the middle of nowhere and put it in the center of everything. And it was the Mafia that got the ball, not to mention a few heads, rolling.

The Flamingo's notoriety, Las Vegas' advertising campaign, a new, postwar liberalization of mores and morality, and a wealthier middle class that placed a higher value on recreation coalesced to bring more tourists to the city. Demand was increasing and new hotel/casinos, almost all mob-backed, were springing up along The Strip.

While many people saw Las Vegas as an opportunity to have a little fun living out a fantasy, mobsters viewed the prospects like kids in a candy shop. Not only could they own the house and rake in the dough, it was the perfect venue for laundering bags full of ill-gotten gains, pumping dirty money into legitimate businesses and skimming off enormous tax-free profits as easily as sucking soda through a straw.

Nevada laws didn't allow individuals with criminal histories or gangland affiliations to have a gaming

license. But the crime bosses were used to evading laws; that was the basis of all their businesses. So was buying people. They paid off police and politicians everywhere they operated. In Las Vegas the mob hired front men who could sail through any legal obstacles.

The sign out front said, Wilbur Clark's Desert Inn, but Wilbur was the boss in name only. Moe Dalitz and his buddies, Morris Kleinman, Sam Tucker and Lou Rothkopf, all of the Cleveland Mayfield Road Gang, were the puppeteers standing in the shadows in this Kabuki play.

Jake Friedman came to Las Vegas from Houston, Texas, with the idea of building a luxury hotel, which he planned to name The Holiday Inn after the popular film staring Bing Crosby and Danny Kaye. Story has it, however, that one day while visiting the construction site on Highway 91 he was asked to give a working name to the project. He said something to the effect that there was so much sand everywhere, even his socks were full of it, that maybe they should call it the Sands.

One of Friedman's partners, Jack Entratter, who had formally been with the Copacabana in New York, had far-reaching connections among celebrities. Entratter helped establish Las Vegas as a venue for top entertainment. The "Rat Pack," Frank Sinatra, Dean

The "Rat Pack," Frank Sinatra, Dean Martin, Joey Bishop, Sammy Davis Jr. and Peter Lawford, frequented the Sands where they often entertained.

Parisian style revues were
the rage in Vegas, here
the Copa Girls perform
at the Sands.
UNLV Special Collections

Martin, Joey Bishop, Sammy Davis Jr. and Peter Lawford, were frequent entertainers and guests. The 1960 film, *Oceans 11* was largely shot at the Sands, and the actors partied into the wee hours of the night in the hotel's showroom and lounge.

Friedman may have built it and had the dream, but Meyer Lansky, Joe Adonis, Frank Costello and Doc Stracher were pulling the strings behind the Sands. Crooner Frank Sinatra owned a piece of the action during the 1960s, and Howard Hughes would sweep it up along with several other properties in the later half of that decade.

Top guns of the Chicago mob, including the Fishchetti brothers, Tony Accardo and Sam Giancana, were the offstage actors at the Sahara and the Riviera. Ray Patriarca, head honcho of the New England Mafia, was taking plenty of gold, rather than sand, out of the Dunes.

Anthony Stralla, aka Tony Cornero, came to Las Vegas with his brothers in 1931 and opened the Meadows, the city's first real nightclub. After California and federal authorities shut down Cornero's gambling ship, the *S.S. Rex*, which he operated off the Los Angeles coast, he returned to Las Vegas and opened the S.S. Rex Club on the first floor of the Apache Hotel.

Tony Cornero paid $650,000 for 32 acres on The Strip in 1954 and set about to build the largest hotel-casino in the world. He would call it the Stardust and emblazon the name on the biggest neon sign to ever rise above The Strip. Cornero planned to finance the entire project through the sale of stock. Selling shares in Stardust, Inc. all across the country, Tony began to build his dream hotel.

Not in the habit of dealing with authorities, at least not through the proper channels, he neglected to register with the Security and Exchange Commission (SEC). The SEC shut down Cornero's sale of stock when the project was about three-fourths complete.

There were so many gangsters running so many casinos that competition became a problem. While the Stardust was still under construction, Moe Dalitz complained that it would cut into his business at the Desert Inn. Irritated, Dalitz was ready to take care of the problem the way mobsters usually do, but Meyer Lansky proposed a diplomatic solution. Tony Cornero represented the Stardust at the meeting. Moe Dalitz and Morris Kleinman sat in for the Desert Inn, and Longy Zwillman flew in from New Jersey to round out the bargaining table.

The wiseguys worked out a kind of profit-sharing deal that interlocked their interests in each other's

casinos. It was a maze of subterfuge that even further obscured the various properties' true ownership.

Not long afterward Cornero was shooting craps at the Desert Inn when he suddenly collapsed and died of a heart attack. Rumors held that the heart attack was induced by a drug injected into Tony Cornero's veins in the Desert Inn's restroom the night he died. John "Jake the Barber" Factor, brother of cosmetics king Max Factor, stepped in to complete the Stardust. Jake the Barber, who was little more than a front man for Sam Giancana, shelled out a reported $10 million.

It was rare for gangland rivalry to end in bloodshed in Las Vegas. None of the crime families wanted to kill the goose that was laying 24-caret omelets. They wanted to keep Las Vegas clean, and there was a code to that effect. People have said that it was like having two police forces, the cops and the boys.

Anthony "Tony the Ant" Spilotro was one of the boys who cooked his own goose. The five-foot-five-inch-tall Spilotro, who was a suspect in 25 murders but convicted in none, was a courier for the Chicago mob. He would carry suitcases filled with cash from Las Vegas to points east. Tony got greedy. While this wasn't unique among gangsters, ignoring the code of keeping the city clean and conducting criminal activity at street level was.

Spilotro formed what was called the "Hole in the Wall Gang," named for their practice of breaking through walls to get to cash hidden inside various businesses. The Mafia kingpins who were pulling in millions weren't about to let one of their underlings upset the apple cart for the likes of petty burglary.

While in Chicago Tony the Ant and his brother, Michael Spilotro, mysteriously disappeared. Some weeks later a farmer who was spreading weed killer over his cornfield in Indiana discovered two bodies. They were identified as the Spilotro brothers.

Jay Sarno conceived and created Caesars Palace, but a Roman legion of mobsters funded it. Sarno's concept was to bring true opulence to Las Vegas. He thought the Flamingo "was sick — like an old storage room," and "the Desert Inn was a stable." Sarno liked to live high and reportedly gambled away $25 million during his lifetime. Extravagance came naturally to the man who said that it wasn't gambling that attracted people but fantasy. Caesars was Sarno's dream, but in reality Tony Accardo,

The swimming pool at the Desert Inn, c. 1950s

Sam Giancana, Ray Patriarca, Jerry Catena, one of Vito Genovese's top aids, and Vincent "Jimmy Blue Eyes" Alo were all major investors in the hotel casino. The Teamster's Union pension fund, under the direction of Jimmy Hoffa, kicked in another $10 million in "permanent" loans.

Whether the mob's subterfuge was sophisticated enough to obscure the true ownership of most of the major casinos in Las Vegas, or if they were hiding behind a wall of payoffs, the gangsters operated with relative impunity. Ironically, authorities outside Nevada were the ones who often discovered the gangsters' involvement.

Ben Jaffe, who headed the Fontainebleau Hotel in Miami Beach, created the Tropicana with its Caribbean ambiance of Old Havana and opened it in 1957. Jaffe's associate, Phil Kastel was originally picked to operate the casino but couldn't be approved by state gaming authorities because of alleged gangland ties. J. Kell Houssels, part owner of the El Cortez and the Showboat and a longtime Las Vegas business-man, was brought in to manage the hotel and ease suspicions.

It was a few months after the Tropicana's opening when Frank Costello walked into the foyer of his fashionable Central Park West apartment house in New York City one evening.

Jay Sarno's Caesars Palace began an age of opulence in Las Vegas.

The "Folies Bergere" show opened at the Tropicana in 1960.

Someone called out, "This one is for you, Frank!" As Costello, known as the prime minister of organized crime in America, turned, a fat gunman opened fire. Frank staggered, blood streaming down his face as he muttered, "somebody tried to get me." He collapsed onto a chair.

They rushed Costello to a hospital where doctors removed a .38 slug from behind his right ear. Meanwhile, detectives searched his pockets and found some interesting handwritten notes. "Gross casino wins as of 4/27/57, $651,284; Casino wins less markers, $434,695; Slot wins, $62,844; Markers, $153,745. The detectives enlisted the help of the Nevada Gaming Control Board who discovered that $651,284 was a perfect match for the gross casino receipts for the Tropicana Hotel for its first 24 months of operation.

The Strip was ablaze in bright neon. Its casino-hotels had over-shadowed downtown, the center of old Las Vegas gambling. But Glitter Gulch wasn't ready to be counted out yet. Downtown's counter punch was the Fremont. Funded by $6.5 million in Teamster pension funds, the Fremont was the first downtown hotel to attract big-name entertainment. At the Fremont a teenager from Arizona who had been performing on the Lew King Ranger Show in Phoenix, Wayne Newton, got his start as a Las Vegas performer.

Soaring 15 stories above the intersection of Fremont and Second streets, the 155-room hotel remained the city's tallest building for several years. During the 1950s the Fremont's roof was a popular place to view the atomic blasts and mushroom clouds rising from weapons tests at the nearby Nevada Test Site.

Delphine "Mom" and C.P. "Pop" Squires officiated at the ribbon cutting for the Showboat Hotel, 1954. UNLV Special Collections

Today's Fremont Hotel opens onto the Fremont Street Experience. Photo by Rex M. Oppenheimer

Blooming with Atoms

The fireball formed at the instant of a nuclear detonation emits a brilliant flash of extreme luminosity. An observer watching the explosion of a 1-megaton weapon from 135 miles away would see a flash of brilliance many times brighter than the sun at high noon. Yet, a showdown with the bomb itself did not dim Las Vegas' prospects.

Las Vegas was gaining a reputation as an extraordinary place, like no other on earth. Its top-shelf entertainment, nonstop gaming, and drinking and carousing had established it as a city without limits. While people elsewhere were building shelters so they could hide from a possible atomic explosion, Las Vegas was billing the nuclear blasts as a tourist attraction.

Las Vegas: Boomtown

The mushroom cloud became a Las Vegas symbol: there were atomic hairdos, atomic cocktails, the Atomic View Motel and a dance featured at the Desert Inn Sky Room called "The Atomic Bomb Bounce." The Las Vegas Chamber of Commerce put out atomic calendars with dates of future tests marked so visitors could plan their vacations around the events. Clark County featured a mushroom-shaped explosion on the county seal for years.

President Truman had approved the opening of the Nevada Test Site at the end of 1950. Between 1951 and 1963 there were 119 atmospheric tests of nuclear devices at the site on the Las Vegas-Tonopah Bombing and Gunnery Range in the desert of Nye County about 65 miles northwest of Las Vegas.

Nobody seemed concerned about any safety risks. The Las Vegas papers didn't take on an investigative role, but rather, as *Review-Journal* editor John F. Cahlan said, "conditioned the local people for the explosions that were to follow." The focus was purely on the benefits of nuclear power.

The Atomic Energy Commission (AEC) summarily dismissed complaints made by victims of the testing. One farmer downwind from the test site claimed his goats had turned blue after one of the atomic blasts. The AEC countered that "The blue color was caused by the goats rubbing against the zinc coating of his fences." Perhaps it was only coincidence that it had never happened before.

A single Republican member of the state legislature introduced a resolution to halt atomic tests at the test site. The *Las Vegas Sun* shot back, "Who shall get out of Nevada, the AEC or the crackpot who makes such a suggestion in public?"

Nevada Senator Pat McCarran and Governor Charles Russell both championed the tests. Said the governor, "We had long ago written off that terrain as wasteland and today it's blooming with atoms."

In Vegas Atomic blasts became tourist attractions: chorus girl dubbed, "Miss Atomic Blast."

CHAPTER SIX

MURDER INCORPORATED MEETS VEGAS INC.

The Strange Days and Ways of Mr. Hughes

Howard Hughes, high-flying, movie making billionaire and businessman, had become eccentric to the extreme. Once a dashing playboy and pilot, designing, building and flying aircraft, setting aviation records, heading up major movie studios and bedding blond bombshells, he had become a drug-addicted, germ-phobic recluse. He refused to shave, bathe, brush his teeth, cut his hair or fingernails and ate only Campbell's chicken soup and banana-nut ice cream. One of the nation's richest men, he had become an emaciated physical wreck, who had taken to storing his expended urine in Mason jars he kept in a closet.

Strange that such a person's financial involvement in Las Vegas should be seen as lending the city an air of legitimacy. Yet, that's what it did.

Despite the city's success, before 1966 almost all legitimate lending institutions either refused to make loans to Las Vegas' casino-hotels, or Nevada's

Howard Hughes, c. 1950s

prohibitive regulations excluded them. This left the door wide open for alternative sources of financing, such as those available to the underworld entrepreneurs who had backed almost every major project in the city.

Hughes had been coming to Las Vegas since the 40s. Back in his more dashing days, he visited the city often and was swept up in its glamour and excitement. He'd make the rounds, flitting from one casino to the next.

When he'd married actress Jean Peters in a ceremony at Tonopah, Nevada, in 1957, he'd already begun to gain a reputation for a variety of eccentricities. He was becoming somewhat reclusive, but his appearance and behavior were still relatively normal.

By November 27, 1966, Hughes' appearance wasn't so normal. At 4 a.m. on that day, a locomotive pulling only Howard Hughes' two private railway cars screeched to a halt on the Vegas outskirts. Hughes, bearded, and with only 120 pounds covering his 6-foot-4-inch frame, was taken off the train on a stretcher, placed into a waiting van and driven across town to The Strip.

His arrival and appearance were unconventional but like most gamblers coming to the city, Howard

Hughes had brought some money with him. About six months earlier, he'd received the largest check ever made out to an individual — $546,549,171 — in payment for his controlling shares in Trans World Airlines. Howard Hughes wasn't a gambler in the conventional sense, but now he was betting on Las Vegas.

Howard Hughes' reasons for moving to Las Vegas may have been many, but primary among them was the desire to minimize his tax burden. By some accounts, the billionaire had not paid a penny in income tax for the past 17 years, a habit he did not wish to break. Nevada was much more tax friendly than California, his former state of residence. Hughes also thought Las Vegas held great business potential. He'd been buying property there since the 1950s. Despite his crazed appearance, strange reclusive manners and customs, his business dealings continued seemingly unaffected.

When he'd decided to make Las Vegas his headquarters, Hughes hired Robert Maheu, a former FBI agent turned private investigator, as his advance man. Through Hank Greenspun, publisher of the *Las Vegas Sun* and owner of KLAS-TV, and Moe Dalitz, the mob-affiliated headman at the Desert Inn, Hughes had arranged to rent the hotel's two top floors.

Dalitz agreed to rent the rooms to Hughes, but only for six weeks. After that the hotel would need the luxury accommodations to house the high rollers who'd be arriving for New Year's Eve. When the six weeks had passed, Hughes was not ready to leave. Dalitz refused point blank to extend his stay. Hughes, who wasn't gambling, was taking up valuable space. He was costing Dalitz money.

Hughes' fixer, Robert Maheu, contacted an old acquaintance, mobster John Rosselli. Maheu knew Rosselli, who had a reputation as a go-between in mob disputes, from when they'd each played a role in a CIA plot to assassinate Fidel Castro.

Rosselli spoke with Jimmy Hoffa, who'd loaned Dalitz the money for the Desert Inn and was then financing Dalitz' new venture, the Stardust. Moe had a change of heart and granted Mr. Hughes a two-week extension. Dalitz, however, felt pressured. He let Hank Greenspun know that he was interested in selling the Desert Inn.

Greenspun suggested to Dalitz that if he wanted to sell the Desert Inn, perhaps he should call Greenspun's former lawyer, Edward Morgan. He might have some ideas. Morgan just happened to be a friend of Maheu's.

Three months later, Howard Hughes paid $6.2 million in cash and assumed $7 million in liabilities for a lease on the Desert Inn until 2022. Morgan made a $150,000 finder's fee, Rosselli got $50,000 and Greenspun took home $25,000.

Howard Hughes wielded enormous power. His penchant to use his wealth to gain control over people and his environment was unleashed on Las Vegas. Hughes was anti-Semitic, anti-black — he opposed the Clark County School District's integration plan — and he hated children so much that he canceled the annual Easter egg hunt on the Desert Inn Golf Course for fear of, "snot-nosed children" running loose. Yet, Nevada Governor Paul Laxalt said of this bearded, skeletal creature, with three-inch plus fingernails curling into his grasping hands and jars of urine filling his closet, "If Nevada ever had a friend, a real friend, it was Howard Hughes."

The billionaire had promised the governor that he would underwrite the cost of a medical school for the University of Nevada. He never did. What he did do, this man who supposedly legitimized the gaming industry in Las Vegas, was skirt the basic safeguards the Gaming Control Board had put in place.

To obtain a gaming license, the rules required Hughes to appear in person before the board, file a financial statement and be photographed and fingerprinted. The recluse refused to do any of them. Yet, the board and later the Gaming Commission approved his application.

Shortly thereafter Robert Maheu remembers getting a call from the boss he'd still never actually met, "How many more of these toys are available?" asked Hughes. Within months he'd purchased the Sands for $14.6 million, the Frontier for $14 million, the Castaways for $3 million, the Landmark for $17.1 million and the Silver Slipper for $5.3 million. The last Hughes purchased because its revolving neon sign in the shape of a slipper shined into his window and disturbed his sleep. He reportedly sent Maheu a telegram that read, "I want you to buy that place, that damn sign is driving me crazy, it goes round and round and round."

Casinos were just part of Howard Hughes' shopping spree. During this same period he also purchased a small airline, an airport, a motel, a restaurant, several gold and silver mines throughout Nevada and almost a

Hank Greenspun (far right) stands with his wife, Barbara, to his left and Frank Sinatra is (far left) with his wife, Barbara.

hundred residential lots and undeveloped land along The Strip. By the late 1960s he'd purchased almost every vacant lot along the 3-mile stretch from the Tropicana to the Sahara. He also bought a television station from Hank Greenspun.

According to Greenspun, it began when Hughes would have his aides calling the station, or its owner's home, every night. He wanted the station to stay on the air all night long. Failing that, aides would constantly call asking that the station remain on the air at least an hour longer. Aides also conveyed Hughes' desire that Greenspun hire someone just to find out what kind of movies Hughes liked. Finally, he just bought the station.

Even after he owned the station, Hughes kept up a steady stream of complaints. He'd whine that the screen was too dark, that sound levels were annoying, or that different films be substituted at the last minute for ones he'd previously selected and which were already printed in the TV listings in the newspaper. When Hughes was informed that other viewers complained when the station deviated from its advertised listings, his solution was to stop printing the schedule.

Hughes' desire to control wasn't limited to television programs. He had plans to reshape the city of Las Vegas. He intended to build the largest hotel-casino in the world and create a new international airport, which he then planned to sell to the city at cost. He had detailed plans to create the world's biggest bookmaking operation. For whatever reason, none of those ideas ever came to fruition.

Howard Hughes left Las Vegas as suddenly and mysteriously as he'd arrived. It began when he read a news story that a hydrogen bomb, 100 times more powerful than the atomic bomb dropped on Hiroshima, would be detonated at the test site. The article stated that persons within 250 miles of the detonation,

particularly if they are on upper floors of high buildings, might feel a slight tremor following the explosion.

The bomb tests had troubled Hughes for some time. He'd had plans to bribe Lyndon B. Johnson, Richard Nixon and Hubert Humphrey to stop the testing. In fact, he'd given $100,000 each to Humphrey and Nixon, who had accepted the cash as campaign contributions but did nothing to stop the testing.

After reading about the hydrogen bomb, Hughes made plans to leave. He told Maheu that in addition to the atomic testing, too many things disturbed him in Nevada. There was, "a mass of miscellaneous problems which mainly seem to be a product of sharing the state with a number of other people. In other words, the unions, the minorities, the threat of overabundant competition."

Then, one day, in a mirror image of his unconventional arrival, aides carried the billionaire by stretcher from the Desert Inn to a waiting van, whisked him away to Nellis Air Force Base, and placed him aboard a waiting Lockheed JetStar aircraft. The plane took off immediately, winging its strange passenger to the Bahamas.

Back at the Desert Inn, the drapes remained drawn around the penthouse windows. Nobody noticed that Howard Hughes was gone.

The Mob Sells Out

Many of the mobsters had had no problem with selling their casinos to Hughes. They were getting on in years. Their operations didn't run as smoothly as they once did; there was always the possibility of continued congressional committee crackdowns, such as those begun by Senator Estes Kefauver back in 1950; and there was the persecution of Hoffa and other mobsters by Attorney General Robert Kennedy. Most of the casinos were aging and well past their prime. Besides, Hughes was paying cash, and a lot of it.

While mob-backed front man, Wilbur Clark, seen here with President John F. Kennedy, was cultivating an air of respectability, the President's brother, Attorney General Robert F. Kennedy, was leading a crackdown on many mob figures.

Howard Hughes' investment in Las Vegas lent legitimacy to the gaming industry, but he did not, as some claim, clean up the city. Mob ownership and participation in Las Vegas casinos continued after Hughes' departure. In addition, the Desert Inn and Sands showed huge losses for every year that Hughes owned them, and the most logical explanation is that skimming operations were taking place inside the famous billionaire's properties.

Perhaps while Hughes was ensconced in his penthouse, hiding from the world, the underworld was hiding things from him. Although renowned as a brilliant entrepreneur, Howard Hughes had made many business mistakes during his career. He reportedly mismanaged almost everything he owned, including RKO Studios and TWA. The former playboy turned hermit had no experience or expertise in casino operation. The reasonable conclusion is that he had his pockets picked the whole time he was in town.

Hughes' stay in Las Vegas did mark, however, the beginning of an important change. Howard Hughes had brought clean money to town. Las Vegas desperately needed capital. Legitimate financing sources had shied away from the city or were excluded by demanding regulations. Mob money had created a burst of growth, but since the completion of the Stardust in 1958, no new casinos had been built until 1966.

Governor Paul Laxalt, pushed by William F. Harrah and Conrad and Baron Hilton, wanted to make it possible for more untainted funds to follow Hughes' lead. In 1967 he began to seek legislation that would remove a key prohibitive restriction to corporate investment.

To regulate gambling more strictly, Nevada law required every shareholder of a corporation to obtain a license from the Gaming Commission. This made it impossible for large, publicly traded corporations to invest in Nevada casinos. The legislature had considered revising this law in 1963 and 1965. Both times, former Governor Grant Sawyer, who had in fact helped strengthen the regulations, opposed any changes. He believed that corporations could serve as shields for organized crime ownership.

Laxalt changed that. In 1969 Nevada adopted the Corporate Gaming Act. This allowed publicly traded corporations to own casinos with only a few key employees, rather than thousands of shareholders, having to be licensed.

Las Vegas hotels and casinos were a booming business. Now the door was open for major corporations with great experience in hotel operation to enter the market. Hilton, Hyatt, Holiday Inn and Ramada walked right in.

The Hilton Corporation purchased the Flamingo and the International from Kirk Kerkorian in 1970. By 1976, Sin City was responsible for 43 percent of the 163-hotel chain's gross revenues.

Laxalt spearheaded another change in the gaming regulations. Until 1969 the Gaming Commission had

Governor Paul Laxalt, seen here with President Ronald Reagan, pushed legislation that helped open the door for corporate investment in Las Vegas.

only two options to punish those who violated regulations. The commission could either deny or suspend the establishment's license to operate. These were harsh remedies, which caused a drastic impact not only on the casino but also on many working men and women. Consequently, the commission was often remiss in meting out penalties. Laxalt's innovation was to empower the commission to levy fines, which it was not reluctant to do.

The millions of dollars of corporate investment flowing into Las Vegas spurred dynamic growth. The inflow of clean capital helped dilute mob power but did not eradicate it.

Sam Boyd (left) who personified the Las Vegas-style Horatio Alger story, accepts an award from Sen. Howard Cannon.

In 1976 the Gaming Control Board uncovered a massive skimming operation at the Stardust. This came at the same time Ned Day, in stories appearing in *The Valley Times* and *Review-Journal*, called "The Organized Crime Treaty of 1977." The "treaty" supposedly gave the Chicago-Midwest mob control of Las Vegas, while the New York and other East Coast families ran gambling operations in Atlantic City.

In 1978-79, FBI wiretaps of conversations between the Tropicana's entertainment director, Joe Agosto, Kansas City mob boss, Nick Civella, and respected hotel executive, Carl Thomas, exposed a plot to skim the Tropicana casino. Gaming authorities uncovered another skim operation at the Stardust in 1983.

Yet, the sustained flow of legitimate capital continued to wash out mob influence. By 1985, Las Vegas was largely free of underworld ownership of casinos.

Is gangland sway finished in Las Vegas? Or has it morphed into a different form? Some critics point out that while Mafia ownership and skimming operations may be history, the city's loose morals and mountains of cash continue to make it a world center for criminal activity, including money laundering, power brokering and bribery. They cite examples such as U.S. Customs officials' 1998 "Operation Casablanca" bust.

Operation Casablanca, which then Treasury Secretary Robert Rubin called, "the largest, most comprehensive drug-money laundering case in the history of United States law enforcement," was part of a covert operation comprising more than 140 arrests across three continents. The investigation uncovered international crime and corruption, with Las Vegas as its nexus, in the hundreds of billions of dollars. The outlaws, who included 12 prominent Mexican bankers, their lawyers and associates, arrived in Southern Nevada by chartered jets and were sitting in chauffer-driven stretch limousines when they were arrested.

The city's unsavory past is well known and there is no doubt much about Las Vegas' atmosphere remains conducive to criminal activity. It is also certain that Sin City has changed.

Wall Street's gamblers have come to see Las Vegas as a safe bet. Most casinos today are part of publicly traded conglomerates. They are run not by gamblers or dealers, wearing eyeshades and garters on their sleeves, who have worked their way to the top or by mobsters in pinstriped suits carrying violin cases. MBAs from Wharton Business School are more likely to be calling the shots at these mainstream companies.

The Magicians

Besides gangsters and buttoned-down corporate types, magicians have been another force primary in Las Vegas' ascent. In other venues they may be called entrepreneurs, but the magic men of modern Las Vegas, such as Jay Sarno, Kirk Kerkorian and Steve Wynn, have waved their wands over the city and manufactured pure wizardry.

Mob money and rule turned what Meyer Lansky first referred to as a "miserable, dinky little oasis town" into an empire of gambling and vice. Corporate investment and management have driven the city's growth beyond epic proportions. Las Vegas has become the entertainment capital of the world.

The city shares something with another entertainment capital, Hollywood. Tinseltown has also grown through the investment of huge, publicly traded companies, but it was the original vision and imagination of individuals that created the kingdom of celluloid illusions.

Many individuals have had great influence on the city. Billy Wilkerson, Bugsy Siegel, Benny Binion, Sam Boyd and Jackie Gaughan each brought their own vision to Las Vegas, and each helped make and remake the city.

Binion's philosophy of getting rich by making little people feel big became a cornerstone of the city's formula for success; his innovations, such as free drinks to players and the World Series of Poker, were important contributions. Gaughan, a Las Vegas pioneer, put an essential part of the formula into practice by instituting mass-marketing campaigns that used contests, promotions and giveaways aimed at the middle class. Sam Boyd personified the Vegas version of Horatio Alger in pre-corporate Sin City. Working as a dealer and croupier at casinos along Fremont Street, he advanced to pit boss, shift boss, general manager, vice president and finally owner.

But the magic of Jay Sarno, Kirk Kerkorian and Steve Wynn catapulted Las Vegas into a fourth dimension, making it so much brighter than other gambling and entertainment venues that it became the first sight visible to astronauts orbiting the earth. Some of it was because of scale, creating the world's largest casino-hotels. Partly it

was outrageousness, where a medieval castle, Cleopatra's floating barge, volcanoes, white tigers and live circus acts cohabited in an environment that was like something out of this world. Indeed, Las Vegas' next step was to virtually become a parallel universe where nations, cities and eras such as Italy, ancient Egypt, Venice, medieval England, Paris and New York were seemingly transported to the Southern Nevada desert.

Although Caesars Palace and Circus Circus had mob backing, they were Jay Sarno's babies. He conceived their splendor and grandiosity, and they definitely ratcheted up the extravagance quotient of 1966 Las Vegas. Sarno had a successful vision. By the time it opened, Caesars had $42 million in advance bookings. It remained the world's most profitable casino for years.

Kirk Kerkorian, a high school dropout, battled his way through stints as a professional boxer and World War II pilot in the Royal Air Force. Then he worked as a crop duster and flight instructor before he built a shuttle service flying gamblers between Hawthorne, California, and Las Vegas into an airline worth $104 million.

The Mirage
MGM MIRAGE

Although more introverted than Sarno or Wynn, Kerkorian had a strong sense of direction that guided much of Las Vegas' development. He was instrumental in furthering corporate ownership of casinos while still implementing his personal vision.

Kerkorian's investments in Las Vegas seemed charmed from the beginning. His purchase of the Flamingo and 80 acres across from the hotel for $960,000 earned him $5 million when he later sold it to Sarno as the site for Caesars Palace.

Statue of Siegfried and Roy

He then built the International, which opened in 1969 as the largest Las Vegas hotel project ever undertaken up to that time. Selling the International and the Flamingo to Hilton, Kerkorian announced plans to build the MGM Grand Hotel, which opened at a cost of $106 million in 1973. The MGM Grand was a huge success right out of the gate. It had a great run for several years before a disastrous fire struck the hotel in 1980, killing 85 people and closing the property for nearly a year. Kerkorian sold the MGM in 1986.

Two years later, he began the new MGM Grand. At nearly $1 billion

the innovative resort comprised four separate gaming areas, each with its own theme, and an amusement park. The new MGM Grand helped pioneer the concept of Las Vegas as a family destination.

The media embraced the marketing campaign of Vegas as a family resort where parents could take in shows and gaming while their kids played on water rides. They trumpeted the family theme as the future of Las Vegas. Other hotels made concessions to family entertainment.

Las Vegas used to be sin city. With society's expanding concepts of individual freedom and choice of lifestyle and a less puritanical view of vice, the city lost of lot of its sin stigma. It was simply adult entertainment. Vegas' pleasures, naughty but nice, were not evil but they weren't necessarily for the family, either.

The MGM Grand closed its theme park. It curtailed family-oriented marketing, and the casino's accouterments took on a decidedly more traditional and adult theme. The city's visitors still include more families and children than in decades past, but with most of the newer resorts promising an indulgent, upscale experience, Vegas' role as an amusement park for parents, rather than children, is fairly well entrenched.

From Oasis to Mirage

Meyer Lansky knew that owning the house was the only lucky side of the gambling equation. Billy Wilkerson had received similar advice from his friend, Joe Schenck.

Steve Wynn learned that lesson watching his father "crumble and lose his self confidence." As Wynn further put it, "The one thing my father's gambling did was to show me, at a very early age, that if you want to make money in a casino… the answer is to own one."

MGM Grand, MIRAGE *MGM MIRAGE*

(Both photos) Treasure Island brought even more fantasy to Las Vegas.

legitimate lending institution willing to make loans to the city's gaming industry. E. Parry Thomas, who ran the bank, was willing to take a gamble in a gambling town. When he met Steve Wynn, he was willing to bet on him.

Parry loaned him the money to buy a liquor distributorship. With profits made from that business plus another loan from the Valley Bank, Wynn purchased a small parking lot next to Caesars Palace. He'd persuaded Howard Hughes to sell him the property, which in itself was quite a feat, since the billionaire was notorious for not selling any land he owned. Soon, Caesars got wind of Wynn's supposed plans to build a competing casino on the land so close to their property. The mighty Caesars paid Wynn $2,250,000 for the parking lot, roughly twice what he had given Hughes for it.

Steve Wynn's association with Las Vegas began when his father, Michael, ran the bingo games at the Silver Slipper and gambled away all his earnings in the casinos on The Strip. The Wynns returned broke to Maryland where the father managed to put together a chain of bingo parlors. Later, when attending the University of Pennsylvania, the younger Wynn would return on weekends to help his dad run the bingo halls.

In 1963 the elder Wynn died on the operating table when doctors tried to repair a damaged aortic valve. Steve was devastated. He said, "My world collapsed that day," but added, "I've never been afraid of anything since."

Steve Wynn took more than courage with him when he left Maryland for Las Vegas in 1967. He brought his lifelong experience with gambling, good and bad, and he carried with him the romantic dreams he'd formed as a child about the city and its primary industry. He remembered the pit bosses wearing "those high collars" and the cocktail waitresses who "were all very beautiful." Steve Wynn remembered it as the only business that offered the "glamour of the movies and the stability of a bank."

The Bank of Las Vegas, reorganized as the Valley Bank in 1964, was for years the only

Owning a casino was always Wynn's goal. Using the profits from his sale to Caesars, he began buying stock in the Golden Nugget. The Nugget was one of downtown's most rundown properties. Not long after he began buying the stock, Wynn discovered that there was rampant skimming going on at the casino. He bought more stock.

Once Wynn gained control, he ousted the incompetent and corrupt staff that was running the casino into the ground. The Golden Nugget's profits began to soar. In the first year Wynn elevated the old casino's take from $1 million to $4.25 million. By 1977 the Golden Nugget's earnings had risen to $12 million. Wynn was on his way.

His next foray was in Atlantic City where he built the 506-room Golden Nugget. Wynn considered other Atlantic City casinos to be too drab. He added a splash of flash to his new establishment with vaulted mirrored ceilings, crystal chandeliers, stained glass, and marble pillars. Though his casino was that city's smallest, it soon became its most profitable.

Steve Wynn had business acumen, good instincts and guts. He also possessed the gift most prized by all gamblers everywhere, luck. Not long before the days of easy profits in Atlantic City were to level off, Bally's offered Wynn $440,000,000 for the Golden Nugget, which had cost him about $140,000,000 to build. Experts have estimated that Bally's paid up to twice what the casino should have been worth considering Atlantic City's prospects at the time.

With his pockets full of money and his head full of dreams, Steve Wynn headed back to Las Vegas. Just as Billy Wilkerson and Bugsy Siegel and latter Jay Sarno had done, Steve Wynn gambled on a vision that would reshape the city.

In 1988 he began building the Mirage. It was the first new casino constructed in the city in 15 years. The Mirage, built on a 102-acre site next to Caesars Palace, was the most elaborate and expensive project ever attempted in the city up to that time.

A volcano, surrounded by waterfalls and lagoons, erupted outside the hotel every 15 minutes. The spectacular casino featured a special habitat for the rare royal white tigers bred by Siegfried and Roy, in an atrium nine stories high. Sharks, rays, surgeonfish and triggerfish swam in a 20,000-gallon, saltwater aquarium just behind the reception desks. An artfully designed marine environment, constructed at a cost of $14 million, housed the world's most expensively maintained dolphins. The Mirage introduced Cirque du Soleil to America.

The top casinos all cater to high rollers. Many offer special perquisites and attractions to lure the big bettors. Wynn spent around $24 million to create eight luxurious two- and three-bedroom villas to please the world's most wealthy gamblers. Billed as residences, the special apartments featured European art from the 17th, 18th and 19th centuries, salons plush with imported wall fabrics and marble floors, hand-loomed carpet, crystal chandeliers, bedrooms modeled after a 17th-century royal chateau, and private kitchens where master chefs prepared the finest haute cuisine dishes.

Wynn had gone too far, was the verdict of many experts. At $630,000,000 the Mirage was too expensive; it couldn't possibly generate the cash flow needed to cover its debt.

Yet, the high rollers came. Within six weeks of the Mirage's opening, 400 people had each bet a million dollars or more on a single visit to the hotel. It wasn't just high rollers who were bankrolling the new casino. The attractions drew the crowds. Cash flow for the first year was close to $200 million. Within two years the Mirage was the world's most successful casino.

Next Wynn created the $430,000,000 Treasure Island, with three 36-story towers and 100,000-square-foot gambling complex. Based on the Robert Louis Stevenson novel, it featured a British man-of-war and a pirate ship, both manned by professional stuntmen, engaged in a full-fledged battle in Treasure Island's Buccaneer Bay.

Vegas had seen opulence and extravagance before, but Wynn's properties were upping the ante, elevating the drama and illusion. When Disneyland first opened in the 1950s, there was nowhere else

The world indeed was coming to Las Vegas.
Photo by Rex M. Oppenheimer

Illusion par excellance:
Paris, France,
Las Vegas Boulevard
*Photo by
Rex M. Oppenheimer*

on earth like it. Now Steve Wynn was creating attractions that were designed to win that same distinction for a gambling town in the middle of nowhere.

Las Vegas glamour had often been criticized as ostentatious glitz and kitsch. The Bellagio, which Steve Wynn opened in 1998, turned the mirage of Vegas' sophistication into reality.

The $2.1 billion Bellagio's European fantasy image included Wynn's $350 million personal collection of fine art. This was not ersatz elegance. Masterpieces by Rubens, Picasso, Degas, Monet, Gauguin and Van Gogh displayed along with pieces by more modern artists such as Warhol, helped once again to transform the city's image.

Steve Wynn's personal vision created the Mirage phase of Las Vegas development. His creative spark spurred investors to assimilate his concepts. After more than a decade without any major casino developments,

the 1988 Mirage gave birth to a new era of casino construction.

Between 1990 and 2000 it was as though a new world was being created in the Nevada desert. Each new property seemed a civilization unto itself.

There was the medieval splendor of King Arthur's Court at the Excalibur and the mysteries of ancient Egypt at the pyramid-shaped Luxor. Hollywood's magic comes alive at the MGM Grand and the legends of rock 'n' roll bring down the house at the Hard Rock Hotel. There is the lofty view from the Stratosphere Tower, the magic of what Steve Wynn called the Monte Carlo's "popular elegance," and New York, New York with a Statue of Liberty beckoning the masses seeking freedom from the cares of everyday life.

This wasn't everyday life. From Mandalay Bay's House of Blues to the Venetian, with gondolas plying romantic canals and a 35,000-square-foot satellite gallery housing exhibitions of fine art provided by the Guggenheim and Hermitage museums, to the Paris, replete with Eiffel Tower and Arc de Triomphe and the Aladdin, the new Las Vegas seemed to defy all laws of time and space. The number of hotel rooms in the city more than doubled during the Mirage decade.

Along with the grand new casinos came shops and boutiques featuring the world's finest designers, restaurants operated by the planet's premier haute cuisine chefs, and shoppers and diners all seeking the best. In a city where once people seldom walked, hundreds of thousands now jammed The Strip, ogling the sights and sampling its wares.

Wynn's sense of fancy and adventure engendered many mimics. Those that flourished weren't just copycats. Each brought its own vision and competitive edge to win a share of trade. Not all were successful.

As corporations have stepped in to replace individual entrepreneurs, some vital creative energy may have been lost. Sometimes unfortunate decisions, such as the construction of towers at the Flamingo that cast the swimming pool into perpetual shadow, have been made. Myopic focus on the bottom line has sometimes driven an enterprise to the bottom.

The Aladdin, which opened in 2000, was in receivership by 2001. This committee's horse/camel failed to carve out an alluring enough identity to compete in a crowded marketplace. It also bucked Benny Binion's formula. Rather than offering a luxury experience at a bargain price, it offered a middleclass experience at a premier price.

The corporate attitude toward casinos as money machines, the focus on inflows and outflows and lack of true vision have still managed to produce a number of successes. Yet, it has left gaps, which a new generation of magicians eager to pull rabbits out of niches, has endeavored to fill.

The behemoth corporations are just not flexible enough to operate successfully outside of their chosen formulaic structure. While they battle to fill huge properties, such as MGM/Mirage, Mandalay Bay and Park Place with more than 10,000 rooms each, they have had to jettison some smaller, still valuable casinos.

Steve Wynn, who lost (albeit a profitable defeat) his Mirage/Bellagio empire in a $6.4 billion takeover bid to Kirk Kerkorian's MGM in 2000, purchased the Desert Inn for $270 million. That was just $70 million more than ITT had spent to renovate the property three years earlier. With his eye on a specialized market segment, which the cumbersome corporations are not nimble enough to service, Wynn will pull out the top hat, cape and wand and once again attempt to make magic.

Photo by Rex M. Oppenheimer

Photo by Rex M. Oppenheimer

The Bellagio, replete with world-class art masterpieces, brought a new level of sophistication to the city.
MGM MIRAGE

Photo by Rex M. Oppenheimer

93
CHAPTER SIX

REAL PEOPLE IN A MYTHIC LAND
BETTING ON TOMORROW

Prospectors bring the gold to this boomtown. The gambling tables keep sucking it up and replenishing the mother lode. Gaming is still Las Vegas' most recognized enterprise. Yet, Las Vegas has also become a tourist attraction for those who gamble only a little, or not at all.

The V in Vegas could stand for variety. The city that changed gambling's name to gaming, has become an entertainment extravaganza. The Las Vegas club scene is hot. Concerts by big-name stars in relatively small venues draw audiences from every corner of the country and the world.

A constant array of talent dazzles — mega stars from every music genre, including rock, pop, country and classical, avant-garde performance art, hit Broadway shows, the conjuring of the world's greatest magicians, pugilistic events such as the heavyweight championship of the world, plus pirate ships doing battle, volcanoes exploding and death-defying high wire acts. The entertainment scene in Las Vegas is crazier than Carnival, more raucous than a Roman circus and busier than rush hour in Hong Kong. And it never stops.

(Left)
Despite the increasing number of new residents, they are far outnumbered by the sea of tourists that washes through the city every year.
Photo by Rex M. Oppenheimer

(Right)
Families are changing the face of Las Vegas: Contrary to the casinos' controlled environments, some of the city's new playgrounds are in the open air.
Photo by Rex M. Oppenheimer

Pundits galore have proclaimed Las Vegas overbuilt, oversold and overdone. The city has repeatedly managed to prove them wrong.

Competition for the gambling dollar is ever increasing. Atlantic City approximates a Las Vegas East. Native Americans have operated Las Vegas-style casinos in California since 1998. As many as 37 other states allow some type of casino gambling, and 48 states offer a lottery. Yet, Vegas is still the draw.

By 1997 nongaming revenues already comprised 52 percent of the city's total income, yet gaming remains the city's 900-pound gorilla. It not only dominates the area's economy, it is the single-largest entertainment-related revenue stream in the United States. Gaming

In the face of increased competition, Las Vegas is still America's favorite place to gamble.
Photo by Rex M. Oppenheimer

proceeds nearly doubled between 1990 and 2000, from $4.1 billion to $7.6 billion. During the same period, visitor volume increased from nearly 22 million people to more than 35 million, and between 1996 and 2000, total visitor spending rose from $22.5 billion to $31.4 billion.

The booming entertainment/gaming industry, combined with ever-increasing nongaming growth patterns — more than 20,000 housing permits per year since 1988 — have caused some commentators to praise the Las Vegas economy as a paradigm others should emulate.

Beyond its economy, however, there is abundant speculation and discussion about the Las Vegas phenomenon. The city's almost logic-defying success, the ability to host conventions for both pornstars and preachers, and its unique role in sanctioning sin as entertainment have given rise to much prophesy about its purpose and place among American cities.

Cultural anthropologists, columnists and authors have declared that through the nation's acceptance and normalization of previously dissolute behavior, Sin City has become more like the rest of the country, and the rest of the country has become more like it. They claim that Las Vegas is no longer an aberrant but a caldron in which evolving social patterns are forged from the nation's desires. Some analysts have announced that Las Vegas is the prototype of 21st-century America.

It is true that on some levels there has been a homogenization of culture,

not just in America but also around the world. The same brands of food and clothing can be found to some degree in Moscow, Paris, Mexico City and Des Moines. In some ways as the world is getting smaller, the notion of community is expanding.

Although an easing of moral standards may be mirrored in the images that flash on movie and TV screens, or in the nation's acceptance of gaming as a national sport, it isn't plain that reasonable people are confusing fantasy with reality or choosing to live more sinful lives. Most of the nation may no longer look upon Las Vegas

People still come to Vegas to escape the ordinary.
Photo by
Rex M. Oppenheimer

as aberrant, but it does view it as different, which is a great part of its attraction. One of the reasons people go to Las Vegas is to escape the ordinary.

Why some pundits believe that Las Vegas represents the wave of the future isn't clear.

What is clear is that Las Vegas is a mythic land populated by real people. While it may not be an archetype of America's future, its own future is changing.

From The New Frontier to The Old Homestead

Las Vegas has changed direction many times. From desert oasis, to Mormon settlement, ranch country, mining center, railroad town, city of vice and entertainment extravaganza, it has successfully reinvented itself again and again. Yet, for years, despite its worldwide renown and big-dollar image, and although millions of people continually passed through it, Las Vegas remained a small, wide-open western town.

People called it the new frontier. The local population, whether they wore boots and jeans or alligator shoes and fedoras, didn't want to be told what to do. They called themselves independent and self-sufficient. They were anti-authoritarian and anti-government.

UNLV former head basketball coach Jerry Tarkanian

Las Vegas had always valued winners above community. The individual's rights reigned supreme and winning was the goal. It seems appropriate that one of the first forces forging Las Vegas' disparate factions into a sense of community was a rogue band of winners.

Jerry Tarkanian, then basketball coach at the University of Nevada at Las Vegas (UNLV), and his championship team, the Runnin' Rebels, became a focal point of identity for the city's residents. Las Vegas always loved sports. Games are a gamble, and there's always a winner. The city loved the Runnin' Rebels because they were fast, flashy and, above all, winners.

The Runnin' Rebels really were rebels of a sort. They came from a small team at a small college in a city without a basketball tradition. Their coach was a rogue, who stood up to authority and backed up his arrogance with victories.

The team was a perfect metaphor for Las Vegas. Flashy upstarts who lacked tradition, they shot to the top of the rankings and emerged NCAA champions in 1990. The city embraced them exuberantly.

Las Vegas was no longer just Sin City, it was an all American city, home to one of the most recognized college basketball teams in the nation. It was a sign of normalization; it was also a badge of community spirit. The tributaries of transience that flowed through the Las Vegas population like flash floods rolling across the desert's surface, merged into a solid stream of community support.

The 1990s were a watershed decade in the city's history. Unprecedented population growth and casino expansion, record numbers of visitors spending record

Having long abandoned attempts to market itself as a "frontier town,"
Las Vegas is now a leading-edge community in the New West.

99
CHAPTER SEVEN

More and more Americans, from retirees to young families just starting out, are coming to Las Vegas to find a place they can call home.
Photo by Rex M. Oppenheimer

Rather than the fast life, many new arrivals are seeking a good life.
Photo by Rex M. Oppenheimer

A stronger feeling of community, although nascent, is developing. Increasing numbers of new residents are advocating a government more concerned with its citizens' welfare. These elements of the populace, who have arrived mostly since the 1990s and have swelled the city's population at a record pace, are considerably different from many of their predecessors. Previous immigrants were often escaping an old life as much as seeking a new one. They were quite content to be left alone. The newer arrivals are demanding services they believe are a citizen's due. They want better schools, parks, libraries, and the public spaces that are essential to form and nurture a community.

The big O of opportunity has always spun through the Las Vegas Valley like a whirlwind. Since the 1990s those swirling opportunities have expanded in an even larger circle. Prospects in Las Vegas are bigger, better and more diversified than ever.

The chance to win big, to escape the humdrum existence of daily life, to latch on to a dream has always pulled people to Vegas. Since the 1990s, however, the opportunity many newcomers seek in Las Vegas does not hang on the flip of a card or shake out with a roll of the dice.

amounts of cash, and the emergence of a significant nongaming economy changed more than the face of Las Vegas. The city was developing a soul. Many newcomers included not just people seeking a dream, but many willing to build themselves a piece of the American Dream.

The city's Old West identity was reduced to image long ago. And today, the only way a mobster might still have a stake in a casino is by owning stock in its controlling corporation. Las Vegas still is a wide-open western town. The spirit of freedom flows through the streets, billows in the breeze and lingers in the air. Many of the city's newer residents, however, while relishing freedom, breathe easier when the atmosphere also offers a sense of security.

Lawyers and bankers, accountants and city executives, shoemakers and veterinarians, people in virtually every occupation under the sun, have streamed into Las Vegas at a rate averaging 60,000 new citizens a year for the past 15 years. They include blue-collar workers displaced from jobs in California and elsewhere. Many find good-paying union jobs in the Las Vegas Valley and enjoy a higher standard of living than they did back home. Construction workers come in their pickups from Idaho, Montana and Oregon to help build the fastest growing region in the nation.

Nevada is a Right-to-Work state, yet many unskilled or semiskilled workers come to Las Vegas and find union-protected jobs with relatively high wages in the service sector. They begin to fashion a solid middle class life. Hal Rothman, in *Neon Metropolis*, writes about a skycap at McCarran Airport making $80,000 per year and dealers at the Bellagio routinely taking home more than $75,000.

Not long ago most of the doctors that relocated to Las Vegas were either gamblers, enthusiasts for the desert lifestyle, or cantankerous cowboys. Today, graduates of the nation's top medical schools are choosing to practice in Las Vegas where they find an ever-growing need for their skills and an expanding array of partnership/practices and hospitals.

Before the 1990s, educated professionals, including teachers, architects, lawyers and financial planners, may have come to Vegas for fun but very few made the city their home. That changed during the 90s. A large number of young professionals relocated to Las Vegas, creating a sizeable upper middle class with, in many cases, only a very indirect link to the gaming industry. These motivated men and women find great demand for their services and enjoy good positions, a high standard of living and continued growth.

An increasing number of retirees are also enjoying the area's relatively low cost of living and high value for the dollar. Retirement communities, such as Del Webb's Sun City in Summerlin, Sun City-McDonald Ranch, and Anthem, have had great success. Retirees and young professionals appreciate the incredible entertainment possibilities, entrepreneurial spirit and cosmopolitan atmosphere, without the dirt and danger so prevalent in America's other big cities.

Multiculturalism

Perhaps the mob first brought multiculturalism to Las Vegas. The gangsters who ran the city for so long represented a melding of various ethnicities, including Jewish, Italian and Irish. Las Vegas and its multicultural makeup have evolved considerably since then.

Between 1990 and 2000 the populations of both Clark County and the city of Las Vegas increased by more than 85 percent, while the city of Henderson grew by a whopping 170.1 percent. Much of the population increase was of various racial and nationality groups. Las Vegas is developing a more eclectic ethnic composition.

The number of Latinos in Clark County increased 264 percent during that decade, from 85,000 to more than 300,000. In 2000 they comprised 20 percent of the population. In Census 2000, more than a third of the students in Las Vegas public schools were Latino.

During the same period, the Asian population of Nevada soared 156.2 percent, or 90,266 persons, with 72,547 living in Clark County and 22,879 of those residing in Las Vegas, comprising nearly 5 percent of the city's population. Census 2000 placed Clark County's African-American population at 124,885 people (9.1 percent), with 49,570 (10.36 percent) living in the city of Las Vegas.

Although the United States has made great strides in reversing past discriminatory practices, people of color continue to encounter prejudice to one degree or another almost everywhere in the country. Southern Nevada's record of race relations is not unblemished. The discriminatory deed restrictions in North Las Vegas and the institutionalized segregation in Basic, Nevada,

(Left)
In addition to a sea of suburbia that now surrounds the city, luxury condominiums, ranging from several hundred thousand dollars into the millions, are going up right off The Strip.
Photo by Rex M. Oppenheimer

(Right)
The desert sands are disappearing beneath rooftops.
Photo by Rex M. Oppenheimer

The first African-American family to move into all black Carver Park in segregated Basic, Nevada
UNLV Special Collections

The Moulin Rouge, 1956, an integrated nightclub in the heart of Las Vegas' ghetto, attracted black and white performers and patrons.
UNLV Special Collections

103
CHAPTER SEVEN

(Left)
Many minority workers who left low-paying jobs without benefits in their hometowns have found the ticket to a good middle-class life in Las Vegas.
Photo by Rex M. Oppenheimer

(Right)
Growth can be a multi-edged sword. In addition to amplified pollution worries, the increasing atmosphere of normalcy created by the influx of families and a growing middle class that derives its living from nongaming sources, can threaten Las Vegas' image as Sin City.
Photo by Rex M. Oppenheimer

which later became Henderson, are recounted in an earlier chapter of this book.

The opportunity to make money lured African Americans to Las Vegas, as it did almost everyone else. In 1940 there were only 178 blacks in the city, but that number had multiplied to 15,000 by 1955. Most of them worked in service and back-of-the-house jobs. Throughout the 1950s African Americans were not permitted to enter Strip hotels through the front door.

African Americans could walk through the front door of the The Moulin Rouge. The famed inter-racial nightclub opened in the city's black ghetto, Westside, in 1955. Black and white performers and patrons partied many a night away at the club, which for a time was the coolest after-hours spot in town.

Many histories credit a 1960 consent decree with integrating the Strip. Dr. James McMillan, who headed the Las Vegas chapter of the National Association for the Advancement of Colored People in the early 60s, offered a different perspective.

In a 1997 article in the *Review Journal*, McMillan recounted that at a time of increasing civil rights aware-ness and action, it was his responsibility to attack the blatant discrimination at the Strip establishments, where blacks washed the dishes but couldn't stay in the hotel or play in the casino. McMillan planned a march, but it never came off. According to McMillian, the mob bosses didn't want black people demonstrating in front of Strip casinos. A few days before the scheduled demonstration, the mobsters agreed to integrate the casinos. The former NAACP leader credits Moe Dalitz's influence as an important factor in the casino's decision to integrate.

While many members of the minorities face dis-crimination and only find low-wage jobs in the Las Vegas

Valley as they do elsewhere in the nation, there are differences. One major variation is the availability of unionized jobs in the service sector, which allow many minority individuals to enter the middle class.

The availability of these jobs has attracted large numbers of Latinos from California. Many of these are women who worked in semiskilled jobs, such as maids or restaurant help, on the West Coast where they earned low wages with no benefits. In Las Vegas they have found unionized jobs as hotel maids, or in the kitchens of the Strip casinos, where they earn a substantial income and receive good benefits. People who could barley get by, and certainly not get ahead, in California are able to purchase homes and enjoy a promising middle-class lifestyle.

One exception to this is the construction industry, which in Right-to-Work Nevada is nonunion. While Latino women are finding union jobs in the service industry, many Latino men are building houses in the city's subdivisions as nonunion labor.

Like most cities, Las Vegas had a traditional ghetto area, the Westside. Also, as in many other cities, new immigrants from some minority groups often seek out communities of people from the same nationality or linguistic group, forming enclaves within the city. Yet, the area's recent, rapid growth and the opportunities to earn good wages in the service sector have helped integrate its many new suburbs far beyond the levels achieved in many other American cities.

Whither Thou, Las Vegas?

Some pundits have prematurely forecast Las Vegas' demise. These doomsayers have often opined that the city had overbuilt its number of hotel rooms and had outlived its uniqueness. These critics often seem to imply that the Las Vegas miracle will peter out, if for no other reason than that nothing lasts forever.

Las Vegas has seen phases of prosperity end. Yet, rather than vanishing, the city has morphed into a new vision of itself. In its journey from desert oasis on the Spanish Trail to the world's most popular destination, the city has had many lives.

For most cities, growth has often been a two-edged sword. Increased population bolsters the economy by attracting additional businesses and fosters greater community development, but it puts great strain on the infrastructure and city services. Traditionally, Las Vegas citizens eschewed services in favor of lower taxes and less involvement, and wanted to be left alone.

The legions of newer arrivals over the past decade have strained the city's existing resources while demanding even greater services. Las Vegas is expanding as never before. Its gaming/entertainment industry is growing, but so is a large segment of the population only marginally associated with that industry if at all.

Many of the city's newer citizens comprise families with children and parents who try to teach good moral and ethical values. These families have formed sound communities and support schools, sports teams, service clubs and groups. They are increasingly challenging Las Vegas' traditional libertarian and libertine environment.

The old Las Vegas took seed in the Wild West; its ethos was branded by hard-chiseled individuality and lawlessness. Meyer, Bugsy and the boys took heed of no one. They catered to people's desires and made anyone who objected an offer they couldn't refuse.

Some commentators have said that Las Vegas has become more like the rest of the country and that America has become more like Las Vegas. They are referring to the city's patina of respectability, its conversion of gambling to gaming, and to the nation's greater acceptance of what used to be considered sin.

Yet, America has changed in other ways, too. While some behavior that used to be called licentious is now considered libertarian, acts that were once thought of as sophisticated, such as smoking, are now seen as taboo. More cities are banning smoking in bars, restaurants and other places where the public congregates. When the mob ran the casinos, they answered to no one. The corporations must answer to their shareholders. The potential exists for the city's increasing normalization, through its growing population and expanding nongaming opportunities, to affect its ability to be Las Vegas.

Despite various marketing campaigns to present Las Vegas as a family vacation center, the town's main lure continues to be decidedly adult entertainment. Casinos cater to the pursuit of easy money. Luck is hailed, cheered and worshipped 24 hours a day.

Will the influx of families, the greater demand for public services and normalization jinx Las Vegas' magic touch? Will the new advocates of community squelch the freedoms that make Sin City such an attractive destination? Or will the city's new image as the whole world's center ring keep the spotlights shining?

It's a gamble. You can bet on it!

Can decadence and suburban family values coexist?
Photo by Rex M. Oppenheimer

BUILDING A GREATER LAS VEGAS

Las Vegas architecture, construction and real estate industries shape tomorrow's city, providing working and living space for area residents.

AMERICAN ASPHALT & GRADING COMPANY

American Asphalt & Grading Company (AA&G) is a leading provider of infrastructure construction services to private and public sector clients in the southwestern United States. The company is the only competitor in the industry to provide a broad variety of integrated site preparation services, including grading, paving, concrete curb and gutter work, pavement maintenance and crushing, mine reclamation, SWPPP (Storm Water Pollution Prevention Program) and material sales.

Service, speed and efficiency: these are the three "products" American Asphalt & Grading Company offers to its clients.

For any and all large development projects, AA&G's contractors busily tend to their specific tasks and duties, carefully maintaining great attention to the grand scheme. AA&G never takes its eyes off the big picture and always works with a vision of the finished project. This commitment and depth is what separates the company from its competitors and what has helped it become a strong and successful organization.

With the addition of its new financial partners and the ongoing support of its construction partners, AAG's management team continues to implement and expand on its existing strategy — becoming the premier provider of infrastructure services for homebuilders and public agencies in the rapidly expanding Southern Nevada marketplace. The nation's fastest-growing population center for each of the last 16 years, Nevada offers an attractive tax environment and a mild desert climate for relocating businesses and new residents.

AA&G's founder, Don Andress, is a native of Nevada and the Las Vegas area with over 30 years of construction experience, a trade he learned from the ground up. It was in 1983 that Andress founded AA&G

and he is proud of the significant contracts his company has won over the years. Las Vegas' Bears Course golf course, the Kaiser Commerce Center in Fontana, California and the Las Vegas Motor Speedway are just three examples of the firm's past projects. They reveal AA&G's ability to tackle a variety of jobs with skill and efficiency. However, these examples don't disclose how prolific the company is: since its inception, AA&G has completed thousands of jobs.

The team of managing partners is extremely qualified, with each principal having worked 15 years or more in the construction industry. Paul Robinson, AA&G's residing president, brought 25 years of heavy construction-industry management and operations experience acquired from Walter Group, Perini Corporation, Moseman Construction and SJ Groves to AA&G. Kirk Scherer, AAG's current chief financial officer, joined the company in 2001, providing 20 years of finance, accounting and tax experience; prior public and private company CFO experience within construction, manufacturing and consumer product businesses; and public accounting experience as a well-versed CPA.

AA&G's Dave Fortner also generously contributes to the practiced management team as the director of sales and business development with a background in estimating and operations; maintaining and aiding the growth of sales relationships; estimating and bidding for private projects; and expanding market share locally and in new markets. The fourth partner, Marty Cook, joined AA&G in 1993 and currently serves as the director of residential grading. Marty is responsible for day-to-day private grading operations, to which he provides a well-versed background in operations and production control.

With this skillful team of experienced individuals, AA&G has been able to secure contracts on multi-billion dollar projects such as the McCarren International Airport. While serving on such projects, AA&G has successfully established longstanding relationships with large, national and local developers, but nothing better illustrates this than AA&G's relationship with the developer Del Webb. In order to complete Del Webb's

Anthem Country Club in Las Vegas, AA&G had to devise a new way of moving large volumes of aggregate and massive rock, a process which led to a partnership between the companies to capitalize on this new system.

For the $50 million Anthem contract, AA&G had to preserve the pristine natural condition of undisturbed land and at the same time, complete three golf courses built in the bottoms of rock canyons. Fill materials were blasted and blended with fines for the course grades and contours, a process that AA&G was able to do on-site, utilizing heavy mining equipment and technology. Not only were the golf courses completed, but the company was also able to employ special surfacing techniques that enhanced the beauty of the development. The ingenuity shown by AA&G resulted in minimal impact on the natural environment and significant cost savings for the client.

It's not uncommon for developers to save money by working with AA&G. When the firm was contracted by Catellus, a major California-based real estate developer, to work on the Kaiser Commerce Center, 8 million-cubic-yards of steel furnace slag needed to be moved, placed and compacted in an extremely short period of time. Working two shifts per day, AA&G not only completed the project on time, but under budget. This 500-acre site is now the premier industrial center in Fontana, California.

While fulfilling its missions to grow core businesses organically through share gain and market growth; to drive market share within existing new business units; to expand its services; and to aggressively pursue operating improvement opportunities, AA&G is unwavering in its dedication to provide quality, on-time and cost-conscious services. This commitment has led to the company's participation in many public projects such as the Gowan Detention Basins, Buffalo Drainage Channel and Vegas Valley Wash.

The list of AA&G's services is extensive and includes paving, excavation, road and bridge construction, detention basins, concrete work and additional services in complete asphalt maintenance and aggregate production. In its primary grading operations, AA&G moved and placed over 105,000 cubic yards of material per day in 2001; and the paving division lays down an annual average of 325,000 tons of asphalt on highways, parking lots and homeowner association streets. As another understandable

point of pride for AA&G, its paving crew is an undeniable champion in its field, having placed 5,200 (195 truck-loads) of blacktop within required specifications in one 10-hour period, with a team of only 11 men — compared to an industry average of 3,500 tons for the same time period.

AA&G also takes a lead role in its professional and civic communities. The management team belongs to homebuilder associations, contractor groups and other allied business organizations, as well as organizations such as the UNLV Foundation, which is a nonprofit group that raises and manages private funds to enhance the university by strengthening its teaching, research and public service capabilities. AA&G also supports the Andre Agassi Foundation, which provides recreational and educational opportunities for at-risk boys and girls, assisting underprivileged, abused and abandoned children.

Service, speed and efficiency: these are the three "products" American Asphalt & Grading Company offers to its clients. As the only professionally managed competitor within the industry, AA&G is sure to continually grow and prosper, while providing a safe environment for its workers and contributing to the healthy growth of the communities it serves.

CARSON TAYLOR HARVEY, INC.

Carson Taylor Harvey, Inc. is a leading construction company with unique operational systems and services developed to meet the needs of specific clientele. These include: pre-construction consultation, cost analysis, general contracting, construction management, finance/build, design/build, program management, building maintenance and other services.

In southern Nevada, Carson Taylor Harvey, Inc. is overseen by a dynamic team of 35 professionals, outstanding people who are committed to improving the construction industry by delivering the highest caliber of construction possible. They accomplish this by working closely with their clients, encouraging them to remain involved throughout the entire construction process, and offering many valued clients warranties that extend beyond the industry standard.

Recently, the company completed several prominent projects in southern Nevada: the Las Vegas Springs Preserve Infrastructure and sound wall, the RTC-RFCD building, the central plant at the Las Vegas Convention Center, and the UNLV Foundation building. Other projects within the public sector include: an additional control tower at McCarran International Airport, infrastructure and a park project for the Aliante Nature

Discovery Park, a public library for the city of Henderson, and three command centers for the Las Vegas Police Department. Within the private sector, projects have ranged from Alamo and Thrifty Rent-a-Car centers to the Panevino Restaurant and several CVS pharmacies, including one located on the Las Vegas Strip.

> ## "We exist to build. And through the process of building, we strive to exceed our clients' expectations."

These projects exemplify the caliber of work performed by Carson Taylor Harvey and its mission to be an organization of dedicated construction professionals who are committed to attaining the highest level of customer satisfaction. They deliver a similar commitment within their community.

The company and its team members serve several organizations within southern Nevada, including the Natural History Museum, Frontier Girl Scouts, YMCA and United Way of Southern Nevada. The company also contributes to "Make a Difference Day" when employees volunteer to feed the homeless in downtown Las Vegas. Doug Carson and Peter Harvey are active participants in such community service projects and both are past AGC presidents.

Such dedication to the industry and commitment to community service has always been an important part of Carson Taylor Harvey's history. Originally founded as Carson Construction in 1946 by Don Carson, Carson Taylor Harvey has played an important role in the development of southern Nevada.

From a small office building for the Teamsters Union following World War II to construction work on some of the earliest gaming establishments in Las Vegas such as the El Cortez Hotel and the Las Vegas Club, Don Carson quickly earned an admirable reputation. In fact, many of the core values first introduced by Don were readily adopted and are still maintained by his son, Doug Carson, who took over the company in the mid 1970s. The company continued to excel as Carson Construction until 1999, when it was acquired by Taylor Construction Group (Des Moines, Iowa) and became Carson Taylor Harvey.

Since 1946, Taylor Construction Group has grown to become a leading national construction company with several subsidiary firms located in 6 states with projects in 25 states. Collectively, Taylor Construction Group's clients include some of the most sought after in the country and in every specialized sector of construction.

Within retail construction, Taylor Construction Group's experience ranges from simple tenant improvement projects to major regional malls. This includes the Coral Ridges Mall, an enclosed 1.2-million-square-foot regional shopping and entertainment center with a 700-seat food court, 10-screen state-of-the-art theater complex, children's play area, and NHL regulation ice arena. The mall is anchored by Dillards, Sears, JC Penney, Younkers, and Target.

With projects ranging from preschools to universities, the company has earned a reputation for new school construction and challenging educational renovations. This includes one of the first law libraries built in the 21st century, which opened on January 2, 2002, at the California Western School of Law. This four-story, 49,000-square-foot facility is home to more than 140,000 volumes.

By employing a proprietary fast track scheduling techniques and rigid budget guidelines, the company has proven invaluable to industrial projects such as warehousing, manufacturing, printing, heavy equipment, food processing, and cold storage. This includes a new 63,000-square-foot recycling center in Boulder, Colorado, a dual-purpose facility highlighted by an administration building and a processing center that are connected by a sky bridge.

Within the health care industry, Taylor Construction Group specializes in new facility construction and renovation that requires partnering with medical professionals and administrators. Within the public service sector, it is best known for medium-security prisons, county jails, detention facilities, police stations, courtroom projects, and parking structures. The latter includes the construction of a multilevel parking structure adjacent to an Olympic-size track and soccer field at San Diego State University.

For religious institutions, the company has completed dozens of churches, synagogues and mosques. For group retirement providers, it has constructed several senior living facilities. And for the hospitality industry, it has worked on many admired properties in the Midwest and across the western United States. In short, if there is an industry that requires specialized construction skills, Taylor Construction Group and Carson Taylor Harvey have the experience necessary to get the job done right.

As summed by Jack Taylor, CEO, "We exist to build. And through the process of building, we strive to exceed our clients' expectations."

Carter & Burgess/C&B Nevada

☐ Carter & Burgess, Inc. was established in Fort Worth, Texas, in 1939 by landscape architect Gene Carter and civil engineer John Burgess. The two childhood friends survived lean years to enjoy sunnier, more successful times together, in the process forging a strong bond that has served as the foundation for their dynamic, continually expanding company.

Gene and John weathered the Depression years working on Works Progress Administration projects in various parts of Texas. Soon they realized they could create a successful partnership by combining their skills; early jobs included military projects as the nation prepared to enter World War II. Both men served their country during the war, Burgess as a Marine in the Pacific Theater and Carter by continuing to work on projects at military bases in the United States.

John Burgess (Left) and Gene Carter (Right) in 1939

During the post-war boom Carter & Burgess grew rapidly as it took on a multitude of new projects. The company planned major residential and commercial developments in Fort Worth, undertook civilian airfield improvements throughout the Southwest, and continued its military work in the region, including air defense

> Today Carter & Burgess is a full-service, multidiscipline consulting firm with more than 2,300 employees in major metropolitan areas across the nation.

systems. During the 1960s the firm was involved in major urban renewal projects, and in 1967 it was selected to help plan and design Dallas/Fort Worth International Airport.

After incorporating in 1967, Carter & Burgess began to expand in its region, opening offices in Houston and Dallas. Although the real estate and financial markets bottomed-out in the Southwest during the 1980s, the company remained strong and active because of the diverse range of services it offered. More geographic expansion occurred in the 90s, and most engineering and architectural disciplines were adopted at this time.

Unlike many consulting firms, Carter & Burgess is organized by market sectors. The company's professionals believe that by continually building expertise in specific market sectors, clients will ultimately benefit because teams better understand the intricacies of their unique industries. These sectors include transportation programs, facilities, retail and distribution, land development, public works, urban design and planning, environmental, acoustic/theatre/communication and survey.

Today Carter & Burgess is a full-service, multidiscipline consulting firm with more than 2,300 employees in major metropolitan areas across the nation.

The Las Vegas Monorail

In 1995 the company acquired MEA in Las Vegas, which had served the Valley since 1979. The Las Vegas office of Carter & Burgess now employs more than 130 professionals and is considered one of the corporation's most highly recognized branches. The office offers a myriad of services including civil, structural, mechanical, electrical and traffic engineering, master planning, survey and program/construction management.

To better meet the needs of clients in Nevada, related entity C&B Nevada, Inc. was created in 2000 to provide architecture, interiors and planning. This combined pool of resources presents a range and breadth of expertise that can benefit any design project. C&B Nevada is recognized for providing expert attention to detail and a level of responsiveness that expedites projects. The firm's roots in sound engineering practices means designs are as solid as they are functional and aesthetically pleasing.

Carter & Burgess and C&B Nevada have helped to design the skyline of Las Vegas from civil design on multiple hotel/casinos to program management and engineering on the Las Vegas Monorail and architecture and engineering on the flashy CVS/pharmacy on the Strip.

Honesty and integrity have become hallmarks of all Carter & Burgess/C&B Nevada client relationships. A strong local presence, coupled with a service mentality, help distinguish the firms among A/E service providers and will lead to more success in the years to come.

CVS/pharmacy on the Las Vegas Strip

CENTURY 21 CONSOLIDATED

☐ Founded in 1983, CENTURY 21 Consolidated was one of the first offices established in Southern Nevada for the CENTURY 21 system. Today the company retains the values with which it operated in the beginning and currently ranks among the top 50 of a total of 6,600 CENTURY 21 offices throughout the United States. CENTURY 21 Consolidated is comprised of a highly knowledgeable and professional staff of experienced and ethical sales associates who are dedicated to imparting

quality service. With a talent for placing its clients first by keeping their best interests in mind, the company has encouraged many repeat visits. Consequently, CENTURY 21 Consolidated has established a reputation for leadership and high standards in the marketplace.

What was once only vast desert in the late 1940s, Las Vegas is now inundated with flamboyance, glitz and glamour. Along with its current environment comes non-stop action, incredible entertainment and luxurious living. Containing the cities of Las Vegas, Henderson, North Las Vegas, Boulder City and other unincorporated vicinities, the greater Las Vegas area totals 1.5 million in population. And with an average of 294 days where sun shines bright in the sky, it's an alluring area no matter what potential residents crave — from high-rise pampering to a sprawling waterside estate. Proud of its home, CENTURY 21 Consolidated has the resources and know-how to effectively find the perfect properties for all of its clients and customers.

CENTURY 21 Consolidated provides "full service" capabilities as a relocation and corporate relocation expert, giving individuals the power to buy or sell their homes. A division of the largest residential real estate sales organization in the world, the company helps customers move across town, across the country, or around the world. Furthermore, as a member of the relocation networks INRELCO, ERC, CGRN and MRN,

> ## CENTURY 21 Consolidated provides "full service" capabilities as a relocation and corporate relocation expert, giving individuals the power to buy or sell their homes.

CENTURY 21 Consolidated has greatly contributed to the professional standards with which relocation-affiliated organizations operate today.

In addition, the company has a property management and leasing department for the convenience of clients and is actively involved with associations dedicated to enhancing the Las Vegas valley. These associations include Nevada Development Authority, Greater Las Vegas Association of Realtors and Las Vegas Chamber of Commerce and Better Business Bureau. Furthermore, the company is one of the top women-owned businesses in Nevada.

As Las Vegas continues to grow, CENTURY 21 Consolidated remains centrally located to competently serve the entire Las Vegas valley. Under the leadership of Owner and Broker Bette Leal, the company and its 150 agents have flourished, earning numerous awards and recognition for their top performance. Bette began her career in real estate in 1968, almost immediately earning top agent status. In 1983 she was one of the first agents to join the CENTURY 21 system in Las Vegas and has been with it ever since, catering to her love of meeting new people and handling a variety of real estate challenges. Moreover, Bette happily takes an active role in the company's day-to-day business operations.

In 1989 Bette's daughter, Desiree, returned to Las Vegas after attending college in Europe and living in Puerto Vallarta, Mexico. Armed with a degree in International Business, she obtained her real estate license to work alongside her mother who also served as her mentor. It was after 24 years as a successful agent that Bette opted to move to the "other side of the real estate desk," which was when she became broker and owner of CENTURY 21 Consolidated in 1992. This enabled mother and daughter to harmoniously corroborate together to propel the company to one of the most successful CENTURY 21 offices in the United States.

As an esteemed facet of the CENTURY 21 system, Bette operates the CENTURY 21 Real Estate Academy, which is a pre-licensing school where students complete 90 hours of pre-licensing instruction to obtain and maintain their license to practice real estate in the state of Nevada. As the only one approved to conduct the academy, Bette manages instruction for those wishing to get started in real estate and those looking to continue practicing.

Both Bette and Desiree believe in treating their clients and customers with an equal amount of respect and integrity across the board. Whether they are in the market to purchase a $100,000 condominium or a $5 million estate, the women believe that all clients deserve equal diligence, hard work and commitment. CENTURY 21 Consolidated looks to engage the steps necessary to fulfill this commitment. With the latest in technology and the most advanced in training, CENTURY 21 Consolidated has a personal and professional integrity unsurpassed in the industry.

Bette and her employees passionately engage in community affairs, looking to enhance the state of the city. Not only does CENTURY 21 Consolidated focus on building a strong, local company within the worldwide CENTURY 21 system network, but it looks to reaffirm its sense of leadership and high standards through heavy involvement and volunteerism with nonprofit organizations

as well. Its work with Easter Seals has helped individuals with disabilities and special needs live improved lives — CENTURY 21 Consolidated supports the organization in addressing its members' life challenges and helping them to achieve personal goals. In addition, the company has worked substantially with Small Paws, an organization solely dedicated to the cause of animal rescue.

Because of its dedication to quality service and its ability to exceed clients' and customers' expectations significantly, the company has seen growth, profitability and success, earning it the Centurion office award year after year.

Believing that its customers deserve the finest service ever offered by any real estate organization, CENTURY 21 Consolidated provides it for them. Because of its dedication to quality service and its ability to exceed clients' and customers' expectations significantly, the company has seen growth, profitability and success, earning it the Centurion office award year after year. This award is given to CENTURY 21 offices that have exemplified the qualities that make the CENTURY 21 system the world's leading brand in real estate.

CHRISTOPHER HOMES

'Southern Nevada's Leading Builder of Luxury Homes'

For more than 22 years, the name Christopher Homes has been associated with excellence in luxury homebuilding. Long known as "Southern Nevada's Leading Builder of Luxury Homes," the company is widely recognized for introducing the newest, most innovative and exciting design concepts to the local housing market.

Christopher Homes was founded in 1981 by company CEO, J. Christopher Stuhmer, a second-generation Las Vegas homebuilder. Originally established as a builder of custom homes, the company soon expanded into building luxurious production homes, with an emphasis on larger and more elegant residential designs, more sophisticated architecture and unsurpassed opportunities for buyers to customize their selected homes.

The focus is on making the entire process as smooth and convenient as possible for each client.

A pioneer in the Southern Nevada luxury market, Christopher Homes has a time-honored reputation for continually raising the bar of excellence in architecture, interior design, design flexibility and client service. From stylish single-family residences to the most opulent multi-million-dollar custom estates, no other builder can offer more elegance, convenience and value.

Over the years, Christopher Homes' innovative residential designs have earned more than 100 awards on the local, regional and national levels, including multiple honors for "Home of the Year," "Best Custom Home in the Nation," "Best in American Living," and "America's Best Builder."

As an industry leader, Christopher Homes has also received a great deal of national media attention. Publications such as the *New York Times, Los Angeles Times, Wall Street Journal* and *Robb Report* have often called on the company for pertinent information regarding trends in the local and national markets. Management representatives of Christopher Homes have frequently

been asked to serve on judging panels for some of the housing industry's preeminent award competitions. In 2003 Christopher Homes was selected to build the show home for the International Builders Show, which was toured by more than 5,000 housing experts from around the world and named "Best Custom Home in the Nation" at the National Sales and Marketing Awards.

A sampling of neighborhoods that earned Christopher Homes the position of Southern Nevada's most successful luxury builder include Country Club Hills, Palisades, Vineyards, and Bellacere neighborhoods in the Summerlin master-planned community and The Christopher Collection, The Villas and The Enclave in the exclusive Southern Highlands Golf Course community in southwest Las Vegas.

Christopher Homes is also building opulent custom and luxury production homes in Park City, Utah. A client can have their custom home built on their choice of home site, or in one of Christopher Homes' exclusive neighborhoods.

The Christopher Homes custom home division continues to build some of the Las Vegas valley's most luxurious custom homes in such communities as Lake Las Vegas, Southern Highlands Golf Club, Seven Hills, Anthem, MacDonald Highlands and Summerlin. Custom home clients can have their personal dream home built on their choice of home site, plus enjoy the advantage of being able to consider architectural features from the many award-winning home designs Christopher Homes has created in the past. The focus is

on making the entire process as smooth and convenient as possible for each client.

The result is a long list of very satisfied homeowners. In fact, Christopher Homes has one of the best referral rates in the country.

Whether it's a luxurious production home or a custom estate, Christopher Homes is the name to trust.

Merlin Contracting & Developing, LLC

From exquisite postmodern palaces to quaint country cottage estates, Merlin Contracting & Developing, LLC has enriched the lives of homeowners throughout the greater Las Vegas region. Guided by founder Stephen Jones, the company has built a reputation as one of the finest high-end custom homebuilders in Las Vegas since it went into business over a decade ago.

The company's success stems from skills and practical construction wisdom that Steve acquired early on as an apprentice builder. For years he worked alongside an old-school craftsman named Audie Coker. Building small homes from the ground up, Steve soon learned to treat every detail with the utmost attention regardless of how small or seemingly insignificant. Working under the auspice that everything was held to the highest standard of quality and professional integrity, Steve and Audie completed numerous projects throughout the Las Vegas valley. During this educational time period Steve gained hands-on experience with each skill and trade of the

construction business. This comprehensive understanding of home building from start to finish is essential to building an outstanding, finely finished custom home and is the main ingredient that has separated Merlin Contracting from its competitors.

When Audie retired in 1989, Steve created Merlin Contracting & Developing, LLC. From the start, the company's main focus was on building custom homes. After finishing numerous homes in Spanish Trails, Merlin Contracting quickly earned a convincing reputation for excellence in custom home building throughout the valley, especially on the fast-growing west side.

Merlin has since completed many elegant custom homes in Las Vegas with diverse and notable achievements in Tournament Hills and Eagle Hills. Other exceptional examples include a large estate in Green Valley, one of only two homes built on Shadow Creek Golf Course, and a dozen elegantly finished units including the developer's penthouse at Park Towers, Las Vegas' most prestigious high-rise condominium. Throughout these projects, the

company's professional execution and meticulous attention to detail has always been at the forefront.

In the late 1990s, Summerlin, a planned community in Las Vegas, created a "Featured Builders Program" to manage and maintain quality control in custom lot development. Merlin was chosen as one of only eight builders that participated in the highly innovative and quality-driven program for a planned community that has since achieved national recognition.

In 1994 Steve brought in his brother, Bart, to share some of the responsibilities of the growing business. The company has continued to grow and currently employs seven superintendents, two finish carpenters, a labor crew and an office staff of five. Its team is comprised of a unique blend of individuals who offer a variety of experience and expertise and are committed to achieving only the finest results. The company collectively reaps its greatest reward in its clients' satisfaction.

In 2000 Merlin Contracting & Developing, LLC completed five custom homes, two commercial projects and numerous remodels. Merlin has also engaged in building and remodeling luxury high-rise condominiums at Park Towers. The Park Towers project represented a

new vehicle through which Merlin and its sub contractors showcased their craftsmanship and commitment to quality. Merlin, along with interior design partner Colours, Inc., were selected to upgrade the first luxury high-rise in Las Vegas.

Since then Merlin has been busy building and remodeling a diverse array of settings from 16,000-square-foot estates on 2.5 acres, to high-end remodels, to a 20th -floor luxury penthouse condominium.

Merlin's commitment to quality and integrity is exemplified in the fact that a number of the multimillion-dollar homes Merlin has completed were realized with a handshake rather than a contract. Old West commitment to quality and the long view as a part of a community create a level of trust special in the homebuilding field.

Merlin Contracting and Developing, LLC and Steve Jones have played a long and active role in Southern Nevada. As a member of the Nevada Homebuilders Association and Rotary Club and supporter of the Boy Scouts of America, Nevada Institute of Contemporary Art and board member of Boys Hope & Girls Hope, Merlin Contracting & Developing, LLC plans to be a supportive part of Las Vegas' growth for many years to come.

RE/MAX CENTRAL

▭ RE/MAX International began in Denver, Colorado, in 1973 as "a pad of paper and a dream" and has grown into a global real estate franchise network that spreads across 44 countries and eight territories, on six continents.

The revolutionary RE/MAX concept of enabling real estate professionals to maximize their business potential has evolved into an organization of more than 100,492 sales associates in more than 5,401 offices worldwide. RE/MAX has 29 franchises in the Greater Las Vegas Area.

One of the top producing franchises is RE/MAX CENTRAL with over 120 outstanding Professional Realtors. Their Outstanding Production makes RE/MAX CENTRAL one of the top producing RE/MAX franchises in the Southwest.

RE/MAX CENTRAL has two offices in prime locations. RE/MAX CENTRAL is the only RE/MAX in Summerlin located on West Charleston Boulevard. The RE/MAX CENTRAL Sahara Office is located on West Sahara Avenue where over 50,000 cars travel daily.

RE/MAX CENTRAL publishes its own Magazine, *LAS VEGAS HOMES BY PRICE*. *LAS VEGAS HOMES BY PRICE* features homes in price order allowing consumers to shop value by comparing areas by price.

RE/MAX Sales Associates, on average, lead the industry in production, experience, and professional designations, and the Las Vegas office is no exception. With thousands of Las Vegas homes for sale, finding the

right home in the Las Vegas real estate market can be a daunting task. RE/MAX CENTRAL can sell new homes and resales throughout the entire Las Vegas Valley, Henderson, North Las Vegas and Summerlin, America's best-selling, master-planned community.

RE/MAX CENTRAL provides a comprehensive "list to sell" service that includes Internet advertising, virtual tours, advertising in *LAS VEGAS HOMES BY PRICE* magazine, and even leader board exposure of over 50,000 cars that pass the Sahara Office every day.

The red, white and blue RE/MAX balloon, with its "Above the Crowd!®"slogan, is one of the most recognizable business logos in the world. With nearly 90 RE/MAX hot air balloons around the globe, RE/MAX has the world's largest balloon fleet. Recognized as an industry leader, RE/MAX sells more real estate than any other real estate organization in the world.

In 1997 RE/MAX Sales Associates were involved in more than 1 million sales transaction sides within a single year in the United States alone — an industry milestone. The audited production figures represent the most transaction sides in a single year ever recorded by any real estate network. The RE/MAX network has repeated the feat since. RE/MAX stands for "real estate maximums." In exchange for paying a management fee and a share of the monthly office overhead, RE/MAX sales associates keep the maximum allowed amount of their commissions and receive the many benefits of RE/MAX programs and services. By offering associates maximum commissions and maximum career freedom, RE/MAX influenced competitors to re-examine and adjust their own policies toward sales agents, thus dramatically changing the industry.

As the network grew, renowned for its top producers and quality service to consumers, so did support programs, making RE/MAX a dynamic force in real estate education and technology.

RE/MAX Satellite Network (RSN) has launched "Review," an online video sales site offering 40 program titles featuring the industry's best educators and trainers. Included in the initial offering are the first five programs from the network's highly successful "RE/MAX Coaching Hall of Fame" with industry speakers, Brian Buffini, Richard Robbins and Howard Brinton. This new service is available only through RE/MAX Mainstreet, the organization's proprietary extranet, where streaming video samples are available for each title. Associates can build a video library, view programs they may have missed, or give them as gifts to prospects and clients. RSN was the first and remains the only proprietary real estate television network. Programs are broadcast over the DISH Network, reaching 60,000 RE/MAX offices in nearly 6,000 residential and office downlinks throughout North America.

In a business environment of mergers and acquisitions, RE/MAX is the only major real estate network still owned and directed by its founders. RE/MAX's commitment to its membership has led to an ever-increasing number of accolades from the business community at large — including selection of RE/MAX as the best in the business. In its annual ranking of top franchises, *Entrepreneur* magazine named RE/MAX the

number one real estate services franchise in 2000. On the consumer front, *Worth* magazine honored RE/MAX in both 1999 and 2000 with its prestigious "Readers' Choice" award as the best real estate brokerage. RE/MAX — now an established industry leader — celebrated its 30th anniversary in 2003.

Community involvement is highly valued at all levels of the RE/MAX organization — from individual associates to RE/MAX offices, regions, and RE/MAX CENTRAL International.

RE/MAX marketing and charity fund raising take on many forms: Most recently, RE/MAX has become a national co-sponsor of the Breast Cancer Survivor Recognition Program at Komen Race for the Cure events. The RE/MAX organization has also been the official real estate sponsor of Children's Miracle

Network since 1992. Each year, about 20 charities host fund-raising golf tournaments at Sanctuary, the private course of RE/MAX International co-founders Dave and Gail Liniger. RE/MAX International is the first major sponsor of The Wildlife Experience, a conservation and community center promoting understanding of the natural world and its conservation through art and education.

RE/MAX CENTRAL — now an established leader in the Las Vegas real estate community looks ahead to even greater development and success in its next quarter century.

All these venues and more represent the RE/MAX CENTRAL network's commitment to community involvement, serving the public beyond its real estate needs.

Among RE/MAX promotional efforts is the RE/MAX World Long Drive Championship, featuring the longest hitters in golf. And you'll find RE/MAX on the speedway as well as the title sponsor for the ARCA RE/MAX Series, a nationwide auto-racing tour viewed by hundreds of thousands of fans live and millions more on television.

The RE/MAX hot air balloon fleet's most unique member – the giant, house-shaped "Soaring Home" balloon – makes appearances throughout the year across the United States.

TSUNAMI PROPERTIES, INC.

☐ Sue Naumann, President and Corporate Broker of Tsunami Properties, Inc., a residential real estate brokerage and property management company, brings nearly three decades of real estate experience and expertise to the table. Sue is trained, experienced, and dedicated and her unique approach to business has allowed her to shine as a REALTOR® and now as an independent business owner.

Tsunami Properties was first established as a sole proprietorship in the summer of 2002. Although the company was new to Las Vegas, Sue was certainly not new to the real estate business. With customer service a top priority and Sue's mentoring nature, the company soon outgrew its small space. Sue, with her partner (also her biggest supporter and fan), her husband John, decided to incorporate and expand the business. Tsunami Properties, Inc. has moved into a beautiful, upscale 2600-square-foot office space in the Marnell Corporate Center, centrally located in the Southeast,

just off Las Vegas Boulevard and Sunset. John and Sue envisioned an office that was state-of-the art and one in which their agents could prosper. When it comes to her agents, Sue believes, "Their goals are my goals. I want them to be as successful in real estate as they want to be."

Sue is an active member of the Greater Las Vegas Association of REALTORS® (GLVAR) where she has served on numerous committees and workgroups through the years and now serves as a Director. She also serves as a Director for the Nevada Association of REALTORS® (NVAR) and is a current member of the National Association of REALTORS® (NAR). She is a 2002 graduate of LeadershipNVAR, a statewide program designed to nurture future leaders. "The LeadershipNVAR program was an invaluable experience," says Sue, "and the friendships forged and the skills and lessons learned in this innovative program will always have an impact on the decisions I make in my life, both personal and business-related."

The tremendous success that Sue has achieved can be directly attributed to the diligent work ethic instilled in her at a very young age by her parents who always encouraged her to do the best job she could possibly do in everything she attempted. Working as a messenger for a title company in Reno might have been a dead-end job for some, but Sue was inspired to excel and eventually advanced to the Chief Title Officer position. She was first licensed as a real estate agent in 1979 but continued to work in the Title Industry. Later in her career, she worked as a paralegal for a bankruptcy attorney who was the attorney for a large mortgage company bankruptcy case. She handled all of the property sale motions for court and anything that was real estate related. The title and bankruptcy experience Sue acquired has proven to be invaluable while working as a REALTOR®. Sue brings to her industry a level of expertise, wisdom, and motivation that is surpassed by very few.

In addition to her volunteer service at the Greater Las Vegas Association of REALTORS®, Naumann has also been very active in the Women's Council of REALTORS® as the 2003 Local Chapter President and, most recently, as Secretary-Treasurer for the State Chapter. The Women's Council of REALTORS® is a national organization with more than 14,000 members. Named #17 of the top 30 organizations for women in the United States, the Women's Council of REALTORS® provides a huge referral network and encourages its

members to "achieve their individual potential for success" by creating business opportunities and providing educational offerings. Sue has also gone the extra mile to earn a bachelor's degree in English Literature with a Business Administration Minor from the University of Nevada, Reno and designations respected in the real estate industry as well: the Certified Residential Specialist (CRS) designation; the Graduate REALTOR® Institute (GRI) designation; and the Leadership Training Graduate (LTG) designation. She is also the only person in Henderson to achieve the e-PRO 500 designation, which was awarded when Sue was chosen as one of 500 REALTORS® nationally to participate in a National Association of REALTORS® pilot program for internet real estate professionals. As 2002 marked the 50th anniversary for the Nevada Association of REALTORS®, Sue was also recognized as one of Nevada's "50 Golden REALTORS®" at the annual convention held at Lake Tahoe.

All the experience and knowledge that Sue has acquired in her career qualifies her to be a mentor to both "seasoned" agents and agents new to the business. She is patient and enthusiastic and prefers a one-on-one approach when training new agents, walking them through each transaction until they feel comfortable and confident, all the while helping more "seasoned," experienced agents troubleshoot problem transactions. She also encourages more continuing education than is required for license renewal so agents can keep abreast of the latest in industry trends. In an effort to keep Tsunami Properties, Inc. on the cutting edge, Sue prides herself in having all the bells and whistles when it comes to the latest in technology to enhance the client's (and the agent's) ultimate experience.

Moving to Las Vegas from Reno in 1991, Sue began working in real estate in the Las Vegas area, first with one national franchise company and then with another, where she remained until 2002 when she decided to venture out on her own. Her friends had called her "Sue-Nami" for years so the name Tsunami Properties seemed a natural progression. As a working Broker, Sue is very in-tune with what is happening "in the trenches" and can empathize with the problems her agents are experiencing on a day-to-day basis.

As Tsunami Properties, Inc. continues its mission of providing the best and most up-to-date service possible, Sue and her agents will continue to offer the professional, personalized service that everyone deserves in

> "We want to be the company one thinks of when considering buying, selling, investing, or renting. We want to build relationships and have clients for life. Whether selling or buying, if they are surfing Las Vegas," says Sue "we want prospective clients to *Surf Tsunami First.*"

each and every real estate transaction. Through her commitment to the real estate industry, Sue will continue to support and protect the professional image of real estate professionals by creating greater customer satisfaction through the ethical, honest, and responsible practice of real estate. "We want to be the company one thinks of when considering buying, selling, investing, or renting. We want to build relationships and have clients for life. Whether selling or buying, if they are surfing Las Vegas," says Sue, "we want prospective clients to *Surf Tsunami First.*"

CENTEX HOMES

☐ Suffice it to say that Las Vegas is a booming city, the jewel of a young and prosperous state. New Las Vegas neighborhoods blossom like a desert rose and their new homes glisten brighter than the desert sun. This marks yet another chapter in the American Dream. And often — in both Las Vegas and beyond — Centex Homes provides Americans with these magnificent new homes.

Centex Homes was founded in Dallas in 1950 and Centex Homes dba Real Homes is a Las Vegas-based division of the company. From the beginning, Centex Homes has embraced cutting-edge technological advances in new home construction. In the 1950s Centex Homes began development on the nation's first master-planned community — Elk Grove Village — in Illinois. As early as 1957, Centex introduced underground utilities and phone lines — amenities that, outside of Las Vegas, are still beyond the reach of many neighborhoods.

In 1968 Centex was incorporated and the company began trading stock publicly a year later. At that time, Centex Homes became a separate business unit focused on residential construction. Historically, Centex Homes has specialized in building neighborhoods of detached, single-family homes, however the company has recently branched out. Centex's products now include residential construction segments like

value-oriented, entry-level homes; on-your-lot homes; active adult communities; resort/second homes; and urban, in-fill neighborhoods. In total, Centex Homes is one of the nation's leading and largest builders and operates in more than 90 markets in 26 states.

Centex Homes' illustrious, 54-year history has been capped by a gamut of awards. In fact, since 1968, Centex has been the only builder to rank within the Top 10 builders on Professional Builder's "Giant 400" list each year running. In 1998 Centex Homes was named "Builder of the Year" by *Professional Builder's* magazine. Centex Corporations is a Fortune 250 Company. Moreover, since 2000, Centex has been named the nation's most admired engineering and construction firm by *Fortune* magazine three times — a testament to the fact that Centex has emerged as a formidable player in the home building industry.

Centex's impressive customer service has become a model for competitors. Why? For starters, during the home-construction process field managers treat each home as if it is custom-built. They make weekly phone calls to customers and conduct pre-occupancy orientations and pre-closing walk-throughs to ensure their homeowners' satisfaction.

Improved quality control mechanisms will continue to underpin Centex's evolution. Today in-line inspection practices range from the verification of the quality of the wood that goes into construction to the assembly process itself. As a result, Centex homes have become more energy efficient and stronger.

Many believe that the main reason people are drawn to Las Vegas in droves is because it offers unparalleled entertainment and good weather. This is indeed true. Yet the fact that Las Vegas' homes and companies such as Centex glisten a little brighter than the rest doesn't hurt either.

PECCOLE NEVADA CORP.

William "Bill" Peccole began turning his imagination into reality in 1949. Envisioning golf courses and homes spanning Las Vegas' vast western valley, he entered into a series of purchases and exchanges with the railroad and the Bureau of Land Management. He eventually acquired over 3,000 acres of land on the west side of the Las Vegas Valley.

Peccole was born in Stockton, California, and moved to Las Vegas with his father and brother when he was 18 years old. On arriving in the area, he helped his father with various business endeavors. Bill went on to graduate from the University of Nevada, Reno, and Springfield College. After serving as a Captain in the Army Air Corp during World War II, Bill returned to Las Vegas and opened Peccole Insurance Company. At the same time, he began to develop real estate in Las Vegas.

In 1949, Bill Peccole was elected to the Las Vegas City Council, and in 1953 he married Wanda Lamb, a member of a prominent pioneer Nevada family. They reared three daughters, and eventually had 16 grandchildren. Together, they went on to build the first enclosed shopping mall in Las Vegas, the Charleston Plaza Mall, followed a few years later by the Westland Mall. Later developments include Canyon Gate, a residential golf and tennis country club development; Peccole Ranch, a master planned community of over 2,000 homes with school and park areas; and several commercial shopping areas. Peccole Ranch is home to a state-of-the-art medical and surgery center, the Thomas & Mack Medical Plaza. As dedicated advocates of education, community safety, and the arts, Bill and Wanda donated the land for the Sahara West Library in Peccole Ranch, the Durango Fire Station, and later established the Wanda Lamb Peccole Center of the Arts at the Meadows School.

In 1993 Bill and Wanda established Peccole Nevada Corporation to carry on their legacy. Two years later Peccole Nevada began Queensridge, its largest project to date. Inspired by Bill's Italian origins, Wanda's eye for aesthetics shaped Queensridge, the Italian themed development situated on 1,000 acres of high desert.

This private, guard-gated enclave includes a 27-hole Johnny Miller/Chi Chi Rodriguez designed golf course. This unique golf course utilizes land which could not support building structures to create a celebrated communitywide amenity. Today, Queensridge is one of the most prestigious addresses in Las Vegas. With large custom and semi-custom homes, the community enjoys lush landscaping, rose gardens, lakes, and breathtaking views of the Red Rock mountains and sweeping views of all of downtown Las Vegas.

The Peccole Nevada Corporation has successfully maintained the standard of excellence established by Bill and Wanda Peccole.

One Queensridge Place, the crowning jewel in Queensridge, will be the first luxury high-rise development in the city. Two-story penthouse residences top the single 14-story tower as well as the three, 18-story towers. These residences, featuring full amenities, incredible city, golf course, and mountain views, will truly be custom homes in a vertical environment.

Peccole Nevada Corporation developed the first suburban "lifestyle" commercial shopping centers in Las Vegas. Home to the first Whole Foods Market in Nevada, these centers feature premier national retailers including Williams-Sonoma, Ann Taylor, The Gap, Pottery Barn, Talbots, Chico's, and others. Each is built in the Peccole tradition, with beautiful design and lush landscaping to insure a memorable shopping experience.

Peccole Nevada Corporation today continues to set standards of excellence. As one of Las Vegas' most prominent real estate developers, they are dedicated to their clients and the properties they develop. They have a vested interest in this desert land that is their heritage and home.

BUSINESS & FINANCE

A wide array of Las Vegas companies and institutions contribute
to the financial growth, security and success of scores of local and
international individuals and companies.

BankWest of Nevada

☐ Endeavoring to provide the highest quality in banking, BankWest of Nevada takes the time to develop direct and valuable business partner relationships with clients. Implementing professional and competent banking through a plethora of personal and business services, the financial institution ensures feelings of security and organization for all customers who entrust their accounts with it.

As one of its available personal services, BankWest offers customers an "Access ATM" card that enables them entry into their checking or savings accounts 24 hours a day, seven days a week. With this card, they can withdraw cash — up to $1,000 per 24-hour period — make deposits at BankWest of Nevada branch ATMs, transfer money between checking and savings accounts and verify account balances at literally thousands of ATMs in the United States and throughout the world. Moreover, a member of the Plus System®, Star System® and Interlink®, BankWest provides the most advanced in convenience banking.

The financial institution also offers a "DirectLine Card," which is a combined ATM and Visa® check card. With this card, customers can expediently make purchases at various shopping locations. Clients' payments are automatically withdrawn from their checking accounts and they are detailed on a regular monthly statement. Similar to the "Access ATM" card, customers can withdraw cash up to $1,000 per 24-hour period, make

deposits, transfer money and verify account balances at ATMs.

BankWest's certificates of deposit come at competitive rates and with maturities ranging from seven days to 24 months. With them, customers can earn a higher fixed rate of interest with the commitment of funds for a designated length of time. As members of BankWest, customers can also access a time deposit open account, which is a time deposit that offers a maturity of 180 days and earns a competitive interest rate. Unlike a certificate of deposit, they may make deposits and withdrawals and still earn a competitive fixed rate of interest.

In the checking account arena, BankWest offers a "Success Account," which is created for individuals who enjoy the convenience of a checking account with unlimited check writing availability. Once customers open a "Success Account" with the bank and maintain a required minimum daily balance, they can conduct banking without paying a monthly service charge.

Supplementary to its array of personal services, BankWest of Nevada also imparts a wide range of financial services for all types of businesses.

With credit cards, BankWest enables the buying power it takes to meet customers' every need. Specifically, those who qualify can apply for the convenience of a VISA® credit card, which permits immediate cash advances at thousands of locations worldwide. In addition, customers receive powerful charge account privileges at over 1 million retail outlets and professional locations throughout the world.

Keeping up with modern capabilities, BankWest offers "NetlineTM," the easiest, safest and most convenient banking available online in the marketplace. Secure and available 24 hours, "Netline" provides:

- Account information including account balances, history, statements, and transaction activity;
- Check images including a view of the front and back of checks paid against customers' accounts;
- Bill payments, which are setup on a recurring basis or as a one-time payment made to businesses or individuals;
- Funds management, where BankWest transfers funds between customers' accounts in different locations;
- Loan payments, where the bank makes payments on customers' loans;
- Order checks, where customers can place check orders directly through Clarke American;
- Stop payments that customers can place on checks to prevent fraud;
- Savings bonds, where BankWest orders savings bonds directly from the U.S. Treasury Department;
- Email access so that customers can submit correspondence directly to BankWest employees;
- Automated alerts, where BankWest sends automatic email alerts for balances or for personal reminders;
- Data export, where customers can export their account history to Microsoft Money, Quicken 98 or higher, Quickbooks 2004 or higher, or spreadsheet software.

BankWest also provides a multitude of home mortgages. With its home purchase loan option, the financial institution helps customers understand all of the advantages of home ownership. In addition, the bank advises them on the home-buying process, provides financing options, calculates payments, helps during the application process and keeps them informed of rates and costs. With a strong team of mortgage loan professionals, individuals and families can obtain the home of their dreams in the most cost-efficient manner possible.

Another personal services option available with BankWest is its "Premium EquityLine," where homeowners can receive a convenient revolving line of credit that provides them with an opportunity for valuable tax benefits, sending kids to college, paying for medical expenses, purchasing new furniture, taking a dream vacation, financing a start-up business, consolidating bills and purchasing a new vehicle or RV.

For those instances where customers need additional cash in a hurry, BankWest permits them to initiate advances against their "Success Account" for any amount up to their credit limit. To help them cover expected or unexpected expenses, they can repay the used portion of the loan in full or in monthly installments. Thus, there is no need to worry about overdrawn accounts.

In addition, BankWest has secured loans where customers can obtain extra cash without disturbing investments — an option ideal for savers and investors that need cash for a variety of reasons. BankWest's unsecured loans, on the other hand, save patrons money on their high interest credit card balances, helping them to pay for major purchases, handle personal expenses, consolidate bills, take luxurious vacations, manage college tuition, or pay an unexpected tax bill.

BankWest's personal savings accounts are a classic investment tool for all ages that earns interest without high balance requirements. By obtaining such an account, customers can make six withdrawals per quarter without a charge and accounts earn a competitive interest rate on all collected balances.

Supplementary to its array of personal services, BankWest of Nevada also imparts a wide range of financial services for all types of businesses. The banking professionals at the financial institution believe that its

clients' businesses come first and as such, employees initially perform a detailed analysis of all their banking needs. Following this analysis, customers then get the competent assistance that they require to fulfill these needs.

As part of its business-service offerings, BankWest has certificates of deposits; time deposit open accounts, which tender a maturity of 180 days; and checking accounts. With its business checking accounts option, the bank provides clients with an earnings credit based on balances to offset monthly maintenance fees. Furthermore, customers enjoy the benefits of unlimited check writing and unlimited deposits.

BankWest of Nevada is highly committed to reinvest in the communities where it conducts business to ensure a brighter future for everyone.

Another type of business checking account, BankWest's "Business NOW Account" allows clients under sole proprietorship and nonprofit charitable corporations or organizations to earn interest on the funds in their accounts. In addition, clients can write an unlimited number of checks as long as they maintain a $2,000 minimum opening balance.

Putting the bank ahead of the competition, BankWest conveniently offers a courier service that comes directly to clients' businesses during regular business hours to pick-up or deliver banking transactions. BankWest's couriers are available to transport deposits, correspondence and other pertinent items to or from its various locations.

Furthermore, BankWest of Nevada offers business clients a VISA® credit card specifically designed to meet every financial need, "NetlineTM" and commercial real estate loans. Commercial real estate loans are term loans that are secured by income-producing real estate for investors or owners and are generally used to finance

or refinance property. Term loans are individually tailored to financing needs and can have either variable or fixed interest rates for a period of up to 25 years.

BankWest's construction loans offer a line of credit for a sum certain. With a construction loan, the money is advanced through a flexible construction management process as funds are needed to pay for hard or soft costs. During the loan's term, clients pay monthly interest only on the outstanding balance. The dollar amount needed for these payments may be included in total costs so that customers do not have to pay "out of pocket." BankWest also offers construction financing for office, industrial, retail and residential subdivisions.

Other loans that BankWest presents are equipment loans, letters of credit, and for any other capital need such as equipment leasing, hard money real estate loans, or those loans funded by mortgage-backed securities. In the area of residential construction, BankWest offers owner-occupants the easiest, most flexible construction loan available — it has very competitive pricing, comes with professional assistance, possesses no application or underwriting fees, is accompanied by flexible construction administration programs, pays monthly interest on the outstanding balance and incurs no pre-payment penalties.

BankWest's revolving line of credit provides the flexibility to take advantage of business opportunities as they arise. Businesses can borrow, repay and borrow again up to the original amount agreed to by BankWest throughout the life of the loan. This type of credit facility is typically repaid from business' operating cash flow. Furthermore, customers can use a line of credit to fund seasonal changes in inventory and receivables, take advantage of vendor discounts and meet unexpected cash needs.

To help small businesses expand, BankWest's Small Business Administration (SBA) offers a variety of financing options to them. For instance, the institution provides long-term loans for machinery and equipment, a general working capital loan, a revolving line of credit and a micro-loan.

A secured commercial loan from BankWest helps to fund its customers' equipment purchases, finance their real estate, extend their working capital and restructure their debt. With such a loan, clients receive customized repayment terms, competitive pricing to meet the needs of all types of situations and assistance from loan officers who bestow the expertise that it takes to help clients make the right decisions for their businesses. With unsecured commercial loans, BankWest also helps to fund equipment purchases, finance real estate, extend working capital and restructure debt.

BankWest's beneficial repertoire also includes merchant services that come with reliable, low-cost processing. With the bank's "Merchant Bankcard," businesses can process their point of sale (POS) and credit card purchases. These services also provide global card acceptance capability — its network accepts MasterCard®, VISA®, Discover Card®, American Express®, Diners Club®/Carte Blanc® and other private label/proprietary cards; competitive pricing; support after the sale; and an enhancement to business image.

BankWest's "Business Money Market Account" is a convenient investment account available to all businesses. This option grants immediate access to money and check writing capabilities while earning competitive interest rates on balances. With a $3,000 minimum opening balance, clients are not required to pay a monthly service charge.

In association with its third-party payroll partners, BankWest offers payroll processing for companies, helping them to avoid in-house processing time and costs that come out of profits. With a quality, cost-effective payroll processing referral service, companies can avoid check fraud losses and can take advantage of BankWest's positive pay service. This pay service is the most secure and operative mechanism to date for controlling check fraud losses. Through a continuously updated issue file, BankWest is able to successfully identify potentially fraudulent checks, enabling early detection and unauthorized-check return prior to the expiration of federally regulated deadlines.

With a business savings account, businesses can build their capital and put excess funds to work. In fact, they can make six withdrawals per quarter without incurring a charge and their accounts earn a competitive interest rate on all collected balances.

Easing the process of banking, BankWest's wire transfer services offer customers expedient, accurate, and secure fund collection and disbursement. Permitting businesses to receive or send funds electronically or via the Federal Reserve Communication System, transmittance is fulfilled quickly with minimal risk. For incoming wire service, the bank has the resources that businesses need to receive wires from their customers, regardless of the systems they use. Secure and delivered promptly, the financial institution reduces risk and puts those funds to work immediately for participating companies. With wire service options, customers receive heightened security and impeccable accuracy in addition to speed. In person, via telephone, fax, or "NetlineTM," through its wire transfer services, the bank helps customers to better manage their cash flow.

Under the Community Reinvestment Act (CRA), BankWest's federal regulator, the Federal Deposit Insurance Corporation (FDIC) evaluates the financial institution on its credit-criteria fulfillment. In its most recent CRA examination, BankWest received an "outstanding" CRA rating on meeting needs.

BankWest of Nevada is highly committed to reinvest in the communities where it conducts business to ensure a brighter future for everyone. Striving both as a company and as individuals, the bank "lends a helping hand to its community with competence and compassion" to improve the quality of life for area residents and business people. With BankWest, it is not only the extensive assortment of services that keep its customers returning, but it is the hearts of its employees and its caring community service that helps them feel confident that their banking issues are being handled by the best.

Las Vegas Chamber of Commerce

Since its incorporation in 1905, the metro area of Las Vegas has doubled in size every 10 years. Although the gaming and tourism industries play a major role in its amazing growth, the greater Las Vegas Valley wouldn't be what it is today without the support and contributions of the Las Vegas Chamber of Commerce (LVCC).

Founded in 1911, the LVCC has established itself as the third-largest local chamber of commerce in the United States. With over 7,000 members, the LVCC creates a cohesive community where big and small businesses alike enjoy a strong local economy. Through

innovative programs, community and business services, lobbying efforts and networking events, the LVCC has helped shape the economic growth of this booming city. It's no wonder *Forbes* Magazine and the Milken Institute voted Las Vegas the "third best place to be to do business in the U.S." in 2002.

Working closely with local and state governments since its inception, the Chamber has played a key role in such projects as:
- The construction of the Hoover Dam in the 1930s;
- The creation of the Livewire Fund (now the LVCVA) in 1944 to help promote Las Vegas as a vacation spot;
- The creation of the Las Vegas Better Business Bureau in 1955;
- The creation of Las Vegas Events — bringing major sporting and media events to the area — in 1982; and
- The 1994 establishment of the Government Affairs Committee that has led the Chamber to many candidate endorsement and legislative victories.

Governed by a volunteer board of trustees, counseled by the Board of Advisors and served by a professional staff of over 60, the LVCC has recently added several noteworthy and award-winning achievements to its track record. Believing that education is the cornerstone of growth and development for Southern Nevada, the LVCC started Workforce 2010, a three-tiered plan to increase the quality of the work force in Southern Nevada. The first tier of the work force preparedness program focuses on supporting K-12 education. The next phase will include identifying and mentoring emerging talent, which will include adult literacy efforts. The final phase will focus on mentoring graduating high school students.

Through its affiliation with Las Vegas Parties, a partnership of local businesses and civic interests, the LVCC has also been highly influential in transportation improvements including the widening of Interstate 15 — the highway that links Southern California and Southern Nevada. Since the free flow of traffic is essential to the Las Vegas economy and quality of life, the Chamber has supported this project from its pre-planning stages.

Also in the planning stages is a high-speed rail line connecting Las Vegas to Los Angeles. So far the Chamber has been instrumental in obtaining approval for construction of this super train up to the state line that borders California.

Preview Las Vegas is an annual event that the LVCC co-sponsors with the Nevada Development Authority. More than 1,750 business owners and executives gather to hear local and national speakers outline their views on the coming year of business in Las Vegas. Covering such topics as economics, real estate and development, gaming and hospitality, technology, education and transportation, Preview Las Vegas has proven to be the No.1 business-forecasting event of the year. Knowing what the future holds helps business executives adapt wisely, leading to greater profitability and growth.

The Chamber hosts over 100 events and services a year including:
- Customer Service Excellence, honoring customer service excellence throughout the county;
- The Community Achievement Awards, recognizing exceptional community leaders in 11 fields; and
- A CEO/Principal for a Day exchange.

The Chamber also offers a variety of executive development programs including the Business Education Series and Leadership Las Vegas.

Since tourism plays a major role in the Las Vegas business community, a significant focal point for the Chamber is visitor services. The Chamber receives over 275,000 page views per month on its Web site. In addition, the Chamber distributes more than 16,000 Wedding Guides and 40,000 Relocation Guides each year.

As a member of the Las Vegas Chamber of Commerce, the list of benefits seems endless. Members have access to cost-effective advertising rates in all of the Chamber's publications including its monthly newsletter, *The Business Voice*, which reaches more than 10,000 business executives. Members are also given a free listing on the Chamber's Web site, instantly opening doors to a global market. The Chamber provides members with monthly reports detailing how many times their business has been referred through the Chamber's information center and accessed via the Chamber Web

site. In addition, the Chamber's Visitor Center staff provides referrals to more than 50,000 phone inquiries and walk-in visitors each year.

Members also benefit from networking events such as luncheons, mixers, seminars and workshops. These events provide members the opportunity to meet and mingle in a pressure free, relaxed environment. The LVCC offers discounted services including group health insurance, workers compensation insurance and discounted office supplies to help businesses reduce expenses.

To help shape the community, the LVCC offers members opportunities to participate in programs whose outcomes have profound effects on the quality of education, transportation, air quality and other social and civic issues. The Grassroots Organization for Action and Leadership (GOAL) is just one such service where members can become more involved with governmental processes. In 2001 the Chamber proclaimed a major victory by defeating a union-sponsored four percent

business income tax initiative. The Chamber's actions spared businesses over $250 million a year in new taxes. The Chamber also supports programs that give members the chance to reach out to the community. Some of these programs are Connect for Kids at the Library, Business Mentorship for the Homeless, Clark County Reads and We Care.

As the Las Vegas Chamber of Commerce continues to be the biggest business lobbying group in the state and the most influential "voice of business" in Clark County, a prosperous future for the Las Vegas Valley is a sure bet.

(Left)
Chamber President and CEO Kara Kelley (left) shown here with Nevada Governor Kenny Guinn. The Las Vegas Chamber of Commerce is a strong political force in Nevada and is active in protecting small business in government affairs.

(Right)
Chamber members enjoy more than 100 networking opportunities each year. The Chamber also offers a variety of professional development seminars to give members the tools they need to succeed in business.

Nevada First Bank

Some companies find themselves attempting to be all things to all people, and over time, they find that's not successful for their customers or themselves. The defining difference for Nevada First Bank is its steadfast commitment to be the business bank of choice in Southern Nevada. By maintaining the focus on serving business customers and their specific needs, Nevada First Bank has developed a loyal following and continues to grow with new customers.

The bank was founded in 1998 by a diverse group of local community leaders. The first financial center opened on Sahara Avenue near Palace Station, and two additional financial centers were added to serve the East and West parts of the Valley. In addition, in June of 2001, Nevada First Bank located its corporate headquarters and an additional financial center near the intersection of North Rainbow Boulevard and I-95. In June of 2004 the bank opened a new financial center in the Green Valley area and is scheduled to open a new branch soon in Reno.

The leadership team at Nevada First Bank includes board members who hold prominent posts at companies around the Valley. While a typical board may meet monthly or quarterly, the board members of Nevada First Bank meet weekly to discuss customers' needs. President and CEO Arvind Menon explains, "Our bank's officers and board of directors not only lend us their business expertise and integrity, they contribute to our ability to advance Southern Nevada's financial growth. And they know how to run a successful bank — like a successful business." Nevada First Bank is comprised of local entrepreneurs who are experienced in running the kinds of businesses that their clients are running.

To serve the changing needs of its customers, Nevada First Bank offers a range of business banking services, including commercial loans, cash management and online banking beyond what might be expected from a community bank. It is possible, for example, for a customer to view cancelled checks and other documents online. Nevada First Bank has introduced a new Positive Pay service that has proven to be effective in preventing fraud by keeping people from duplicating or forging checks. These are the types of services that truly benefit the bank's customers and add genuine value.

All of these services are presented by an outstanding group of Nevada First Bank employees. Menon and the mangement team are extremely proud of the banks 75+ associates and the personal service they provide to customers. "It's an incredible group that we have attracted to work here," beams Menon. "As we grow, we'll continue to attract the best of the best."

The bank customizes a package of services for prospective business customers, many of whom are referrals from other customers, and expands or adjusts those services as the business's needs change over time. Able to handle all their banking needs either via the telephone, speaking directly with associates here in Las Vegas, or FirstNet — the bank's online banking program — some customers rarely need to visit a financial center. Many customers use the extensive, free courier services offered by the bank, saving valuable time for controllers or other employees.

The primary goal is to successfully grow the bank with high-quality businesses by providing banking services that the Nevada First Bank board members would like to receive in their own businesses. At Nevada First Bank, the focus shall remain on each individual business it serves, and its employees are enthusiastic to provide them with this customized and personalized level of service.

Nevada First Bank is an active member of the community and contributes time and resources to a variety of local charities. Among the organizations that have benefited from Nevada First Bank's benevolence are the Clark County School District, Big Brothers/Big Sisters of America, Junior Achievement, the Juvenile Diabetes Research Foundation and the University of Nevada, Las Vegas College of Business.

UNLV College of Business

The UNLV College of Business is the primary choice for business education in Nevada. The administration, faculty and staff are committed to the mission: to advance the knowledge and practice of business develop business leaders and foster intellectual and

economic vitality through the creation and dissemination of knowledge and outreach.

The College of Business and the accounting department each hold accreditation from the Association to Advance Collegiate Schools of Business (AACSB) International. Accreditation ensures the college is meeting the highest standards for excellence in education and is important for students pursing advanced degrees.

The college offers undergraduate degrees in:
- Accounting
- Economics
- Finance
- Human Resource Management
- International Business
- Management
- Management Information Systems
- Marketing
- Real Estate

Graduate degrees include Master of Accounting, Master of Arts in Economics, Master of Business Administration (MBA), Executive MBA, Master of Science in MIS.

Responding to local demands the college expanded the MBA programs to include three dual MBAs:

MBA/JD, MBA/Dental Medicine Doctorate and MBA/Master of Science in Hotel Administration.

The current student population consists of over 300 graduate students and nearly 4,000 undergraduate students. The college grants over 500 degrees each year.

This translates into a stream of talented employees for companies regionally, nationally and abroad.

Through the efforts of the Center for Business and Economic Research, the Lied Institute for Real Estate Studies, and the Nevada Small Business Development Center, the college provides a range of services and expertise to regional businesses.

Alumni continue to help the college to extend its reach and enhance its reputation by joining the College of Business Alumni Association. The Alumni Board of Directors is composed of graduates from each decade since the forming of the college.

The college seeks the support of individuals and businesses in the community, like Nevada First Bank, who share a vision for the college.

Sun West Bank

In the 1980s the face of banking in Nevada began to change. Large organizations acquired other large banks, allowing small institutions to prosper and build market share. However, during the 1990s the acquisition movement shifted to small community banks; as many as 20 were acquired, leaving only five to serve the Las Vegas metropolitan area. There was opportunity and need for a locally owned bank with strong local ties and a commitment to its community. An institution that could meet the needs of customers — especially business customers caught in the "merger mania" and left under-serviced and overlooked.

Organized in early 1998, Sun West Bank was founded with the intent of bringing back the face of the community bank, offering a high level of service and a promise to remain long-term and make a difference in its regions.

Sun West's founding president and CEO, Jackie DeLaney, was one who was caught in "merger mania." She was the chief operating officer and executive vice president for Sun State Bank, being groomed to become the president. When Sun State was acquired in 1997, DeLaney realized she had an extremely important decision to make: "I could stay on board with the acquiring organization or continue to pursue my dream of being a bank president and truly making a difference." In her mind the choice was clear and a new community bank was created.

DeLaney set a precedent that had nothing to do with dollars and cents, loans or profits — Sun West is the first Nevada-based bank founded and organized by a woman as its president and chief executive.

It took less than five months for Sun West to organize and open its first two branches, easily a record in Nevada. It also began with a generous $12 million in capital, enabling a strong lending limit and the resources to build a solid banking organization.

DeLaney was fortunate to have an experienced team help her get Sun West up and running. Developer and former Sun State Bank Chairman Ken Templeton became and remains the chairman of Sun West. In fact, all of the outside directors from Sun State moved to the new bank, bringing with them a level of professional experience, entrepreneurial spirit and strong community ties that enable them to understand banking and Nevada's diverse market.

Sun West has increased its profits annually since its inception and continues to expand. In its first six years of operation, it grew to over $250 million in assets with five Nevada branch locations serving the Las Vegas and Reno metropolitan markets.

Sun West strives to make a positive difference in its communities, with a passion to better the lives of youth in Nevada. In June 2002 the bank was honored by Big Brothers-Big Sisters of Nevada for its continued support of the mentoring program. The bank has also aligned itself with organizations and programs such as the Boys & Girls Clubs, YMCA and Project Literacy. In 2004 the staff was recognized nationally for its dedication to the five promises outlined in General Colin Powell's America's Promise initiative.

"Service Above the Rest" is not just Sun West Bank's motto, it's a very real commitment made by the staff and board — it's what sets it apart from its competitors. Sun West intends to remain a common name and a familiar face as it continues in its quest to be Nevada's No. 1 independent community bank.

MANUFACTURING & DISTRIBUTION

In addition to producing exceptional goods for individuals and industry, regional manufacturing and distribution companies provide employment for residents.

Nevada Beverage Company

Entrepreneur Pat Clark, Sr. earned his place among the 20th century pioneers of Las Vegas, a city that is now among one of the fastest growing in the nation. Arriving in Las Vegas from New York in 1938, Mr. Clark devoted his life to his family, service to his community and the development of several successful businesses in the automobile, beverage distribution, construction and banking industries.

Clark's first local businesses included two used-car lots and a full-service garage that were natural extensions of Mr. Clark's lifelong interest in cars. On November 27, 1942, Clark was awarded the Southern Nevada Pontiac franchise, the result of which is the present day Pat Clark Pontiac·GMC.

For Mr. Clark, one job was never enough and in May 1941, Mr. Clark was asked to run for city commissioner. He strongly believed in knowing the people he was going to represent and giving them the opportunity to meet him, often saying that a politician who did not "wear out shoe leather" would not and should not be elected. During his campaign, he knocked on the front door of every home in his district. Clark was elected and served two consecutive terms as commissioner while also serving as mayor pro tem, police commissioner and safety commissioner. It was a tremendous honor for him to hold the positions of trust that the people of Las Vegas accorded him. He was dedicated to the well-being of all Las Vegans and was determined to make Las Vegas a great place to live, work and raise a family.

Mr. Clark was responsible for a number of improvements in the Las Vegas valley including the very first traffic light that was installed on the corner of Fremont Street and Las Vegas Boulevard, now one of the city's busiest intersections in the downtown resort corridor. He was instrumental in getting the road from old Tonopah Highway to Mt. Charleston paved so that the community would have access to the mountains surrounding the valley. During his term as commissioner, Mr. Clark installed water lines to give the city's west side running water and was behind having the first community swimming pool built in his district.

While his public works thrived, Mr. Clark's dealership faced difficult times during and after World War II. However, he tackled each new day with a renewed determination and reminded his small sales staff that

Pat Clark Pontiac·GMC

the essential element for their business' success was to provide customers with quality service at all times. To attract attention to the dealership, Clark, put his Tucker automobile on display, one of fewer than 20 cars ever made by maverick automobile designer Preston Tucker. The event drew a crowd of 500 people and eventually became an annual tradition.

Nevada Beverage Company is presently an exclusive distributor of Anheuser-Busch products and the sole distributor in the Southern Nevada region...

In 1948, while operating his car dealership, Mr. Clark founded Nevada Beverage Company, a liquor wholesale distributorship. He initially opened the business in a small warehouse behind his house on Third Street in downtown Las Vegas. Days filled with long hours and hard work followed, during which time Mr. Clark would help unload the delivery trucks himself. Three years after opening the business, Mr. Clark moved his business next door to DeLuca Importing, which was owned by his friend John DeLuca. The two companies eventually merged, with each partner remaining executive officer of his respective business operation. The merger allowed Mr. Clark to devote more capital to the expansion of the company while sharing overhead expenses. This partnership would prove pivotal in Nevada Beverage's history.

By 1956 Mr. Clark found himself with two growing, diverse businesses. His Pontiac dealership had 33 employees and had moved into a larger space that had previously been used to sell Studebakers. At the same time, Nevada Beverage had become the dominant distributor of beer and spirits in Las Vegas and yet, Mr. Clark still found time for other professional ventures.

Together with Robb Johnson, Mr. Clark founded a construction company in the mid-1950s called R.C. Johnson and Associates. The company was responsible

Pat Clark in front of the Nevada Beverage Company Headquarters

for building the round main tower of the Sands Hotel and for the construction of the Romanesque Caesars Palace, hailed at its grand openings as the most unique and magnificent resort on the Las Vegas Strip. R.C. Johnson and Associates worked throughout the Western United States and around the world until 1978, when Robb Johnson passed away and the company closed.

In 1959 Mr. Clark, along with several local dignitaries, organized Nevada State Bank. They raised the necessary capital and surplus required to open the bank by selling 24,000 shares of corporate stock to local residents at $31.25 per share. From that amount, $600,000 was put into capital, $100,000 into surplus and the remaining $60,000 into a reserve for contingencies. The bank opened for business on December 9, 1959. After 26 years, in December 1985, the bank was sold to Zions Bank Corporation and after the sale, the new owners requested that Mr. Clark hold the office of vice-chairman of the board, a position he proudly maintained until the early 1990s.

Nevada Beverage Company together with DeLuca Importing took a significant step in 1964 when the companies moved into a 75,000-square-foot building and was maintaining a fleet of 20 trucks. By 1972, 85 percent of all distilled spirits, wine and malt beverages in the Las Vegas market belonged to the two companies. In 1976 Mr. Clark sold his interest in the partnership, divesting himself of the liquor and wine products while still maintaining full ownership of Nevada Beverage Company, which concentrated on Anheuser-Busch beverages.

Following the dissolution of the Clark/DeLuca partnership, Mr. Clark moved Nevada Beverage Company to its current facility on West Tropicana Road, a 50,000-square-foot building with a fleet of 15 trucks.

Ensuring a quality product and exceeding service expectations has earned Nevada Beverage Company a 44.1 percent market share in the Southern Nevada beer market as well as award-winning status among Anheuser-Busch distributors. In 1984 Nevada Beverage Company was one of only 50 Anheuser-Busch Distributors to attain the level of Ambassador, the highest honor a distributor can receive.

Mr. Clark also received recognition for operation of Pat Clark Pontiac as a two-time recipient of the *Time* magazine Quality Dealer Award, an award that recognizes "exceptional performance in dealerships combined with community service." Mr. Clark was nominated for the award by the Nevada Franchised Automobile Dealers Association, which he helped found in 1963.

On March 20, 1985, at a special ceremony in the state capital of Carson City, Nevada, Governor Bob Miller and the state Senate, Mr. Clark was honored for all of his contributions and outstanding accomplishments with State Senate Resolution #6 and the declaration of November 20, 1992, Pat Clark Sr. Day, on the anniversary of his 50th year in the automobile business and "in appreciation for his selfless service to our community." At the time of Mr. Clark's death in 1995, he had maintained his relationship with Pontiac for 53 years and was the only remaining original active Pontiac dealer in the country.

Mr. Clark established a tradition of quality and excellence in customer satisfaction at both Nevada Beverage Company and Pat Clark Pontiac that his son, Pat Clark has continued since taking the reins of both businesses following his father's passing. In addition to maintaining the integrity of the businesses his

Nevada Beverage Company Headquarters

The Nevada Beverage Company's expanded warehouse

father founded, Pat continues in his own right to provide quality products and superior service to customers and clients. Under his leadership, Nevada Beverage Company remains among the top 10 in sales volume in all Anheuser-Busch regions in the United States. In 1997 Nevada Beverage Company won Region 10 Anheuser-Busch Wholesaler of the Year award, the highest recognition the company gives to its family of wholesalers. Recently under Pat's direction, Nevada Beverage Company streamlined its operations and increased the efficiency by becoming an exclusive distributor of Anheuser-Busch products and extending the Tropicana warehousing capabilities by 10,000 square feet. In 2002, Neveda Beverage Company added a 75,000-square-foot warehouse on Cheyenne Avenue.

As the sole distributor in the Southern Nevada region, the company supplies an area that encompasses approximately 44,000 square miles and includes Clark County and the outlying Nevada counties of Lincoln, Nye and Esmerelda. Nevada Beverage Company currently maintains a fleet of over 150 trucks with sales topping 10 million cases of product annually and has a capacity of storing hundreds of thousands of cases of beer at 40 degrees Fahrenheit, even when the temperature outside soars up to 115 degrees.

In January of 1997 General Motors formally awarded Pat Clark the Pat Clark Dealership as a dealer-operator and he, his father and the dealership were lauded by then Mayor of Las Vegas, Jan Jones, for continuing to offer "good, honest service" to Southern Nevada for more than 50 years. Pat Clark has served as a member of the Nevada Franchised Automobile Dealers Association board of directors since 1987 and served as their president in 1998 and 1999. In that same year, Pat Clark Pontiac was awarded a GMC franchise, following a yearlong study of the dealership's sales and customer service performance. In 2001 Pat Clark was honored by *Time* Magazine and the Goodyear Tire and Rubber Company and like his father before him, was named a recipient of the 2001 *Time* Magazine Quality Dealer Award in Las Vegas, Nevada.

As they have for more than 50 years, Pat Clark Pontiac·GMC and Nevada Beverage Company continue to be strong community partners and actively support numerous local civic and charitable organizations with both time and resources. In addition to advocating social responsibility with respect to alcoholic beverage consumption and working to increase alcohol awareness, Nevada Beverage Company and its employees have also contributed generously to organizations that benefit the well-being of children in the Las Vegas Valley. A specific example is their commitment to Boys Hope Girls Hope of Nevada. This organization provides a family-like home environment and college preparatory educational opportunities for academically capable, yet at-risk youth. Another is its longtime support of the local chapter of Make-a-Wish Foundation. Together, the company and its employees have been able to assist in the granting of numerous wishes to seriously ill children. Pat Clark Pontiac·GMC has also played an important role in community and charitable events, committing to regular participation in the General Motors Safe Kids program, a project that focuses on helping parents ensure that their child safety seats are installed correctly and meet all safety standards.

Nevada Beverage Company together with DeLuca Importing took a significant step in 1964 when the companies moved into a 75,000-square-foot building and was maintaining a fleet of 20 trucks.

As a student of his father's business practices, Pat Clark learned that people are the key asset to the success of a business and over the years he has ensured that both Nevada Beverage Company and Pat Clark Pontiac·GMC maintain not only quality service for their customers, but that his employees are rewarded for their dedication and hard work. One example of his commitment to his employees is the development of a state of the art workout facility that is open to all Clark employees and their families. The facility is located at the Las Vegas headquarters of Nevada Beverage Company. Complete with free weights, weight machines,

Nevada Beverage Company gym at the company's headquarters

and a variety of state-of-the-art cardiovascular machines, the 4,000-square-foot gym is also equipped with showers and locker room facilities as well as a tanning facility and juice bar stocked with water, sports drinks and juices. The gym is staffed with a personal trainer, to help employees create fitness goals and develop training programs to help them reach their objectives. The gym has not only played a role in boosting morale; it has helped reduce on the job injuries. Every year, Nevada

Beverage Company's gym plays host to an employee health fair to promote healthy lifestyle choices.

In addition to carrying on the tradition of quality service and attention to customer needs, Pat Clark continues his father's legacy of making family a priority. As the father of three, Patrick, 14, Christopher, 13, and Caitlin, 9, Pat has made it a point to be involved in their lives and interests. Over the past several years, Pat's children have developed both an interest and

Patrick Clark, Caitlin Clark and Christopher Clark

skill level in several sporting arenas leading to the development of Pat Clark Sports, Inc.

Patrick and Christopher began racing in Bandolero Circle Track, Junior Drag and Karting competitions. Patrick has recently changed direction and has begun competing nationally in American Trap Association and local club shooting events. Pat Clark Sports-Trap & Field was formed to support Patrick's endeavors and is actively involved with the Las Vegas Gun Club. Although this is his first year, Patrick shows international potential.

Christopher's skill in both Kart and Drag racing led to Pat Clark Sports-Racing, designed not only to further develop his career but to eventually create youth racing opportunities in Southern Nevada. The racing division consists of a support staff of five, including a director, technicians, coach and office support. Christopher has earned a spot among top junior racers. Pat Clark Sports-Racing will focus on developing sponsorships and racing opportunities as they take their young team on the road. Christopher is currently competing in SKUSA Pro Moto and Stars of Karting tours.

Caitlin has just begun to develop her equestrian skills but in preparation for trials and competitions, the formation of Pat Clark Sports - Equestrian is under way.

In late 2003 Pat further expanded his interests, opening Pat Clark Motorsports on East Sahara Avenue adjacent to Pat Clark Pontiac. Motorsports is a full sales and service motorcycle dealership selling Big Dog and Victory motorcycles as well as a full line of Xingfu All Terrain products.

Like Nevada Beverage Company and Pat Clark Pontiac·GMC, Pat Clark Sports, Inc. has evolved from the personal dedication to and the interests of the Clark family. Carrying forward the traditions of the Clark family, Pat Clark Sports, Inc. symbolizes the new generation of ingenuity and entrepreneurial spirit in the Clark family of businesses.

The core values of providing quality products, commitment to customer service and satisfaction continue to be at the heart of every venture launched by the Pat Clark Family. The living legacy of a tradition of good business, community involvement and belief in the people that work for you, is the backbone of the two landmark Southern Nevada companies, Nevada Beverage Company and Pat Clark Pontiac·GMC and the new venture, Pat Clark Sports, Inc encompassing Motorsports, Racing, Trap & Field and Equestrian.

Pat Clark in front of a racing kart at Pat Clark Sports, Inc., racing shop.

Federal Heath Sign Company

According to experts in the business, 1979 was not a good year to start a sign company, even in Las Vegas. A small group of energetic, experienced sign professionals ignored the doomsayers, however, and gave birth to Sign Systems Incorporated (SSI) in April of that year.

SSI's founders began their careers with a large, well-established sign company in the area. They had been well trained and educated in how to operate a successful sign company. In addition to their formal backgrounds in the industry, they brought to their newly formed company a shoot-from-the-hip, trust-your-gut attitude that was a sure recipe for success.

Over the next 10 years, SSI's enthusiastic team did make a dent in the Las Vegas market, building a solid reputation for designing, manufacturing and installing high-quality sign products. The growing young company also earned a reputation for providing its customers with excellent service, and for tackling new and unusual challenges.

The first major project SSI undertook was the complete remodel of the Frontier Hotel fascia. This was an ambitious and challenging project for a start-up sign company. There followed a long string of other successful projects — from the Westward Ho "umbrellas" to the remodel of the Stardust fascia — that established Sign Systems Incorporated as a force to be reckoned with in the Las Vegas market.

In 1989, SSI became a part of Federal Sign Company, a major national player in the sign industry. Based in Illinois, Federal Sign Company had secured a large job in Las Vegas: the complete renovation of the appearance of the world-famous Riviera Hotel Casino. Federal Sign needed a local company to install the new Riviera displays and came to SSI to negotiate a partnership arrangement.

One thing led to another and toward the end of 1989 SSI became part of Federal Sign Company.

Federal Sign Company's Las Vegas team not only worked on the Riviera project but acquired and began work on a number of other prestigious jobs, including the mammoth remodel of Harrah's. These professionals operated on the assumption that in order to survive and prosper in a competitive industry, they had to build strong relationships with contractors, architects and Las Vegas hotel casino operators.

Recently, Federal Sign and Heath Sign became Federal Heath Sign Company (FHSC) in May 2003. With the joining of these two major, premier national sign companies, FHSC now has a combined total of more than 160 years of experience and is able to provide more options, enhanced value, greater speed and increased flexibility to existing and prospective customers.

Federal Heath Sign Company/Las Vegas can proudly point to a long and growing list of quality work in Las Vegas and elsewhere. These include major projects at many of Las Vegas's most notable hotels and casinos and in many Native American casinos around the country. FHSC's Las Vegas team has completed projects as far away as Saipan.

As one founder said, "It's been quite a journey, and it ain't over yet."

MILGARD WINDOWS

Las Vegas may be known for its dazzling lights; however, its spectacular blue skies, desert flora, and scenic mountain backdrops also contribute to its essence. Because of so many breathtaking views and frequent extreme weather conditions, good windows, both in businesses and in homes, are essential. Milgard Windows knows the importance of reliable windows, and for more than 40 years it has provided the West with the highest-quality windows available and the service to go with them.

Founded in 1958 by Maurice Milgard and son, Gary, Milgard Windows began as a small glass shop with five employees in Tacoma, Washington. By 1962 Gary's entrepreneurial spirit directed him to found Milgard Manufacturing. Shortly thereafter, Gary's brother, Jim Milgard, joined the team, and under their leadership, the company experienced steady growth. Since then, Milgard has become the largest window manufacturing company in the Western United States. With expansion into the Midwest and Atlantic states, Milgard Windows employs over 3,500 employees in nine states. Along with sister companies, Milgard Tempering and Milgard Vinyl, Milgard Windows is a leader in the window industry, selling its products in the United States, Canada, Mexico and the Pacific Rim.

Arriving in Las Vegas in 1991, Milgard Windows quickly established a reputation in the residential construction industry for quality products, quality service and a commitment to excellence. Part of an expansion of Milgard Windows, the Las Vegas location became the eighth facility to build and distribute Milgard products. Pursuing a new direction, the Las Vegas location was the first Milgard facility to implement direct sales to new construction home builders.

Milgard Windows also sells replacement windows and doors through local dealers and home improvement stores. This was the result of growth of the local replacement window market, which encouraged the development of local dealers to assist in the sales and installation of Milgard's replacement windows and doors.

Named one of the top six employers in the state of Nevada, Milgard's presence in Nevada continues to grow. Employing over 200 in the greater Las Vegas area, Milgard is recognized specifically for its benefits, training, community involvement, quality working conditions and employee recognition. As a result, Milgard Las Vegas continually attracts job seekers from outside the state.

Another outstanding achievement for the company was the 2002 Neighborhood Impact Award given by the cities of Las Vegas, North Las Vegas and Henderson for outstanding efforts to improve the community. The MG/CAT (Milgard's Community Action Team) volunteer program provides continuous support for the Boys and Girls Club, the Juvenile Diabetes Research Foundation and many other local charities.

After 11 years in Las Vegas, the facility relocated to nearby Henderson where the business will enjoy the benefits of a new, 140,000-square-foot building. The increase in size will allow Milgard Windows to continue its growth in the market, provide increased capacity for production, and promote better customer service and care.

As the greater Las Vegas area continues to blossom, Milgard Windows will continue its mission of providing the best value-added window technology to residents and businesses, always with an emphasis on customer care and quality service.

MARKETPLACE & ENTERTAINMENT

Retail establishments and the entertainment industry
offer an impressive variety of choices for residents and visitors.

MGM MIRAGE

□When MGM Grand Inc. and Mirage Resorts Inc. joined forces on May 31, 2000 — closing the deal a mere 87 days after the merger was announced — they formed the foremost player in the gaming industry, MGM MIRAGE. Upon the merger, MGM Grand Inc. acquired all outstanding shares of Mirage Resorts Inc. for $21 per share in cash. The transaction resulted in a total equity value of approximately $4.4 billion and MGM Grand Inc. assumed the outstanding Mirage Resorts Inc. debt of approximately $2.0 billion.

the MGM Grand Detroit Casino; the MGM Grand Hotel and Casino in Darwin, Australia; and it managed casinos in Nelspruit, Witbank and Johannesburg, Republic of South Africa. While MGM Grand Inc. brought these aforementioned hotels and resorts to its marriage with Mirage Resorts Inc., the company has since divested itself of its South African and Australian holdings.

Mirage Resorts Inc. brought many of the world's most successful and acclaimed resort properties to the merger as well. First licensed by the Nevada Gaming

Prior to the acquisition, MGM Grand Inc. commenced operation on December 18, 1993, owning and operating several major hotel and resorts throughout the world. Among its holdings were the MGM Grand Hotel and Casino in Las Vegas, Nevada; New York-New York Hotel and Casino in Las Vegas; and Whiskey Pete's, Buffalo Bill's and Primm Valley Resort in Primm, Nevada. Outside of Nevada, MGM Grand Inc. owned

Commission in 1946 under the name Golden Nugget Inc., the organization changed to Mirage Resorts Inc. in June 1991, but maintained its status as the oldest established gaming company in the state. As Mirage Resorts Inc., the company consisted of Bellagio, The Mirage, Treasure Island and the Golden Nugget in Las Vegas. Outside of Las Vegas, Mirage Resorts Inc. included the Golden Nugget in Laughlin, Nevada; Beau Rivage in

Biloxi, Mississippi; and Borgata, a resort in Atlantic City, New Jersey. MGM MIRAGE sold Golden Nugget Las Vegas and Golden Nugget Laughlin to the Poster Financial Group in 2004.

With its newfound cohesion, MGM MIRAGE developed a mission. Its plan: create resorts of memorable character, treat its employees well and provide superior service to guests. Because of its commitment to these goals, MGM MIRAGE has successfully fulfilled its mission, offering 21,154 guest rooms and suites, 75 restaurants — among them AAA Five Diamond winners, nearly one million square feet of casino space, 818,946 gross square feet of meeting and convention space, and 12,166 showroom and 22,866 arena seats since its inception.

In total, MGM MIRAGE owns and operates 11 casino-resorts throughout Nevada, and in Mississippi and Michigan, and has investments in two other casino-resorts in Nevada and New Jersey. The company's leading resort-casino brands in Nevada are:

MGM Grand Las Vegas

Known around the world as "The City of Entertainment," MGM Grand opened in December 1993 as a multi-themed destination resort. Located on 116 acres along the Las Vegas Strip, guests encounter a 50-foot-tall polished bronze lion sculpture, which is the largest of its kind in the United States. The resort features more than 5,000 art deco-themed guest rooms and suites, and a plethora of entertainment facilities, including the 16,766-seat MGM Grand Garden Arena. The gigantic venue has headlined major special events, boxing and superstar entertainers such as Barbra Streisand, the Rolling Stones, Madonna, Paul McCartney, Tina Turner, Neil Diamond, Jimmy Buffett, Janet Jackson, the annual Billboard Music Awards and VH-1's Divas In Concert, just to name a few. The resort also houses the 746-seat Hollywood Theatre that has showcased entertainment headliners including David Copperfield and Tom Jones, among others.

MGM Grand's 343-seat La Femme Theatre is home to "La Femme," direct from the original Crazy Horse in Paris; its popular nightclub Studio 54 is named in honor of and modeled after the original; and a Cirque du Soleil production opened in 2004. In addition to these alluring attractions, MGM Grand's signature restaurants feature celebrity chefs such as Emeril Lagasse, Wolfgang Puck, Michael Mina and Tom Colicchio. The resort has a 380,000 square-foot, state-of-the-art conference center for meetings and conventions; and an inviting 6.6-acre pool and spa complex.

Bellagio

Bellagio was inspired by the breathtaking lakeside villages of Northern Italy; created with elegance and sophistication in mind. The resort offers visitors an impeccably decorated, lavish environment. A Mediterranean-blue, eight-acre lake features world-famous dancing fountains performing a magnificent aquatic ballet choreographed to music and lights. Once guests enter, they are greeted by an array of upscale shops at Via Bellagio — Giorgio Armani, Gucci, Chanel, Tiffany & Co., Prada, Fred Leighton, Hermés, Yves Saint Laurent and other style-savvy shops. Also within Bellagio are the finest of dining establishments, seasonal exhibits, exquisite gardens, Cirque du Soleil's stunning performance of "O," luxurious spa services, an art gallery and an elegant casino.

Danny Gans, featured at the Mirage, is an entertainment legend known as "The Man of Many Voices."

Treasure Island (TI) features a free outdoor show with a group of beautiful, 17th-century "sirens" who clash with renegade pirates.

The Mirage

Welcomed by an erupting volcano at its entrance, guests of The Mirage encounter a lush, tropical-themed resort with a 20,000-gallon aquarium and dense foliage in the lobby. Visitors can enjoy Cravings, the Ultimate Buffet Experience; stroll through Siegfried and Roy's captivating "Secret Garden", visit exclusive boutiques and participate in state-of-the-art conventions. The engaging entertainment includes Danny Gans, "The Man of Many Voices."

Treasure Island (TI)

Adjacent to the Mirage, Treasure Island (TI) entertains visitors with its free show "The Sirens of TI." Found at the resort's entrance, the show features a 17th century clash between a group of beautiful, tempting "sirens" who lure a band of renegade pirates to their cove. Showgoers enjoy Cirque du Soleil's astonishing "Mystere" production and guests satisfy their food cravings at the high-energy Isla Mexican Kitchen and Tequila Bar, the casually elegant Steak House, and other delightful dining options.

Primm Valley Resorts

Arriving or leaving Las Vegas, visitors find three hotel-casinos directly off of Interstate 15 at the California/Nevada state line in Primm, Nevada. Buffalo Bill's Resort & Casino, Primm Valley Resort & Casino, and Whiskey Pete's Hotel and Casino make up the Primm Valley Resort family. Together, the three operations offer a premier destination gaming spot for motorists traveling in the 13 million vehicles that pass through Primm each year. With an array of amenities and attractions — including "The Desperado" roller coaster and the "Turbo Drop" thrill ride; its 6,100-seat Star of the Desert Arena, which has hosted top-name entertainers and major special events; and the nearby Primm Valley Golf Club, which includes two 18-hole championship courses designed by renowned golf course architect Tom Fazio, visitors enjoy their stay no matter which Primm Valley resort they choose.

New York-New York Hotel & Casino

Designed to replicate the famous New York City landscape, New York-New York Hotel & Casino features 2,023 guest rooms and suites set in 12 New York-style skyscrapers. The property's most popular landmarks include a 150-foot replica of the Statue of Liberty and a Brooklyn Bridge reproduction, which bring the urban excitement characteristic of the "Big Apple" straight to Las Vegas. For entertainment, New York-New York

> In total, MGM MIRAGE owns and operates 11 casino-resorts throughout Nevada, and in Mississippi and Michigan, and has investments in two other casinos-resorts in Nevada and New Jersey.

Hotel & Casino houses Cirque Du Soleil's "Zumanity" show in the Zumanity Theater and Rita Rudner in the Cabaret Theater. The resort is not without fine dining — between Gallagher's Steakhouse, Il Fornaio, the authentic Irish pub Nine Fine Irishmen, the themed Village Eateries corner and ESPN Zone, all who pass through the resort find something to suit their tastes. As an exhilarating bonus, the resort's Manhattan Express roller coaster weaves through the hotel and hovers above the pool for both riders and observers to enjoy.

On the Las Vegas strip, MGM MIRAGE offers 16,665 rooms and suites, and a total 19,037 rooms in Nevada.

Shadow Creek Golf Course

MGM MIRAGE owns the esteemed Shadow Creek Golf Course, located amidst the barren Nevada desert on the outskirts of Las Vegas. The golf course has achieved national recognition — perennially ranking among *Golf* Magazine's top 20 courses in the world and earning the title of "The Best Golf Course in the World" in *Robb Report*'s "Best of the Best" issue. Also designed by renowned architect Tom Fazio, the course's stunning mystique, natural beauty, rolling terrain, glistening

brooks and ponds, flourishing gardens and mature trees consistently astonish visitors worldwide.

MGM Grand Detroit Casino

MGM MIRAGE also offers Michigan residents and tourists the popular MGM Grand Detroit Casino, which reigns as Detroit's first casino, opened in July 1999. The art-deco themed resort features a 75,000 square-foot gaming facility with more than 2,600 slot machines and a stirring range of table games. For dining, the resort accommodates a replica of the celebrated Hollywood Brown Derby, the American sports bistro Lion's Roar Sports Bar, an international buffet and other casual dining venues.

Beau Rivage, Biloxi, Mississippi

In Mississippi, MGM MIRAGE's Beau Rivage Resort & Casino is a destination resort pleasantly situated on the Mississippi Gulf Coast in Biloxi that offers the utmost in casual elegance. French for "beautiful shore,"

Studio 54 at MGM Grand is modeled after New York's original Studio 54 nightclub.

(Far right) The variety of restaurants and lounges at MGM MIRAGE provide friendly surroundings for meeting and greeting.

Beau Rivage combines the charm of the Mediterranean with the character of Southern hospitality throughout the resort. This is especially reflected in its front entryway with 31 majestic oak trees. Guests enjoy 1,740 elegantly appointed rooms and suites — including AAA Four-Diamond accommodations unrivaled throughout the Southeast.

Beau Rivage also includes 12 restaurants, a spa and salon, an upscale shopping promenade, Mississippi's first microbrewery, a state-of-the-art convention center and a 31-slip marina. For entertainment seekers, the resort offers a 1,550-seat showroom that features headline entertainment and various productions.

MGM MIRAGE does business in New Jersey as well — with Borgata resort-casino — as a 50-50 joint venture partner with the reputable Boyd Gaming Corporation. Borgata is ideally situated in Atlantic City and gives guests 2,002 guest rooms and suites to choose from, as well as a 135,000 square-foot casino — with 145 gaming tables and 3,650 slot machines. For the most delightful of stays, the resort also houses 11 destination restaurants, a full-service European-style spa, specialty boutiques, a 1,000-seat theater, 70,000 square feet of event space and parking for 6,300 automobiles.

MGM MIRAGE's respected family of assets and brand identities not only include Bellagio, a AAA Five Diamond Award winner, but the Picasso and Le Cirque restaurants at Bellagio as recipients of the AAA Five Diamond award; The Mirage Hotel and Casino as a AAA Four Diamond Award winner; The Mirage's Renoir restaurant as a AAA Five Diamond winner; Treasure Island (TI) as a AAA Four Diamond Award winner; and Beau Rivage as a AAA Four Diamond Award winner.

The company is ideally prepared and eager to pursue future opportunities on an international scale. The management team has an operational program designed to enhance revenues and minimize volatility, reduce operating costs, maintain financial stability, promote the company's reputation for providing world-class service, and position the company for growth by renovating and expanding existing properties and developing new destination resorts.

With approximately 40,000 employees, the company provides unmatched service and amenities to its guests. MGM MIRAGE values and cultivates diversity among its employees, provides a variety of opportunities for them and encourages their participation in the surrounding community; in turn, operating and maximizing value for its shareholders.

MGM MIRAGE empowers all of its shareholders, employees and business partners through its Diversity Initiative, which extends employment, purchasing and construction opportunities to minorities, women and disadvantaged enterprises. The Diversity Initiative launched in May 2000 when the two companies merged. MGM MIRAGE values diversity as an essential tool both morally and in business, and in response, imbeds diversity into its core values and operations. The company developed a diversity committee in 2002 to guide the initiative for the board. A multi-disciplinary team of company executives report to the committee.

MGM MIRAGE is a strong philanthropic advocate and major community representative. The MGM MIRAGE Corporate Charitable Giving Program serves as

Cirque Du Soleil shows, including "Mystere" at Treasure Island (TI) have emerged to play a prominent role at MGM MIRAGE properties.

economic development, professional and personal employee growth, and the availability of community resources; and education — funding efforts that strengthen public education from kindergarten through higher education.

Within each of these areas, MGM MIRAGE gives special attention to groups comprised of at-risk/at-purpose youth, socially or economically disadvantaged populations, and those who collaborate closely for the good of the community.

Supplementing its corporate philanthropy program, the MGM MIRAGE Voice Foundation structures its employee and charitable efforts as a 501(c)(3) non-profit organization. As such, MGM MIRAGE funds charitable organizations located in its businesses' respective cities. The campaign also encourages employees to give to charities directly or to donate through payroll pledge deductions.

Throughout its many highly-regarded properties, MGM MIRAGE's guests enjoy top accommodations, reputable restaurants, spectacular shows, a plethora of leisure activities, shopping at the finest names in retail, extensive meeting/convention facilities and exciting attractions. These amenities complement many gaming options offered at the resorts. Along with its commitment to serving the industry and its communities, MGM MIRAGE remains a leader in delighting the millions of guests that its outstanding resorts attract from all over the world.

> Along with its commitment to serving the industry and its communities, MGM MIRAGE remains a leader in delighting the millions of guests that its outstanding resorts attract from all over the world.

the principal funding entity for the company's community and social investments. The company makes financial donations to the area of childhood development — giving to community-based programs that provide for the overall development and well-being of children; and to community development — giving to programs that resolve community issues. MGM MIRAGE also utilizes its financial viability to invest in diversity — giving to programs that aid diversity-related efforts; and encouraging

Ethel M Chocolates

Aspiring to create the world's finest chocolates, Forrest Mars Sr., through his unwavering dedication to superior quality and exquisite taste, created a confection company that stands in a class of its own. Luscious and luxurious, Ethel M® Chocolates have won the loyalty of millions of customers around the world who are devoted to the unique and incredible chocolates created with only the finest, freshest ingredients in the world.

Although the company dates back less than two decades, the story actually began in 1911 when Forrest's parents, Frank and Ethel Mars, began making and selling chocolates from their kitchen in Tacoma, Washington. Ethel Mars perfected unique recipes for her homemade confections, which she and Frank sold to local businesses. As a result of his parents' early influence Forrest developed a lifelong passion for chocolate and became the driving force behind Mars, Incorporated, the world's largest manufacturer of high-quality snack foods — among them "M&M's"® Chocolate Candies, SNICKERS® Bar, and MILKY WAY® Bar.

After Forrest retired from Mars, Incorporated in 1976, he settled in Las Vegas. But his well-deserved life of leisure was short-lived as he missed doing what he enjoyed most — making fine chocolates. He set about creating a new company that would equal his vision of perfection. Inspired by his mother's early recipes, Forrest named the company Ethel M® Chocolates in honor of his mother Ethel. In 1979 construction began on the new factory in Henderson, located just a few minutes from the Las Vegas Strip. Many of Ethel M's chocolates are made with Ethel's original recipes, and some, notably the legendary lemon satin cremes, are Forrest's own creation. There are more than 60 exquisite chocolates in the Ethel M collection, all made with nature's finest, freshest ingredients: the richest cocoa beans, the most flavorful fruits, fresh cream, whole eggs and real butter. Innovative and delectable, these confections appeal to everyone's taste. The satin cremes include raspberry, chocolate, butter rum, maple walnut, strawberry, vanilla and the signature lemon satin creme — made with fresh-squeezed lemons. The nut

selection includes almonds, macadamias, peanuts and pecans. The special Almond Butter Krisps® (the most popular), cooked in small batches in copper kettles, consist of buttery toffee and chunks of almond coated with rich milk chocolate and sprinkled with almonds.

Ethel M's Liqueurs are world-renowned for their premium liquor brands, which are mixed into a creamy buttery base and covered with rich milk or dark chocolate. Dreamy White® Confections, Silky Truffles®, and mouth-watering fudge are also popular pieces in the collection.

The Ethel M® Chocolates factory is efficient and modern, but many of the steps of preparation and assembly are still done by hand. The nuts are hand-sorted to ensure only the finest quality, the peanuts are hand-ground to create creamy peanut butter chocolates, and the lemons are hand-squeezed to prevent the possibility of seeds or peels affecting the juice. By performing these steps of preparation by hand, the quality of each chocolate is ensured.

Every morning a specially trained taste panel meets to test the chocolates that were created the previous day. Good enough simply won't do. Perfection alone is the only standard of acceptance. By imposing such exacting standards, the taste panel follows the lead of Forrest Mars. Early in the company's history, while touring the kitchen, Forrest quizzed a young associate about the texture of a satin creme batch. "Young man," said Forrest, "what do you think about this satin creme?" "I think it's good, but I don't know if it's perfect," was the reply. "Well, let me tell you something," replied Forrest. "If it's not perfect, you don't push it to the next level. We are creating chocolates with the finest ingredients and best recipes and it is our responsibility to assure our consumers perfect quality with each and every piece." To this day, the entire staff of Ethel M® Chocolates is dedicated to achieving perfection, ensuring that every piece of chocolate is exquisite in texture, appearance and taste.

Forrest Mars wanted to share his love of chocolate-making with visitors to Las Vegas and local residents, so he created the Ethel M® Chocolates factory tour. Thousands of people visit the tour each week to witness the world of chocolate-making, experience the wonder of the botanical cactus garden and sample Ethel M's delicious chocolates. Tour buses returning from Hoover Dam and the Grand Canyon, along with visitors from the Las Vegas Strip, have been visiting the chocolate factory for over 17 years.

At the end of the tour visitors enter the chocolate shop where they are invited to select a sample from the vast array of chocolates beautifully displayed in a glass showcase. Of course, all of Ethel M's collections are available and visitors rarely leave empty-handed. At the end of the tour, guests are invited to sign the guest book so they'll receive the Ethel M® Chocolates mail-order catalog. In fact, it is primarily through the enthusiastic word-of-mouth of millions of visitors that Ethel M has built such a loyal customer following. Although the company's retail stores are primarily located in Las Vegas, Ethel M® Chocolates can be ordered and shipped nationwide.

It's not just the chocolate factory that attracts the visitors to the company's headquarters. Forrest Mars was enamored with his desert surroundings and was inspired to create a beautiful four-acre botanical cactus garden adjacent to the factory. To do so, he enlisted the assistance of the world-famous Huntington Library and Gardens in San Marino, California. Ethel M's Botanical Cactus Garden, considered one of the world's finest and most beautiful, features more than 350 cacti and succulents from around the world. Irrigation is accomplished with clean water that is purified through a unique, state-of-the-art "Living Machine" — a chemical-free wastewater treatment system.

Forrest Mars officially retired, for the second time in his career, from Ethel M® Chocolates in 1988. Ever the inventor and entrepreneur, his commitment to quality, creativity, and community continues to inspire everyone at Ethel M® Chocolates. Ethel M associates work with dedication to create what they believe are the world's finest chocolates. Forrest Mars left a unique and lasting legacy to the company he founded and the desert environment he loved so much.

GES Exposition Services

□ GES® Exposition Services is a leading provider of exhibition and event services, staging some of the world's largest tradeshows in the convention industry. Headquartered in Las Vegas and servicing every major convention market, GES designs and produces world-class events across North America for show organizers and their exhibitors. True to its Las Vegas roots and style, GES never fails to light up its clients' stage.

International CES

Integrity is at the forefront of GES' internal and external business practices. GES attributes its retention success to the ability to match its core values to employee values. The company has attracted individuals who share the belief that personal development is a fundamental priority. Consequently, its employees benefit from the opportunity to grow and to learn on the job perpetually. GES has made continued investments in comprehensive training, both to facilitate job performance and to allow employees to meet their individual goals.

GES' core values also shine through when one considers its impressive record as a corporate citizen. Paul Dykstra, president and CEO of GES, is especially proud of its contributions to the University of Nevada, Las Vegas (UNLV). Through its support for education at UNLV, including financial contributions, curriculum design, the provision of teaching tools and an innovative internship program, the University has been able to increase its offerings within its College of Hotel Administration.

GES dates back to 1939, with a Kansas City company called Manncraft, which specialized in signs, window trimmings and small displays. In 1969 Greyhound Corporation (now Viad Corp) purchased Manncraft. Greyhound entered Las Vegas in 1973 with the purchase of the Las Vegas Convention Services Company. When compared to the modern convention and tradeshow standards spearheaded by GES beginning in the early 1980s, the conventions of yesteryear seem simple and ordinary. Because most of Las Vegas' conventions were held in hotel meeting rooms during the 50s and 60s, old-fashioned manpower preceded forklifts as the method accoutrements. In the old days booths tended to be modular; readymade to open up on-site. Thus, during the early days of Las Vegas conventions, the primary role of GES was to provide carpet and pipe-and-drape for booths. By contrast, in today's high-tech world, tradeshows involve sophisticated designs and tireless technical support.

GES produces 80 percent of the largest tradeshows in Las Vegas, orchestrating large volumes of people, freight and furnishings in an efficient and customer-conscientious way. There is no doubt that the company's tradeshow niche, specializing in the biggest of the big shows, accurately reflects its hometown image.

Yet it is not only size that sets the company apart and highlights its Vegas style. Another hallmark of the GES convention model is the sophistication of the tradeshows it produces. Its 2002 consolidation of all tradeshow components under one roof at its 860,000-square-foot Las Vegas flagship facility has enabled the company to smoothly manage tradeshows that have become increasingly complex. For example, to produce the Consumer Electronics Show, GES painstakingly creates an elaborate floor plan months in advance of the event. This blueprint maps out everything from the conduits that make high technology happen, to the actual day that specific exhibits will move into the convention center.

As GES has grown to provide a one-stop shop for increasingly sophisticated expositions, many of

GES Flagship Facility
Las Vegas, NV

unprecedented size and complexity, it has tackled several challenges involved in the design and management of these "mega" tradeshows. For example, during the giant CONEXPO-CON/AGG tradeshow held every three years, cement batch plants of colossal proportions are erected. Onlookers are often awestruck by these monoliths: large-scale machinery so immense it must be showcased in the convention center parking lot.

It may be surprising to some people that a non-gaming company can stand out in a city like Las Vegas. Yet GES manages to leave a lasting impression on attendees and exhibitors, as well as the local business community. High-value customer service and innovative custom design is the hallmark of GES, a modern and efficient company capitalizing on cutting-edge technology to orchestrate large, sophisticated events.

As for what lies in the future, GES sees still brighter horizons ahead. The company has begun to create the groundwork for future innovation in the industry, harnessed by its ability to design and build exhibits in ways that allow exhibitors to effortlessly market their products. In this vein, GES has led the industry with innovations like the Wireless Ambassador®, hand-held computers that allow staff to access up-to-the-minute data right from the exhibitor's booth. Additionally, the company continues to develop technology that will elevate industry standards in tradeshow logistics in the years to come.

Finally, GES will continue to respond to the demand of its customers, among them the companies and organizations that put on the largest and most recognizable shows in the industry. In this sense, it demonstrates continuity with the past — GES has always specialized in offering high-value services to exhibitors and show organizers, and still continues this tradition of excellence today.

HARRAH'S ENTERTAINMENT, INC.

Inevitably, at some point during its lifetime a company arrives at a critical juncture. It must decide whether to continue down the path of least resistance — to stick with the status quo — or to change course in the hopes of greater success. Companies that are a cut above the rest usually opt for the second path: They choose change before change chooses them. Yet even "bold" companies tend to forego monumental change, preferring to take tentative and calculated risks instead. On the other hand, companies like Harrah's Entertainment are endowed with the vision and courage to rewrite industry standards. Harrah's did so, with flair and ended up building the world's largest casino company.

Harrah's faced the proverbial fork in the road nearly a decade ago. Typifying the boldest of the bold companies, it forged a radically new path. By investing heavily in technology in the late 90s, rather than bricks and mortar, Harrah's began to drastically distance itself from others in the gaming industry. At the time competitors were engaged in a casino building arms race, each vying to outdo each other's latest architectural feat. Today Harrah's casinos are elegant and welcoming, rather than imposing and garish. And because its brand name has endeared itself to customers like no fancy new edifice could, Harrah's revenues have steadily outpaced those of its rivals.

Harrah's introduced the groundbreaking Total Gold (today called Total Rewards) loyalty programs in 1997, allowing gamers to earn free trips, meals and hotel rooms by inserting a colorful card into slot machines before playing. Members rack up valuable points that can later be exchanged for meals, trips or suites at any one of Harrah's 28 properties nationwide. Total Rewards also allows Harrah's to create customer profiles that give it the ability to respond quickly and flexibly to its customer needs.

Gary W. Loveman, President and Chief Executive Officer, Harrah's Entertainment, Inc.

Harrah's data based system has revolutionized the gaming industry. In addition, since slots account for the majority of Harrah's $4.3 billion in revenue and more than 80 percent of the company's operating profit, it is also a critical business strategy.

This helps explain why Harrah's has come to monopolize the Casino Player Best of Gaming Awards every year — awarded on the basis of gaming customer voting totals — for the last five years. Because most of its customers are avid slot players, Harrah's has sought to establish exclusive relationships with slot manufacturers. This allows the company to bring new slot machines to market before other casinos do. In recent years, games such as The Price is Right and the Game of Life have been introduced and — because they offer excitement and a familiar brand — resoundingly embraced by customers.

These innovations underscore Harrah's overall strategy: to attain market leadership through changes that improve customer service. Along these lines, securing a loyal customer following hinges on polite and quick service. For this reason all of Harrah's employees complete training that prepares them for a career of customer friendly service before starting work.

Since a majority of American adults now view gaming as an opportunity to enjoy a fun night out, the stigma associated with gambling has receded significantly. Harrah's is proud to promote the important role it has played in the acceptance of gaming. In part, Harrah's has made this possible by spreading its wings beyond Las Vegas; Harrah's tripled the number of casinos in its portfolio between 1990 and 1997. Today, its bevy of riverboats and land-based casinos are a testament to responsible and fun entertainment.

By the same token, Harrah's has pioneered efforts to promote responsible gaming. In 1988 Harrah convened a task force of employees, recovering problem gamblers and clinicians to study the issue. "Operation Bet Smart" was the first of its kind, an initiative devised to help employees, guests and the public learn how to tackle gambling addictions more effectively. In step with its commitment to civic-minded gaming, Harrah's recently launched a responsible gaming campaign in which President and Chief Executive Officer Gary Loveman encourages gamers to gamble prudently and to seek help if they have a problem.

In Las Vegas, Harrah's works with a number of charitable organizations, including Meals on Wheels. It has contributed donations valued at more than $1 million since 2002 to Meals On Wheels programs nationwide. In addition, Harrah's employees are active in philanthropic events. For example, they recently spearheaded United Way fundraising drives across the nation. Also, for the past four years, Harrah's has taken the lead on senior citizen issues. During National Make a Difference Day Harrah's and its employees contributed both money and manpower to the renovation of lower-income senior citizen housing in Las Vegas and helped launch the Harrah/Rio Senior's Coalition alongside more than 12 Nevada organizations and businesses, the Nevada attorney general and the Nevada State Commission on Aging.

Harrah's track record of success is enviable; it has developed unparalleled brand recognition through technological innovation and excellent customer service. In the wake of Harrah's recent success, other casinos have been forced to rethink the gaming industry's traditional business model. Meanwhile, Harrah's remains ahead of the game, with various technology-centered developments in the pipeline that promise to transform the Harrah's gaming experience into an even more convenient and responsive form of entertainment. As always, these innovations will be customized to satisfy customer preferences.

Through its 28 locations nationwide, Harrah's is able to reach customers who have never visited Las Vegas and who have never viewed gaming as a viable entertainment option. In a short time Harrah's has become a convenient drive from every corner of the continental states. On the other hand, Harrah's sundry casinos actually encourage gamers to visit Las Vegas, as many Harrah's customers find it attractive to satiate their interest in gaming with a trip to the mecca of their preferred recreation.

In July 2004, Harrah's moved to drastically increase its presence in Las Vegas, announcing the purchase of Caesars Entertainment, Inc. for $9.4 billion in cash and stock. Once the deal closes, Harrah's will become one of the two largest operators on the Las Vegas Strip with six casinos, including such famed properties as Caesars Palace, Paris Las Vegas and the Flamingo. The deal will also firmly cement Harrah's position as the world's largest casino operator, with more than 50 casinos in 12 states and five countries.

With a well-known industry name and a wealth of loyal fans, Harrah's accomplishments speak for themselves. Whether one likes to gamble or abstains from it, whether one is a Harrah's employee or competitor, it is hard not to admire Harrah's accomplishments. The company took the road less traveled and maneuvered it with panache.

The Jewelers of Las Vegas

☐ Las Vegas has always been associated with gold and silver, so it's not surprising that the city boasts more than its share of jewelry stores. But within this crowded, competitive market, one company has become so identified with Las Vegas that it is known as The Jewelers of Las Vegas.

The Jewelers has 14 Las Vegas locations in casino hotels, regional and outlet malls throughout the city.

The company was founded in 1976, but owner Mordechai Yerushalmi's association with the jewelry business dates back to his childhood in Natanya, a suburb of Tel Aviv, Israel. Mordechai and his brothers, Yehuda and Yossi, spent their summer vacations working in a diamond-cutting factory in Tel Aviv. He moved to Toronto, Canada, in 1973 and developed a business wholesaling Israeli diamonds. During a business trip to New York City he met the manager of a jewelry store in the Las Vegas Hilton hotel who convinced Mordechai to come to the city.

Mordechai took the man's advice, but after arriving in Las Vegas he was surprised by the high prices some hotel jewelry stores charged. It was then that he decided to go into business for himself. To maintain his supply of merchandise, he created a jewelry chain that spans three continents. In Belgium, rough diamonds are purchased, cut and polished before being shipped to the United States.

In Israel, Mordechai established a diamond operation in the city of Ramat Gan. The Israeli facility exports more than 5,000 carats of diamonds, valued at $5 million, to Las Vegas every year. The Jewelers of Las Vegas is also a complete jewelry manufacturer designing and creating a variety of jewelry items to customer specifications.

What began with one store has grown into the largest wholesale discount jeweler and manufacturer in Nevada, in terms of both sales and number of stores. The Jewelers has 14 Las Vegas locations in casino hotels, regional and outlet malls throughout the city. The company also has locations in Reno, Nevada; San Jose, California; Phoenix, Arizona; Dallas, Texas; Kansas City, Kansas; Detroit, Michigan; Baltimore, Maryland; and Orlando, Florida.

Recently the family opened a few upscale boutiques that showcase selections of the finest products available in Las Vegas. Designed to cater to clientele with distinctive tastes, the shops of Venetzia Fine Jewelry at The Venetian or Le Paradis Fine Jewelry at Caesars Palace dazzle visitors with sheer elegance.

An emphasis on diamond wedding and engagement rings is found throughout the company's stores, but each location also offers a wide selection of merchandise, including diamond necklaces, gold jewelry, bracelets and chains, gemstone rings and watches.

In an effort to provide the finest products, the family established partnerships with many of the world's top producers of fine jewelry and leading timepieces including Chopard, Audemars Piguet, Gucci, Concord, Rado and John Hardy. The Jewelers has recently expanded its selection to include Montblanc writing instruments and accessories, Dupont lighters and Lalique and Daum crystal.

Mordechai Yerushalmi (left) who designed all the jewelry for the 1995 motion picture, *Casino*, is visited by one of the film's stars, Sharon Stone.

Photos of celebrities and prominent athletes line the walls of Mordechai's stores, a testament to his reputation as "Jeweler to the Stars." In 1973 he met his first celebrity client, Elvis Presley, who was performing at the Las Vegas Hilton. Presley asked that a selection of jewelry be brought to his dressing room. He ended up purchasing nearly $25,000 worth of jewelry to give as gifts. On another occasion, Elvis paid a visit to Mordechai while wearing a cape and fake beard. He wanted jewelry that conveyed his favorite motto — "Taking care of business. The jeweler made T.C.B. pendants with lightning bolts going through the letters, covered in diamonds. When Presley later revealed his desire to own a flawless black diamond, Mordechai contacted his diamond factory in Israel to be on the alert. Several years passed before a suitable specimen was found. Sadly, Elvis died before Mordechai could present him with the 6.5-carat gem.

A list of the company's celebrity clients includes pianist Liberace, for whom Mordechai made a $16,000 piano-shaped diamond pin combining mother-of-pearl, onyx and white diamonds. Other patrons include Bill Cosby, Tom Cruise, Julio Iglesias, Heather Locklear, Muhammad Ali, Jennifer Love Hewitt, Deion Sanders Shaquille O'Neal, and Chuck Norris, who has been known to step behind the counter and help sell jewelry to surprised customers.

> ## Photos of celebrities and prominent athletes line the walls of Mordechai's stores, a testament to his reputation as "Jeweler to the Stars."

Mordechai's reputation is such that he was a logical choice to make customized pieces for Robert De Niro, Sharon Stone and Joe Pesci for the film "Casino." Most jewelers would have needed to do research to keep things authentic for the 70s period piece. Mordechai, on the other hand, had already designed jewelry for most of the real-life people who were portrayed in the movie.

As few of today's casino executives go to the sartorial extremes of bosses of the past, Mordechai's customizing business has seen a new light as the flamboyant lifestyles of rappers and athletes have boosted business ten-fold. Everything, from eye-popping "iced" Rolexes

> ## The Jewelers of Las Vegas will continue the tradition of quality, value and service ensuring that it maintains its status as Las Vegas' premier jeweler.

covered in diamonds to outlandish pendants flaunted around the necks of present-day record company execs, is customized by Mordechai and his team of skilled artisans. Customers are continuously amazed to see their original pieces/designs brought to life.

However, being rich or famous is not a prerequisite for shopping at The Jewelers. Most of the diamonds sold by the company measure one carat or less in weight, and the diamond-cutting business in Israel provides a secure source of merchandise at prices below wholesale. This abundant supply allows Mordechai to achieve his goal of creating and selling jewelry that satisfies all tastes and budgets.

The Yerushalmi family takes pride in the city that has afforded them great joys, and has made it a point, year after year, to give back to the community. Family members and employees regularly contribute to such organizations as Nathan Adelson Hospice, the Nevada Cancer Society, the American Heart Association, the University of Nevada at Las Vegas, the Henderson Boys' Club, and Players for the Cure tennis fund-raiser benefiting the National Ovarian Cancer Coalition.

With the family's next generation working alongside the founding fathers, The Jewelers of Las Vegas will continue the tradition of quality, value and service ensuring that it maintains its status as Las Vegas' premier jeweler.

Sundance Helicopters

It is no surprise that Sundance Helicopters has been voted Best Helicopter Tour Company in Nevada by *Nevada Magazine* for four years running. By placing a premium on quality and exceptional service, the company has positioned itself at the top of the industry.

Sundance began operating out of Sky Harbor Airport in Henderson, Nevada, in April 1985 with one small piston-powered helicopter. The company was known as Helicopter Services of Nevada (HSN) and flight training was its primary business. In 1986 owners Fred and Karen Cleeves purchased a used Bell JetRanger, moved their operation to a hangar on the north end of McCarran International Airport, and conducted tours of the Las Vegas Strip from the Landmark Hotel parking lot.

In January 1988 HSN initiated a Grand Canyon tour that featured a champagne picnic inside the canyon. This became the most popular helicopter tour in Las Vegas and, thanks to extensive media exposure, one of the best known tours of any kind worldwide.

Rick Eisenreich, Jim Granquist and John Sullivan purchased the company in September 1992. By then HSN had six helicopters, and business had expanded to include military support, firefighting, external load, power line survey, and traffic reporting. Tours to the Grand Canyon were a rapidly growing component of the business. The name was changed to Sundance Helicopters in July 1994, reflecting an increased emphasis on tourism.

Business increased steadily under the new ownership and the company outgrew one operating facility after another. In late 1997 Sundance broke ground on the west side of McCarran Airport for a new hangar, passenger terminal and office facility.

This move triggered further growth, doubling the company's size in four years.

Today, tourism accounts for three-quarters of Sundance's business. Customers can enjoy a champagne picnic inside the Grand Canyon, a boat ride on the Colorado River and a Hualapai Indian Bar-B-Q. Bryce and Zion national parks, exotic dinner retreats and the Las Vegas Strip at night are also popular tours. Sundance remains committed to its charter and utility customers. During the summer months up to four helicopters are dedicated to firefighting. Video and film production is also a growing market for the company. Sundance has been featured in several major films and national television pieces, and has been employed for filming projects by many production companies including Warner Brothers, Paramount and Disney.

Sundance is conscious of its civic responsibilities and generously contributes services to a variety of charitable and nonprofit organizations. A particularly rewarding part of the company's charitable work is its contributions to the Make-a-Wish Foundation. During the Christmas holidays, Santa Claus frequently arrives on a Sundance Helicopter to meet special groups of children.

Looking ahead, our objective is to continue growing in Las Vegas while remaining true to our mission: "Every day serving our customers at a level beyond their expectations."

NETWORKS & TECHNOLOGY

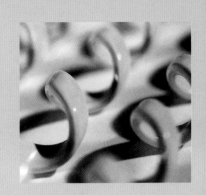

A premier location for cutting-edge communications, media, electronics and utilities, Las Vegas is home to a wealth of organizations that keep information, people, products and power moving throughout the region and the world.

SWITCH COMMUNICATIONS GROUP/THE NEVADA NAP

While surfing the Internet, people may not ever wonder how a specific site eventually reaches their computers. In many instances, collocation facilities house the servers, switches and routers that make Internet browsing possible. Collocation facilities provide the access to high-speed connections and the safeguards needed to protect the operating equipment.

"Switch offers every service that we had before, plus collocation, at such a huge cost savings."

"In the early years of the Internet, Silicon Valley housed 40 percent of the Internet delivery systems," states Rob Roy, CEO of Switch Communications Group, the management of the Nevada NAP.

Since Roy's company was founded in 2000, it has grown by a phenomenal 100 percent every year.

"Switch Communications Group continues to experience strong demand for our high-performance Internet hub where a critical mass of networks, enterprises and content companies can operate and directly exchange traffic with each other," said Roy.

Nevada NAP facilities are built and managed to advanced data center standards. Its footprint will soon be more than 80,000 square feet of space in four buildings with dozens of diverse fiber entry points.

The Nevada NAP is a collocation gateway and carrier-neutral facility for interexchange carriers (IXCs), Competitive Local Exchange Carriers (CLECs), Internet Service Providers (ISPs), Internet Business Exchange (ISXs), Metropolitan Digital Subscriber Line Providers (MDSLPs), Regional Internet Service Providers (RISPs), National Network Service Providers (NNSPs) and businesses that need the best bandwidth services in North America.

Carriers in the Nevada NAP family include MCI UUNET, 360 networks, Cox Communications, Level (3) Communications, Broadwing, Electric Lightwave,

Qwest, Time Warner Telecom, IDACOM, Sprint, WilTel Communications, XO, NovaTel, Xspedius, switchnet, SBC and more than 100 other telecommunications interconnect companies.

The Nevada NAP facilities are designed specifically for high performance Internet activity and provide the perfect environment for mission-critical applications and services. It is becoming the leading disaster avoidance network access point in America.

The Nevada NAP provides access to the most advanced telecommunications products and services in the Western United States and will continue to grow exponentially while it provides superior service to a host of companies.

All of the Nevada NAP facilities are interconnected through redundant fiber links so clients in any one facility can leverage the benefits of directly connecting with clients or carriers in the other centers. Roof rights for wireless access are available as well. The equipment area affords the highest level of protection in terms of security, environment, power backup and fire defenses.

Las Vegas is an emerging technology market experiencing tremendous growth. Nevada's great tax benefits, its close proximity to the West Coast, low level of natural disasters, a world-class airport, abundant power and low cost of living make Las Vegas a perfect location for mission-critical systems.

As issues of disaster avoidance, redundancy, unfavorable regulatory environments and increasing costs push companies out of larger markets, The Nevada NAP offers state-of-the-art collocation facilities located in the heart of the Las Vegas telecommunications corridor. It is

Nevada's only bandwidth commodity exchange with 132 providers and more than 3,000 fibers connected to network access point.

In addition, The Nevada NAP's partner company, SwitchNet, uses advanced carrier-class equipment, BGP, multi-homing, and multiple tier one providers to deliver the best bandwidth product available in Nevada.

Because of its access to so many carriers Switch has created a commodity exchange that allows them to offer the most competitive pricing in the country.

Russ Ketchum, Director of Information Technology for the Four Seasons Resorts and Hotels, explains, "Switch offers every service that we had before, plus collocation, at such a huge cost savings."

"Many fortune 500 companies are surprised to learn that we have better buying power than they do," said Roy.

KINC-TV Channel 15

KINC-TV Channel 15 UNIVISION has served Las Vegas Spanish-speaking audiences since 1992 with cultured and diversified programming. Initially KAFT Channel 27 UNIVISION, the station ultimately changed its call letters to KINC and upgraded its position to Channel 15. These modifications aside, KINC-TV Channel 15 has always offered the same quality programming, making it the first Spanish-language television station to serve Las Vegas' Hispanic community. It proudly appeals to all different ages with everything from news, game shows, variety shows, sports, to telenovela (soap opera) programs.

Through such programs, shows, commercials, community involvement and public service announcements, KINC-TV Channel 15 truly represents the city of Las Vegas and what it stands for.

As an ever-growing segment, the Hispanic market makes up 23 percent of the Las Vegas Television Market Area. According to the 2002 Nielsen Universe Estimates, a demographic study conducted through relevant survey distribution, Las Vegas ranks as the 24th-largest Hispanic market in the United States. As a full power station with cable coverage, KINC-TV Channel 15 reaches this segment within both centralized and remote locations throughout the city and adjacent communities of Mesquite, Pahrump and Laughlin.

The television station is owned and operated by Entravision Communications Corporation, a major media company geared toward the Hispanic audience that encompasses television and radio. Furthermore, Entravision ranks as the largest affiliate group of both the top-ranked Univision television network and Univision's Telefutura network. The company also operates one of America's largest centrally-programmed Spanish-language radio networks through its numerous stations located in 21 of the nation's top 50 Hispanic markets — two of which operate in Las Vegas. As part of this larger media entity, KINC-TV Channel 15 has built itself along with an expanding Hispanic population. Between 1990 and 2002, household growth was 443 percent and KINC-TV Channel 15 supported and became part of that expansion. As a result, KINC-TV Channel 15 has grown significantly through increased ratings and a growing market share.

KINC-TV Channel 15 has catered to its loyal following by providing them with quality entertainment and community-enriching information. The station has informative programs such as its local news at 6 p.m. and 11 p.m., which makes it a highly regarded information source within the Spanish speaking community of Las Vegas. As a huge competitor in the market, KINC-TV Channel 15 leads in ratings of adults 18-34 and competes aggressively as a leader in the age 18 to age 49 adult demographic as well. In addition, the television station has promoted worthwhile artistic and cultural events such as Philharmonic Orchestra performances, sponsored competitive soccer events of the Nevada Soccer Association and its adult leagues, as well as conscientious causes such as water conservation — a crucial act in the American desert locale of Las Vegas. Moreover, the television station has earned a significant reputation and capacity for advertising, due to the amplified purchasing power that Hispanics embody.

Through such programs, shows, commercials, community involvement and public service announcements, KINC-TV Channel 15 truly represents the city of Las Vegas and what it stands for. Perhaps most importantly, though, the television station genuinely supports and successfully communicates to the ever more significant Hispanic community that resides within it.

KVBC-TV

James E. "Jim" Rogers, chief executive officer of Valley Broadcasting Company, which acquired KVBC-TV on September 30, 1979, is almost as much a Las Vegas institution as KVBC itself — and that is saying a lot.

KVBC, the NBC affiliate in Las Vegas, was founded by Donrey Media on January 23, 1955, as KORK-TV and operated until a landmark ruling by the Federal Communications Commission revoked its operating license on October 27, 1978, thus paving the way of KVBC-TV. The station is licensed to the city of Las Vegas and serves approximately 600,000 households in the Las Vegas Designated Market Area, which includes all of Clark, Lincoln and Nye counties in Nevada. KVBC-TV employs 202 persons.

Jim Rogers founded Valley Broadcasting Company (VBC) in 1971, a wholly owned subsidiary of Sunbelt Communications Company, when VBC applied to the Federal Communications Commission for its broadcast license. A 1956 graduate of Las Vegas High School, Rogers went on to earn a bachelor of science degree in accounting and a LL.B. degree from the University of Arizona, and a master of laws (LL.M.) degree from the University of Southern California. He holds honorary doctorates from the University of Arizona, Albertson College, Idaho State University, Kentucky Wesleyan, Carroll College and University of Nevada-Las Vegas, and is also a member of the state bar associations of Nevada, Arizona and California.

Rogers was a teaching fellow at the law school of the University of Illinois in 1963 and 1964, and was engaged in active law practice in Las Vegas from 1964 through 1988, when he ceased practicing in order to devote his energies totally to the development of Sunbelt Communications Company. Rogers owns 98 percent of the stock of Sunbelt Communications, which owns and operates a number of NBC affiliate television stations in Las Vegas, Reno, Winnemucca and Elko, Nevada; El Centro, California; Yuma, Arizona; Helena, Havre and Lewistown, Montana; Jackson, Casper and Cheyenne, Wyoming; Pocatello-Idaho Falls, Idaho; and the Fox affiliate in Twin Falls, Idaho.

In Las Vegas, KVBC has forged a reputation as the market leader. The station's mission statement sets the tone for the more than 200 employees who work both in front of and behind the cameras, creating the station's identity: "We are Channel 3. Each person in every department works as a team member to serve the needs of the Las Vegas community. We lead by providing viewers and advertisers with the highest quality news, information, entertainment and customer service."

Operating a television station in one of the fastest-growing cities in the country can be a challenge. To stay ahead of the pack, KVBC originates more than five hours of locally produced news programs daily, using the latest in technology and resources to keep Las Vegas informed. In the area of entertainment, Channel 3 is NBC for Southern Nevada, pairing this top network with some of the most popular syndicated television programs available.

In addition to his law practice, Rogers has been a founder and director of a number of Nevada and California banks. He became a board director of Nevada National Bank, Nevada's third-largest bank, in 1981, served as a member of the bank's loan committee for 10 years and was chairman of the board from 1985 to 1987.

KVBC originates more than five hours of locally produced news programs daily, using the latest in technology and resources to keep Las Vegas informed.

He was involved in the purchase of Nevada National Bank by Security Pacific Bank of California in 1989 and served on the board of directors of Security Pacific Bank, Nevada, until Bank of America purchased it. He was a founder and served on the board of directors of Community Bank of Nevada and was chairman of its loan committee until he left that bank to form Nevada First Bank in 1998, where he now serves as chairman of the board.

Rogers and his wife, Beverly Barlow Rogers, are enthusiastic individuals who are passionately dedicated to making the world a better place in which to live. As active supporters of education, they have made substantial financial contributions to various colleges and universities. Their gift of $135 million to the University of Arizona College of Law is both the largest gift to the University of Arizona and to any American law school. In November 1998, the Arizona Board of Regents renamed the University of Arizona's college of law The James E. Rogers College of Law. Time magazine has listed Rogers as one of the top 12 philanthropists in the nation.

Jim Rogers is active in all the communities where Sunbelt has television stations. He served as Campaign Chair of the Capital Campaign at Idaho State University, which with a goal of $102 million, raised $155 million. He served as co-chair of the University of Arizona Campaign that had a goal of $1 billion. Rogers helped raise more than $1.1 billion.

He also serves as a board member of the Motion Picture and Television Fund and Board Member of the Golden Boot Awards. Jim serves on the Board of Trustees for nine universities and colleges.

Besides their philanthropic pursuits, Jim and Beverly Rogers have many personal interests. One of them, a long interest in classic cars, has resulted in the Rogers creating one of the best collections of classic cars in the United States. The 240 automobiles they own range from Cadillac V16s to 1976 Rolls Royces. The collection has been shown throughout the Western states and has been used in numerous events such as parades, marches, advertisements and local affairs.

(Left)
The Sunbelt Classic Car Museum, founded by Jim and Beverly Rogers, contains one of the best collections of classic cars in the United States.

(Right)
The University of Nevada-Las Vegas and the University of Arizona have honored Rogers' generosity to their institutions.

SIGMATRON INTERNATIONAL, INC.

For over a decade, Sigmatron International's Las Vegas division has been serving the electronic manufacturing needs of the greater Las Vegas region and beyond by providing exceptional customized services that cater to clients' individualized needs.

The Las Vegas division operates under the direction of Sigmatron International, Inc. — a worldwide electronic manufacturing service (EMS) provider for assembling printed circuit board assemblies (PCBA's), mechanical assemblies and wire harness/cable assemblies.

Sigmatron International, Inc. was originally formed in 1990 and currently maintains its headquarters in Elk Grove, Illinois. In addition to its production facilities both in Elk Grove and Las Vegas, Sigmatron International operates two international production facilities, one in Acuna, Mexico, and another in Mainland China. The company also maintains a limited partnership in Fremont, California, and a purchasing office in Taiwan.

The company serves a diverse marketplace that includes OEMs in the gaming, fitness, industrial electronics, consumer electronics, telecommunications industry and appliance industries.

As its commitment to diversity keeps Sigmatron at the forefront of its industry, it also stands out in its dedicated and individualized customer care. Since the company operates in regional markets, where a local customer service representative is assigned to each individual account, it is able to offer custom service and support resources as well. All of its customer service representatives have a strong background in manufacturing, which enables them to understand customers' production needs.

The purchasing of millions of dollars worth of components and subassemblies needed per year is also managed locally in conjunction with cooperation from the Taiwan office. This relationship allows quicker access to Pacific-Rim supply chain vendors, which are critical to meeting on-time schedules.

As part of Sigmatron's continuing commitment to its customers, it recently significantly increased its production capacity of its ISO 9K2K and UL certified Las Vegas plant with approximately 50,000 square feet of production and office space. This capacity enables Sigmatron to respond to customers' needs with speed, flexibility and reliability.

Specifically at the Las Vegas division, the focus is decidedly on its gaming customer base. However, the facility also services non-gaming customers. The Las Vegas production facility has a staff of just under 150 people that provide customers with customer service, purchasing, production, product repair and engineering services to fit their product needs.

The fully automated factory is capable of assembling PinThrough Hole (PTH) and Surface Mount Technology (SMT) PCBAs in either small proto-type runs or high-volume production builds. Wire harnesses and cable assemblies are also built-to-order utilizing fully automated equipment and processes. Mechanical assemblies ranging from as simple as a metal bracket with a light socket on it, to an assembly as complicated as a slot machine, are also built to customer specifications. Testing is performed either with functional fixtures or on fully automated In-Circuit Test (ICT) systems.

Sigmatron's mission is to provide a single source for comprehensive manufacturing, assembly, test and component sourcing with world-class quality, delivered on-time at competitive pricing. Sigmatron's capabilities will continue to evolve to meet the expectations of its customers in an ever-changing marketplace.

PROFESSIONAL SERVICES

Las Vegas offers premier professional services that meet
the most complex needs of the area's businesses and residents.

Dempsey, Roberts & Smith, Ltd. PrePaid Legal Services®, Inc.

From left to right: Attorney Joseph F. Dempsey, Kenneth M. Roberts and Billy Smith Jr., of Dempsey, Roberts & Smith, Ltd., in Las Vegas, Nevada.

Dempsey, Roberts & Smith, Ltd. Is not like most law firms. For starters, it includes a customer service department. At the end of each day, the firm's employees are rated on 10 different areas of customer service. Anyone hired by the firm's three partners must fit into its corporate culture, which emphasizes a strong work ethic and deep commitment toward helping people. From its inception, the firm implemented a policy whereby all telephone calls from existing or potential clients would be returned that same day.

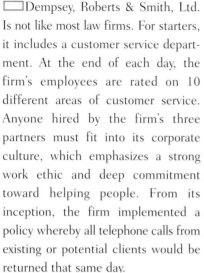

Customer service is clearly its specialty, which is one of the key reasons behind the firm's growth in recent years. Attorneys in this full service firm practice in the areas of personal injury, wrongful death, divorce, child custody, adoption and related family law matters, military law, business, corporate and partnership, collections, entertainment law, international and foreign trade, and real estate.

The Las Vegas firm was established in 1992 by Joseph Dempsey and Kenneth Roberts. The following year, their third partner Billy Smith, Jr., joined the firm.

The law office of Dempsey, Roberts & Smith, Ltd., in Las Vegas, Nevada.

The three attorneys mostly handled corporate bankruptcy and family law matters. Then in the mid-1990s, they received two phone calls that would forever change their practice.

The first call was from a potential client asking if the firm would provide legal services via PrePaid Legal Services®, Inc., a national organization that designs, underwrites and markets legal service plans that are similar to medical healthcare plans. Intrigued by the idea, the fledgling firm contacted the organization and soon began receiving referrals.

Little by little, new clients began trickling in, enabling the firm to grow its client base and profits. Then in 1995, it was designated as PrePaid Legal's provider law firm for the entire state of Nevada.

The other call was from a man seeking legal representation for the wrongful death of his ex-wife, which at the time, was not part of the firm's service offerings. Still, the firm accepted the case, then added wrongful death and personal injury to its service menu in 1995. The case ended up being settled for more than 1 million dollars, which enabled the firm to expand its office space and hire more staff.

In 1994, in an attempt to build upon the partners' international legal experience, the firm introduced the category of international law in the Las Vegas Yellow Pages directory. Today its international legal services are quite comprehensive and include preparing international joint venture agreements and distributor and sales representative agreements.

Due to the firm's philanthropic nature, it frequently donates funds to local charities such as Child Haven and performs a significant amount of pro bono work primarily in family law. In 1999 and 2000, it was recognized by Clark County's pro bono program for its outstanding community contributions. In 2000, and again in 2002, it also received an award for excellence from PrePaid Legal Services®, Inc., making it the company's No.1 U.S. law firm in all categories of customer service.

Equal Justice

Since it introduced legal service plans in 1972, PrePaid Legal Services® Inc., (PPL) has been quite selective about its provider law firms.

Attorneys must possess at least two years of legal experience, be in good standing with their state bar association and community, understand the legal issues facing most middle-income families and place their customers' concerns first. On-site evaluations of prospective attorneys are conducted and the firm's location, parking facilities, support staff and level of office technology are assessed.

Over the years, PPL has worked with North American attorneys to provide more than 1 million households with access to quality legal counsel for a low monthly fee. Plans consist of a wide variety of commonly used legal services such as will preparation, contract and document review, letters and phone calls to third parties, motor vehicle legal services, as well as phone consultation and advice on any legal matter. Additionally, the company's online resource center provides free legal contracts, legal documents and legal forms.

When members need legal assistance, they can contact provider firms such as Dempsey, Roberts & Smith, Ltd., directly and an attorney with experience in the appropriate area of law will return their call.

The company sends a monthly report card to its providers, rating them on various categories such as promptness of return phone calls, the number of complaints received, their skill and conduct in delivering legal services to members and the number of cancelled memberships. Member surveys of provider law firms also are conducted on a regular basis. Like Dempsey, Roberts & Smith, Ltd., PPL provider law firms consistently receive very good and excellent ratings by members.

The company provides services to members in 50 states, the District of Columbia and the Canadian provinces of Alberta, Ontario, British Columbia and Manitoba. It was launched by Harland Stonecipher in 1972, and his quest began to provide equal access to the justice system for middle-income Americans.

By 1984 PPL was available in 17 states, had processed 30,000 member claims and was publicly owned and traded on the NASDAQ exchange. In 1986 it moved to the American Stock Exchange (AMEX). In 1988 PPL made memberships available to Nevada and named Ted and Olga Burke regional vice presidents for the state.

During the 1990s, the company's annual revenues steadily increased by over 100 percent, surpassing the earnings per share predicted by Wall Street analysts for 35 consecutive quarters. The company went international in 1999, offering legal expense plans in Canada and opened on the New York Stock Exchange under the symbol of "PPD" on May 13, 1999.

Throughout its history, the company has achieved major recognition. In 1996, the *Dallas Business Journal* named PPL founder, Harland Stonecipher, a finalist for Entrepreneur of the Year. Two years later, the company was listed in Wall Street's Picks for 1998 and named No. one performing AMEX stock by *Equities* magazine. In 2000 it made the *Forbes* list of the 200 Best Small Companies in America for the fifth consecutive year.

Since their inception, PrePaid Legal Services®, Inc., and Dempsey, Roberts & Smith, Ltd., have been in constant growth mode and have never lost sight of their original goal: equal justice for all.

Harland Stonecipher, founder CEO and board chairman of Pre-Paid Legal Services®, Inc.

An artist's rendition of Pre-Paid Legal's new corporate office in Ada, Oklahoma.

DENNY WEDDLE & ASSOCIATES

Since 1988 Denny Weddle & Associates has provided southern Nevadans with expertise and excellence in the fields of advertising, marketing, public relations and government affairs. Guided by the vision of Dennis (Denny) R. Weddle, the award-winning company has emerged as a true leader in all of its endeavors and community outreach services.

Denny Weddle & Associates began as Weddle/ Caldwell Advertising, Inc. when Mr. Weddle joined with Tom Caldwell and Rick Dale and became its president. Through Weddle's dedication, the agency eventually became Denny Weddle & Associates in May 1993.

Today the firm prides itself in providing targeted, measurable strategies, which achieve objectives in a substantive and professional mode. Working closely with clients, the agency offers consistent professional and personalized service designed to meet their specific needs. Offering a comprehensive range of communications services, the agency is considered a one-stop service provider where "you can have it all."

Among its present capabilities are:
- Public Relations
- Advertising
- Media Placement
- Image Development and Enhancement
- Direct Mail
- Video and Television Production
- Collateral
- Special Services
- Special Events
- Market Research
- Computer Graphics Services
- Executive Training, Consultation and Make Overs
- Sales Training
- Governmental Affairs Representation
- Crisis Intervention
- Meeting Planner
- Travel Agency Services

The agency's diversity came out of Mr. Weddle's rich background in service to both the public and private sectors, where he acquired a wealth of knowledge and experience in many areas of media relations and communications. Mr. Weddle's initial experience began while earning his BFA from Drake University in 1963, and simultaneously working as a commercial television director, radio announcer, professional emcee and actor. Although his passion was in the arts, Weddle later went on to receive his MS degree in college counseling from the University of Southern Mississippi in 1967.

After graduation, he was commissioned in the Air Force, which brought him to two tours of duty at Nellis Air Force Base in Southern Nevada - first as information officer for the USAF Thunderbirds from 1969 to 1972 and later as director of protocol from 1980 to 1983.

Commissioned through the Air Force ROTC program, Lieutenant Colonel Weddle's assignments carried him

> Since 1988 Denny Weddle & Associates have provided southern Nevadans with expertise and excellence in the fields of advertising, marketing, public relations and government affairs.

to over 25 foreign countries and all 50 states. Other highlights of his military career include: selection as a public affairs officer for "Operation Homecoming" at Clark AFB, Philippines and one of only 16 public affairs officers to land in Hanoi and escort American POWs back to freedom; Director, Radio and Television Department at the Defense Information School; and assignment to the USAF Academy as Chief, Cadet Wing Media and director of protocol. He is also the author of the book "I Would Have Gave My Life ... But I Don't

Think My Parents Would Like It," for which he donated all sales profits to POW/MIA children for educational scholarships.

> ## Its staff also brings to the agency dynamic backgrounds that when meshed together create great products.

In addition, Mr. Weddle was an honor graduate of the Defense Information Officer short course at the University of Oklahoma. His decorations include the Bronze Star, Meritorious Service Medal (4), Joint Service Commendation Medal, Air Force Commendation Medal, Vietnamese Cross of Gallantry and others. He is also a rated parachutist.

After selection as Chief, Air Force Protocol, working for the chief of staff, USAF, the Pentagon 1983-1985, Weddle retired after 20 years of service from the United States Air Force effective December 1985, with the rank of lieutenant colonel.

After leaving the Air Force, Weddle went on to serve as director of corporate public affairs for Summa Corporation where he was responsible for press coordination, media and community relations, political action matters, marketing and advertising coordination for the Howard Hughes Estate properties. He departed that executive position to launch Weddle/Caldwell Advertising.

He is a member of Who's Who Among Students in America Colleges and Universities; Who's Who in Tau Kappa Epsilon Fraternity; International Order of Characters; one of the Jaycees' Outstanding Young Men in America in 1977; and a member of Omicron Delta Kappa, Phi Delta Kappa and Theta Alpha Phi Honorary fraternities. Mr. Weddle also serves as a political consultant/lobbyist for a variety of clients and was named No. 8 of the "Top 20 Lobbyists" by The Nevada Republican in 1991.

Customer satisfaction is always at the top of the agency's agenda. It's goal is to present and implement an advertising, marketing, public relations or governmental affairs plan, which accomplish client's objectives in the most favorable and cost-effective manner possible. Its staff also brings to the agency dynamic backgrounds that when meshed together create great products.

With a deep pool of services to pull from, the agency has been able to serve a diverse group of businesses such as Caesars Palace, Greater Las Vegas Association of Realtors, Anheuser-Busch, Summa Corporation, Aeroauction.com, Nevada Federal Credit Union, Desert Springs Hospital, Las Vegas Chamber of Commerce, Delwebb Corp., American Heart Association, Nevada Symphony Orchestra, KRLV Radio Station and American Honda Motor Company.

In an effort to support the community, Denny Weddle is a past chairman or board member of several organizations. Some of these include Nevada Opera

> ## Looking toward the future, Denny Weddle & Associates will continue to provide cutting-edge, value-oriented communications services designed to help companies and organizations grow and prosper that will ultimately enhance the lives of all in Southern Nevada.

Association, United Way, Nevada Public Radio Corporation, Nellis Support Team, Bay Area Public Affairs Committee, Boy Scouts of America and Clark County Community College Foundation.

Looking toward the future, Denny Weddle & Associates will continue to provide cutting-edge, value-oriented communications services designed to help companies and organizations grow and prosper that will ultimately enhance the lives of all in Southern Nevada.

LandAmerica Lawyers Title

☐ As a leading provider of residential and commercial real estate transaction services and title insurance, LandAmerica (NYSE:LFG) operates more than 700 offices through a network of over 10,000 agents in the United States, Canada, Mexico, Central and South America, Israel and the Caribbean.

Founded in 1925, Lawyers Title Insurance Corporation is one of the largest, national title insurance under-writers in the United States, operating as a subsidiary of LandAmerica Financial Group, Inc. The company has been dutifully servicing Las Vegas and Southern Nevada since 1958. Once owned and operated by a prominent local and state politician as Lawyers Title of Las Vegas, the company became a direct operation in 1986 and was renamed Lawyers Title of Nevada.

As the national company grew, so did Lawyers Title of Nevada. With 14 branch locations and 200 employees, Lawyers Title of Nevada changed its name to LandAmerica Lawyers Title. The new name reflects Lawyers Title's nationwide impact that has resulted from aggressive acquisitions and development.

On the local level, the direct operation serves both Clark and Nye counties with offices in Pahrump, Las Vegas, Green Valley, Henderson, Summerlin and Mesquite. The company is a dominant player in the Southern Nevada real estate market, controlling 12 percent of all title insurance business. In addition to existing offices, the company has current plans to open branch operations in Carson City and Reno by 2005.

LandAmerica's Business Purpose

LandAmerica is a family of companies whose mission supports the growth of home ownership and commercial real estate investments. Its business expertise, information services and financial assurances are critically important to the process of real estate transfer. To address such needs, the company is dedicated to continually improving

upon the efficiency of real estate transfer interests and the protection of those interests.

LandAmerica's Commitment

LandAmerica wants to be recognized as one of America's truly great national organizations. To achieve this prestigious acknowledgment, the company perpetually develops its resources and builds on its strengths. Through talent, technological innovation, teamwork and financial strength, LandAmerica strives to deliver unparalleled service and value to customers and agents, provide long-lasting protection to policyholders, create opportunities and growth for employees, and increase value for shareholders.

Education on the Benefit of Title Insurance

For most people, buying a home is the most substantial, single investment that they will ever make. Knowing this, most homeowners provide for the security and safekeeping of their homes by insuring them against hazards such as fire, theft and weather damage. Yet, another hazard that can pose an even greater risk to homeownership is defects in the title.

Title defects can cause a homeowner to lose part or all of the investment in real property. Fortunately, there is a way to protect this investment from these title defects, and it comes in the form of title insurance.

LandAmerica's companies have been in the business of protecting homeowners and their real estate investments with title insurance since 1876. To truly understand the importance behind title insurance as an essential real estate investment, it is helpful to comprehend particulars such as: Land is permanent and the usage of land can change over the years. A landowner can transfer various rights from the title such as mineral, water, or utility rights. Even if the land is vacant upon purchase, it may have a history not immediately evident, so it is first necessary to search the title to determine if any defects or encumbrances are outstanding and to clear the ones that are not acceptable to the buyer or the lender.

LandAmerica Lawyers Title has been servicing Southern Nevada for nearly 45 years demonstrating its commitment and longevity to the community.

What is Title?

Title is a collective term that involves a person's legal rights to own, possess, use, control and dispose of land. Title takes into account all previous ownership, uses and transfers. In order to legally transfer real estate property, a title search must be performed, and in most cases the title must be determined as clear or free of defects or encumbrances.

A title defect is something missing from the title, for example, an undisclosed heir from a previous owner who is entitled to making a claim for the land. An encumbrance is a claim made upon the land but not by the landowner. For instance, a local power company may have an easement for a power line that serves a house residing on the land in question and could, accordingly, make a claim for it.

To override such a possibility, one can purchase title insurance money to ensure clearance of any outstanding defect or encumbrance before the land is transferred.

What is Title Insurance?

Title insurance is an insurance policy that protects against future loss should the title condition be any different than when the policy was written.

Why is Title Insurance Necessary?

There are two types of title insurance policies: a lender's policy (also called a loan policy) and an owner's policy.

The lender's policy financially covers the amount of a loan and provides protection to the lender. Typically, such a policy does not represent the full property value. An owner's policy protects the landowner and can financially cover the full property value. While a loan policy is often required as a part of a real estate transaction, an owner's policy generally is considered optional.

With an owner's policy, the landowner is protected against any title loss, which ensures the value of the property. Because a title policy is considered insurance, if a claim is made against the title, the title insurer must pay any and all costs associated with defense against the challenge and, if unsuccessful in that defense, reimburse the landowner for any reduction in the value of the land.

Where Can One Get Title Insurance?

One can obtain title insurance from any licensed title insurance company or its agents operating within the same state. When choosing a title insurer, it is important to look for a company with expertise and experience, as well as enough financial strength for protection should a claim arise. Real estate brokers or mortgage lenders can recommend such a company.

LandAmerica Lawyers Title has been servicing Southern Nevada for nearly 45 years demonstrating its commitment and longevity to the community. During those 45 years of doing business and influencing Las Vegas, the company has witnessed the growth of a city.

LandAmerica looks forward with anticipation towards its next 45 years serving the real estate needs of all of Nevada and hopes to play a major role in its great state's development and continued future growth.

Orgill/Singer & Associates, Inc.

Orgill/Singer & Associates is a well-respected full service insurance agency that provides a vast array of comprehensive services from Employee Benefits and Physician Services to Personal Insurance and Investment Services, and Surety and Fidelity Bonds. Principled upon a standard of excellence, the agency not only markets and distributes health plans to the Las Vegas community, but more importantly, Orgill/Singer uses its expertise as a tool to educate and empower its clients.

After becoming owners in 2001, partners David Dahan and Eric Springall have worked diligently to cultivate the growth of their business by broadening its customer base and expanding its staff to over 60 multi-disciplined individuals. Stemming from nearly two decades of direction from founders Robert R. Orgill and Steven P. Singer, the firm of Orgill/Singer has earned a solid reputation for its integrity, professionalism, and dedicated service. Today, Orgill/Singer maintains its foundation made even stronger by keen leadership, focused vision, and a steadfast commitment to its clients.

Orgill/Singer has long recognized that one of its highest priorities is meeting the risk management needs of its clients. With a team approach that combines expert advise, quality products and customer service, Dahan and Springall believe that in order to do business in Las Vegas, one must manage risk, not judge it. "Our goal is to enable the small group market to make well-informed health care and insurance decisions," affirms David Dahan, CEO. "Our clients are supported by knowledgeable sales assistance, advocacy and service made possible by the caliber of professionals who work in our organization."

Independence and large premium volume enables Orgill/Singer to represent a number of major insurance carriers and provide the right policies and programs that best suit its clients' needs. As the managing broker for the Las Vegas Chamber of Commerce health and workers compensation insurance plans, Orgill/Singer has been successful in providing "large business benefits" to small businesses in Southern Nevada. Innovative to form strategic alliances and partnerships with various industry-related companies, Orgill/Singer has brought about accessible, cost-effective solutions to smaller-size businesses, such as CONEXIS for COBRA compliance and Flexible Benefits Administration, Employers Shield for EPLI coverage and WorldDoc, an online health decision support service. These meaningful products and services, typically made available to and created for large group employers, are offered as value-added benefits for the agency's small-group clients at substantially reduced, pre-negotiated rates.

Orgill/Singer is proud of its financial profile and fiscal responsiveness to drive job and profit growth. Its budding client base has resulted in the proportional growth of its work force, effectively doubling in size since 2001. To accommodate

Voted Best Place to Work by the Southern Nevada Human Resource Association

Corporate Headquarters serving the Southern Nevada Business Community

the growing firm, Orgill/Singer occupies a state-of-the-art building and continually invests in technology, equipping its staff with necessary tools, training and resources. By utilizing the best software and technology the industry has to offer, the firm operates its systems and processes in the most modernized and streamlined way possible. This translates to improved efficiency and time management, allowing the agency to better serve its customers. Orgill/Singer was recognized for its efforts as a superior place to work as recipient of the 2003 Southern Nevada Human Resources Association Workplace Excellence Award.

David Dahan, CEO (left); Eric Springall, President

Orgill/Singer has long been committed to the interests and advancement of the Las Vegas community through its long-standing involvement with civic and professional organizations. Many of its contributions to the community are the result of participation with local philanthropic organizations and established community service programs, while others are by taking active roles in leadership and professional groups that identify industry needs and challenges. "We believe our agency serves as an advocate for the needs and concerns of our clients in the Las Vegas Valley community," said Dahan. "Together we can apply experience and knowledge to work toward bringing about resolution with integrity and determination."

A 33-year resident of the Las Vegas Valley, Dahan served as vice president and managing partner of Orgill/Singer & Associates for nearly 12 years before becoming the company's chief executive officer and co-owner. Dahan is licensed in life, health, disability, property/casualty and variable annuity in Nevada. Dahan emigrated from France as a child and was educated in the United States. Prior to joining Orgill/Singer, he worked in independent insurance sales and through the years has earned his place in the community as an empowering leader and mentor. Dahan brings more than 18 years of experience in the insurance industry to the Orgill/Singer team and continues to be a driving force in its promising future. Dahan serves on Nevada's Committee for AffordableHealthcare as well as the Las Vegas Chamber of Commerce President's Club and the Henderson Chamber of Commerce Board of Directors. Dahan also serves on the governing board of North Vista Hospital.

Springall, co-owner and president since June of 2001, previously served for 12 years as vice president and managing partner of Orgill/Singer. His 22 years in the insurance industry have added to his exceptional knowledge and contributed to his visionary leadership of the agency. Born in Idaho, Springall moved to Las Vegas in 1963 and attended the University of Nevada in Las Vegas. Springall has extensive experience in a wide array of insurance and investment products and services, including life, health, disability, variable annuity, property/casualty, surety and surplus line brokerage. He is considered an expert on the medical malpractice issues facing Nevada. Dedicated to his community, Springall serves on the Board of Advisors for the Las Vegas Chamber of Commerce.

Dahan and Springall clearly understand the responsibility and level of trust that their clients expect and deserve from choosing Orgill/Singer as their insurance advisor and broker. "It's a road we've chosen," asserts Springall. "We strive daily to be the benchmark for service and professionalism in our industry...our clients and staff recognize that drive and passion."

Through its solid management and visionary leadership, coupled with a committed professional staff, Orgill/Singer is well positioned to take its place in Southern Nevada's history as a flourishing and successful full line insurance and investments agency in the Las Vegas community.

Quirk & Tratos

☐ A chemical engineer. A ballerina. A cellular and molecular geneticist. An aeronautical engineer. A casino chief financial officer/CPA. An artist.

All turned lawyer.

The attorneys at Quirk & Tratos meld unparalleled legal expertise in intellectual property, entertainment and Internet law with a depth and breadth of understanding that comes only from those who have studied and practiced in the industry they represent.

Headquartered in Las Vegas, the Quirk & Tratos name has gained recognition and respect through its representation of innovative businesses, technology companies and creative individuals from around the country. The firm's clientele ranges from Fortune 500 companies to some of the nation's most renowned scientists, celebrities and artists.

Quirk & Tratos is focused upon the development, protection, licensing, and enforcement of creative works for the companies and the individuals who own them. It is the firm's underlying philosophy that all great achievements begin with a great idea. This inspires the attorneys at Quirk & Tratos to protect, nurture and develop the kind of ideas that determine creative entrepreneurs, artistic expression and scientific success.

With practice areas in trademarks, patents, copyrights, art law, entertainment law, litigation, Internet law, technology, trade secrets, rights of publicity, rights of privacy and media law, many of the firm's attorneys are licensed in multiple states and have represented clients before state and federal courts, the United States Patent and Trademark Office, the United States Copyright Office, as well as the International Trade Commission.

Jerry Seiler and Ted Quirk founded the firm in 1969 as Nevada's first patent attorneys. With the addition of litigation and copyright attorney Mark Tratos in 1983, they began to represent authors, artists, songwriters and performers who needed help negotiating contracts and solving disputes. Over the years, as scores of publicly traded gaming corporations and entertainment production companies came into existence, the firm represented companies involved in the design and development of major resorts and stage shows as well as the conception, development and production recordings and television series.

As technology pervaded the culture, Quirk & Tratos added expertise in cybersquatting and Internet law to its capabilities and practice areas.

Product and service branding, as well as development of intellectual property assets, have become primary areas of focus for the firm. To that end, Quirk & Tratos conduct intellectual property audits for its clients, helping the firm formulate worldwide asset management strategies and rights clearances.

The firm also developed unique expertise in the areas of the personal rights of privacy and publicity and has greatly influenced the legislative process in Nevada and other states. For example, the firm's attorneys helped author the Nevada Right of Publicity statute, Trademark statute, Trade Secret laws and related acts.

Quirk & Tratos represents approximately 80 percent of the gaming industry in Nevada, helping its clientele protect innovative creations, devices and games, such as the popular multiple-action blackjack game. Although the firm's Las Vegas location has allowed it to develop great expertise in the protection of gaming-related technologies, it is equally knowledgeable in many non-gaming technologies. Quirk & Tratos attorneys have drafted and filed patent applications for DNA structures, mechanical apparatuses, business methods and complex electronic computer storage devices and broadcast transmissions.

Recently, Quirk & Tratos brought a groundbreaking copyright infringement case in Nevada resulting in the decision that scanning a copyrighted work constitutes unlawful copying under the U.S. Copyright Act — a ruling that has had important implications for the Internet Age. In addition, firm attorneys have served as lead counsel in intellectual property cases for gaming industry giants MGM MIRAGE, Palms Hotel & Casino, Station Casinos, Boyd Gaming Corporation and WYNN Resorts. It also represents non-gaming corporations such as Your Vitamins, Milliken, Nevada State Bank and many others.

With extensive litigation experience involving trademarks, copyrights, patents, trade secrets, rights of publicity and privacy, and general commercial disputes, Quirk & Tratos attorneys have successfully litigated cases in federal and state courts throughout the country. They also have appeared before administrative tribunals such as the Trademark Trial and Appeal Board and the International Trade Commission.

The firm also has developed expansive experience in privacy policies for websites, domain name registration and enforcement, and web-based licensing agreements.

Quirk & Tratos litigates extensively in the cybersquatting and domain name areas across the United States.

In addition to maintaining an "AV" rating for the firm for more than three decades, Ted Quirk and Mark Tratos are both listed among the Best Lawyers in America.

Quirk & Tratos is one of a handful of law firms in the United States that offer expertise in art law, a field that encompasses copyright, contract and authentication issues ranging from identifying the provenance of world-class paintings to structuring and negotiating important traveling art exhibitions. In this vein, attorneys have represented major visual artists, well-known collectors, art institutions, galleries and museums.

Qualified as experts in the field in third-party litigation for more than 20 years, Quirk & Tratos lawyers have represented the holders of various celebrity rights, including the estates of Orson Wells, James Dean, Marilyn Monroe, Buddy Rich, Humphrey Bogart, Malcolm X, Anthony Quinn as well as working artists like David Cassidy, Rich Little, Charo, Steve VanZandt and Michael Jackson.

Quirk & Tratos attorneys teach numerous continuing legal education programs in entertainment and intellectual property across the country. Firm attorneys teach, or sit on the Boards of Advisors for four law schools in the Western United States, including Southwestern University School of Law, Northwestern University School of Law at Lewis & Clark College, the College of Law at Arizona State University and the William S. Boyd School of Law at University of Nevada, Las Vegas.

(Left)
Mark G. Tratos

(Center)
Lauri Thompson

(Right)
Rob L. Phillips

Sierra Health Services

Sierra Health Services, Inc. represents a diversified network of subsidiaries providing a vast array of health care products and services, including managed care benefit plans for employers, government programs and individuals.

Traded on the New York Stock Exchange under ticker symbol SIE, the company serves some 1.2 million people in various parts of the country. One might assume that Sierra was the offspring of a huge conglomerate based in a large metropolitan area. Actually, Sierra's roots are easily traced back to a visionary cardiologist, Anthony M. Marlon, M.D. In 1972 Dr. Marlon was recruited by what is now University Medical Center in Las Vegas, Nevada, to head up the new division of cardiology. Ten years later, with his own private practice thriving, Marlon founded Health Plan of Nevada (HPN), a health maintenance organization (HMO) providing comprehensive health care services at a fixed, prepaid fee. In 2002 Dr. Marlon's original private practice, now known as Southwest Medical Associates (SMA), celebrated its 30th anniversary, having grown to become the largest medical group in Nevada. Also in 2002, HPN celebrated its 20th anniversary as the state's largest HMO.

Although there are many competitors in the health care industry, ever-evolving services and innovations help Sierra Health Services maintain its ongoing commitment to quality and cost-effective health care. According to Dr. Marlon, who serves as the company's chairman and chief executive officer, "Sierra is actively involved in the delivery of health care. First and foremost, Sierra is a health care company. We continue to provide an integrated delivery system that includes a broad spectrum of health care services. Our continuum of care is expanding, not shrinking."

Service is the very cornerstone upon which all the other pieces of this elaborate structure rest. Not surprisingly, Sierra discovered that accessibility to physicians is one of the most important aspects of health care for its members. At SMA "Same Day Access" is the true definition of a "city that never sleeps"; daily hours of clinic operations were broadened, with patients responding enthusiastically.

Sierra also exemplifies the epitome of a proactive, fully committed corporate community citizen. Sponsoring public/private partnerships to prevent youth smoking, encouraging appropriate use of antibiotics and promoting early prenatal care are just a few examples of the many health care-related initiatives that have been sponsored and/or supported by the company. Many civic and charitable causes are beneficiaries of Sierra's considerable financial and human resources support, including student mentoring and school partnership programs.

Twin Lakes Elementary School in Las Vegas enjoys a unique relationship with Sierra. A pioneering mentoring program matches company employees with students for special one-on-one interaction. The program has resulted in an increase in student attendance, academic performance and appropriate behavior. During the company's 12-year partnership with Twin Lakes, Sierra has purchased books and equipment, sponsored field trips, provided free medical/vision examinations and immunizations, underwritten costs for special parent and teacher education and provided necessary financial resources for many additional needed items and services.

Sierra used the 20th anniversary of HPN to host a fund-raising gala to benefit Clinic on Wheels (COW), a mobile clinic program that provides needed medical services and referrals to children in disadvantaged neighborhoods. HPN underwrote the entire cost of the gala so that every dollar raised went directly to COW. The $125,000 gala proceeds enabled COW to purchase, retrofit, and launch a third mobile clinic service in Southern Nevada.

In 2004, Sierra and HPN contributed over $1.3 million to the University of Nevada Las Vegas Foundation toward the construction of the Science, Engineering and Technology building, scheduled for groundbreaking in the spring of 2005. Recognizing that many of the most important discoveries in science, health and technology begin in university laboratories, the company felt it important to help provide facilities that enable students to learn and work in an environment that encourages quality study and research.

The Nevadans for Antibiotic Awareness campaign was recently organized by Sierra in cooperation with state and local health agencies. Its aim is to reduce the number of inappropriate antibiotic prescriptions, thus reducing resistance to this important class of drugs.

Sierra and its subsidiaries employ approximately 3,000 medical and technical professionals, managers, administrators and support personnel. Since its inception in 1984, the corporation has grown — branching out to include Sierra Health and Life Insurance Company, a home health agency known as Family HealthCare Services, Sierra Health-Care Options, a third-party administrator for self-insured employers, Family Home Hospice, and Behavioral Healthcare Options, which provides mental health and substance abuse services.

In its 20 years, HPN has grown to become the largest health maintenance organization in the state, with over 60 percent of the available market in Nevada and 75 percent in Las Vegas. Under the direction of its president, Jon Bunker, HPN has maintained a unique ability to balance affordability for its employer group customers while assuring access to quality medical care for the employees of these groups. This successful

strategy should assure HPN's continued strong market presence into the future. HPN has some form of contractual relationship with every hospital in Southern Nevada and with over 2,000 physicians. Additionally, the presence of Southwest Medical Associates, with 13 clinical locations and nearly 200 primary and specialty care physicians, allows convenient access for HPN members in Las Vegas and southern Nevada, no matter where in the area they may live.

Skeptics might look at such unprecedented growth and wonder how "service" could still remain a pivotal point of concern. To this Dr. Marlon responds, "At Sierra we realize that effective customer service is not simply answering the phone promptly, but creating a total environment to ensure the best possible delivery of health care. In concrete terms this means listening closely to our customers' needs and responding to their concerns. It requires raising the bar higher... and then raising it again."

Raising the bar for Sierra means emphasizing early access to care, sponsoring community outreach programs, hospice care, behavioral health care, home health care and much more. It means making a commitment to benefit the entire community, not just its employees, customers and shareholders. In an industry that represents constant change, growth and discovery, Sierra thrives on innovation and service.

CRAIG A. MUELLER & ASSOCIATES ATTORNEYS AT LAW

Craig A. Mueller, Esq. is a native of Las Vegas, Nevada, and a graduate of Eldorado High School. He is one of only a few Nevadans who has been accepted to, and graduated from the United States Naval Academy. After graduation from the Academy, he served on active duty in the United States Navy on the U.S..S Julius A. Furer. His duty assignments in the Navy included being a Personnel Officer, Deputy Project Manager of the Space and Naval Warfare Systems, and as the Missile and Fire Control Officer on the *U.S.S. Julius A. Furer*.

Craig has traveled extensively throughout many parts of the world thanks to his time with the Navy. His destinations included exotic ports-of-call such as Australia, Asia, the South Pacific islands, the Persian Gulf, the Panama Canal, and numerous other locations in both the Atlantic and Pacific oceans. Craig has since become an active-duty member of the United States Naval Reserves and has achieved the rank of Commander.

While still on active duty with the Navy, Craig attended law school at the University of Baltimore, graduating in 1990. He was admitted to the Maryland

State Bar in 1991 and then to the Nevada State Bar in 1992. He began his legal career in 1991 as a Legislative Assistant for a senior State Senator in the Maryland State Senate. Later that same year, he became a Judicial Clerk for the Circuit Court for Baltimore City in Baltimore, Maryland.

In 1992 Craig returned to Las Vegas to begin work as an associate attorney with the law firm of Beckley, Singleton, Delanoy, Jemison and List. His practice areas included commercial litigation and insurance defense. He then went to work for the Clark County District Attorney's Office in 1993. Craig felt that his experience as a Naval Officer would help him in serving the county as a Prosecutor. During his tenure as a Deputy District Attorney he was appointed as a Special Prosecutor for the DUI Division. He worked on a variety of interesting cases as a Prosecutor, including winning a major jury verdict in a casino theft case.

Both personally and professionally, Craig has found that the city of Las Vegas has offered him so many priceless opportunities over the years. One of those opportunities was opening his own law firm in Las Vegas in 1997. The firm's main areas of practice include DUI defense, criminal defense, personal injury and general civil litigation.

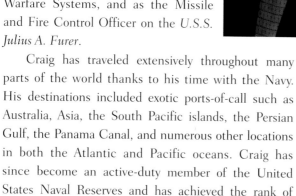

Since opening his office, Craig has found that he has finally been able to give something back to the community. His practice affords him the opportunity to truly "counsel" his clients, not just in their legal issues, but personally as well. He is proud of the fact that he has been the catalyst for change in many people's lives. He earns the trust of his clients and inspires the loyalty of those who work with him.

Craig is a true leader and a dedicated public servant. He is a keen student of world affairs and a vigorous and effective advocate for his clients.

LUCCHESI, GALATI ARCHITECTS

"Engage the imagination!" That's what Lucchesi, Galati Architects challenges its employees and clients to do as part of the firm's vision to help define and enrich the soul of the Las Vegas valley. The firm believes that creating sustainable places where organizations and people thrive requires specialized skills and knowledge; but most importantly, it requires a commitment to research, organizational understanding, a "people-centered" design process, and an ethic of environmental responsibility — especially in the Mojave Desert where resources are scarce.

Lucchesi, Galati Architects has evolved from a small partnership founded in 1986 to a thriving 23-person cross-disciplinary design firm where social and architectural theories are merged with sound environmental practices. This approach results in the creation of places that engage the spirit of the individual, enrich organizations, and contribute to the cultural and natural landscape. The firm's work is its passion and is borne of a sincere desire to merge the two faces of Las Vegas — one an evolutionary international entertainment destination, the other an ever-expanding community of interconnected citizens — into a single, cohesive entity.

Lucchesi, Galati Architects is comprised of talented individuals with varied backgrounds in architecture, interior design, and sociology, all lending their dynamic abilities to the enrichment of their work. The staff has contributed to the community on many levels, earning accolades for their involvement with such groups as the American Institute of Architects (AIA), American Cancer Society, Las Vegas Committee on the Environment, Boys Scouts of America, City of Las Vegas Planning Commission, and Las Vegas and Henderson Chambers of Commerce. These organizations have honored the firm with numerous awards including the AIA Nevada's Firm Award, Service and Associate Member Awards, and Silver Medal; and the Las Vegas Chamber of Commerce's Circle of Excellence and Community Achievement Awards.

Over the past 18 years, Lucchesi, Galati Architects has provided design and consulting services to a myriad of public and private organizations throughout Las Vegas, contributing to the area's culture and growth through education, research, recreation, commerce, public works, religion, and infrastructure. The results of these collaborations include St. Vincent Plaza, R&R Partners Corporate Headquarters, Grant Sawyer State Office Building, St. Elizabeth Ann Seton Catholic School & Parish Center, River Mountains Water Treatment & Transmission Facility, and numerous branches for Nevada State Bank. Additionally, as a result of its community-based approach, the firm was selected to facilitate an "Education and Outreach" program for the City of Henderson Neighborhood Services Division.

The firm also designed the Desert Living Center at the Las Vegas Springs Preserve — an action-based public outreach and applied research facility designed to promote sustainable life in the Mojave Desert. Through dynamic, ongoing education programs, the center will serve as a catalyst for individual and community change from being *"in* the desert" to being *"of* the desert." Lucchesi, Galati Architects is proud of its contributions to this groundbreaking facility, which not only support the firm's vision for the future, but also Las Vegas' ability to *"engage the imagination"* as the city evolves and solidifies its identity as a premier community in which to live, work, and play.

R&R Partners
Corporate Office
Photo by
Cava Photography, Co.

QUALITY of LIFE

Diverse service organizations and medical and social institutions contribute to the health and well-being of residents and visitors, providing countless benefits and opportunities that help define the Las Vegas lifestyle.

The Dental Implant Institute

Las Vegas may be home to some of the world's most spectacular lighting configurations and famous casinos but most people would be surprised to learn that it is also a widely-known center for implant dentistry and periodontics. Las Vegas is the home of Dr. Leon Chen — a world-renowned periodontist and pioneer in his field. With the opening of the Dental Implant Institute in April 2003 along with his existing well-established private practice, Las Vegas Periodontal Care & Dental Implant Center, Las Vegas' best-kept secret may be out of the bag.

Advanced periodontal surgeons Dr. Chen and his partner, Dr. Jennifer Cha, have brought to the table an impressive portfolio of achievements and expertise in the dental field. The team has dedicated their lives to their practice, patients and the science of periodontics and implant dentistry. Together they developed their private practice with a focus on periodontics and implant dentistry, strongly believing that periodontal disease is the reason for 85 percent of tooth loss situations. Since then, they have pioneered tools and procedures and have now built two state-of-the-art learning centers that attract practitioners and speakers from all over the world.

Through his invention of numerous surgical instruments and techniques, Dr. Chen has been the key figure in transforming dental implant surgery from a specialty service to a standard treatment. This gives patients who would normally choose cumbersome bridges a viable alternative. In fact, Dr. Chen's procedures have proven to be so monumental that what once took up to two years of office visits and re-visits now takes merely a few months from start to finish. Through this revolutionary process, tissue never has to be grafted from other parts of the body and there are far fewer surgical incisions performed. Following implant surgery, patients can actually go back to work the same day with little discomfort.

The Dental Implant Institute, with locations in Las Vegas and Henderson,

provides two key services: advanced surgical training for dentists on implant dentistry and an information center for the general public. Under the direction of Dr. Cha, the institute allows Dr. Chen to demonstrate his breakthrough procedures in treating periodontal diseases and the placement of dental implants. Dr. Chen's primary goal is to elevate surgeons' practices to the next level. Twice a month Dr. Chen also gives a free seminar to the general public, answering their questions and concerns about implant dentistry and other related topics. In addition to Dr. Chen and Dr. Cha, the Institute's board members also include famous world speakers who lecture throughout the year.

When Dr. Chen was a small boy in Michigan, he enjoyed arts and crafts. Later this evolved into a liking for interior design. This talent is best shown at his personally decorated, award-winning Dental Implant Institute of Las Vegas. The institute was featured in *Home and Garden* magazine and on national television as the most spectacular privately owned medical center in the United States. By merging his talents for art and his parents' desire for him to be a doctor, Leon Chen entered dentistry after graduating from the University of Michigan. He completed a dental degree summa cum laude at Harvard University School of Dental Medicine, where he received a full scholarship, and Northwestern University Dental School for periodontal specialty residency and masters of science. After graduating, Dr. Chen began his professional career working in Chicago, Illinois, and Boston, Massachusetts. Other career highlights include: clinical instructor, Department of Periodontics, Northwestern University Dental School; assistant instructor, Harvard University School of Dental Medicine; research assistant in toxicology, American Dental Association; and research assistant in microbiology, Forsyth Dental Center.

Along the way, Dr. Chen has been the recipient of many awards and honors including: Award for Excellence in Periodontics of Northeast Regional Periodontal Society, Harvard University School of Dental Medicine summa cum laude in 1993, and Academic Merit Scholarship to the University of Michigan. In addition, he is a consultant for numerous implant companies for the concept of new designs, and he holds a number of patents on implant-related surgical instruments. He is one of the most experienced dental implant and sinus surgeons in the United States. Patients from all over the world seek out Dr. Chen for his ability to successfully perform complex sinus augmentation procedures that other doctors believed were impossible.

For Dr. Chen there is never a dull day as he is also an affiliate professor in the Implant Department of the Harvard School of Dental Medicine; the CEO and Founder of the Dental Implant Institute of Las Vegas; a main podium speaker for the American Academy of Periodontology; The International Implant Symposium; The American Academy of Implant Dentistry; The International Congress of Oral Implantologists; and The European Federation of Periodontology. Additionally, Dr. Chen acted as an advisor for the German and Italian Journal of Implantology, as well as the Journal of International Implant Dentistry and a board trustee for ACC-PAC (Asian Chamber of Commerce-Political Action Committee).

Despite his credentials, Dr. Chen's practice wouldn't be what it is today without the assistance and guidance of his partner, Dr. Cha, who is also a periodontist and clinical dentist specializing in the treatment of gum diseases. Throughout her practice she has built a reputation for being one of the best surgeons in her field internationally and is also acknowledged as the "best of the past 10 years at Northwestern University." Her precise and expert ability has proven to be a true asset.

Dr. Cha has been a resident of Las Vegas since 1975. After graduating from Clark High School, she attended UNLV on a full scholarship and later the Washington University School of Dentistry. She began working as a general dentist in 1988 in Chicago, Illinois, Las Vegas, Nevada, and St. Louis, Missouri. After realizing an interest in periodontics, she went back to school to further her education. By the time she moved back to Las Vegas in 1993 she had developed a remarkable reputation as a successful periodontal surgeon. Dr. Cha is also an affiliate professor of the Implant Department of Harvard University School of Dentistry and is a member of numerous scientific boards.

Together the husband-and-wife team has been voted as two of the top dentists in Las Vegas and have developed a growing practice with six locations — all operating under the philosophy that all patients are to be "treated like family," and receive warm, friendly and exceptional service. In addition to overseeing the locations and institute, they are also the proud parents of five children, an accomplishment they place second to none.

The Dental Implant Institute and Las Vegas Periodontal Care has always made an effort to give back to the community through sponsorships of various organizations including the American Heart Association, The American Cancer Society and local charities.

Committed to excellence in periodontics and implant dentistry, the Dental Implant Institute and Las Vegas Periodontal Care will continue to serve the Las Vegas community as a valued provider of dental care and education and a center for scientific advancement.

FREMONT MEDICAL CENTERS

Good Medicine for Fast Times

A newcomer to the Las Vegas area in 1975, J. Corey Brown, M.D. has accomplished a feat that is both geographically and historically noteworthy: Fremont Medical Centers (FMC), a local medical services company that has grown as spectacularly as the population it serves.

"Quality healthcare is really very simple," says Dr. Brown. "It's all about the patient, and listening to the patient."

A man of quiet intensity, Dr. Brown established Fremont Medical Centers after many years of service as an emergency room physician, Director of the Emergency Department at Valley Hospital, and the first medical director of the valley's Flight for Life program. In 1985 FMC opened its doors to the Las Vegas community. Dr. Brown and three of his colleagues cared for approximately 125 patient a day in FMC's early days.

As the Las Vegas community has grown, so has the need for medical care. Within the first 10 years, Dr. Brown added more physicians and a physical therapy department. In 1988, FMC opened a second location at the intersection of Flamingo and Arville. This office eventually relocated to a state-of-the-art facility at the corner of Tropicana Avenue and Wynn Road.

By 1995, the Las Vegas suburb of Henderson was becoming the fastest growing city in the United States. Seeing the need, the FMC executive team chose to locate the next medical center in Henderson. Soon after, in an effort to keep up with the demand for healthcare in Las Vegas' northwest sector, FMC opened its fourth medical center in Summerlin. The company now offers nine clinic locations and employs more than 60 physicians and 450 allied heath workers.

Despite the company's rapid expansion, the medical staff at FMC has never abandoned its original mission: to consistently exceed the expectations of its patients. By treating patients better than they expect; displaying a friendly, motivated, and caring attitude; using initiative and creativity to make the medical experience a pleasant one; and demonstrating integrity, trust, and respect for

confidentiality, FMC's medical staff strives for excellence in every aspect of healthcare.

Internally, FMC's mission is to consistently exceed the expectations of medical staff by treating them better than they expect. FMC's medical staff is provided with opportunities for growth — both professional and personal — within the company. FMC's company culture places a high value on its employees encouraging annual goal setting, weekly meetings, keeping a Professional Journal of Success, educational reading, and outside activities that promote teamwork, such as participation in Clark County Parks and Community Services Adult Volleyball League. Last year, these management practices earned FMC a nomination for the 2003 Workplace Excellence award from the Southern Nevada Human Resource Association.

The values of growth, teamwork, and the provision of excellent healthcare are recognized in the medical staff's efforts to make each medical appointment as convenient as possible for the patient through prompt delivery of services. FMC offers a total healthcare package to patients who need diverse medical services. On-site radiology services are available at all FMC primary care locations.

For further convenience, FMC's primary care physicians staff FMC clinics throughout the Las Vegas

Valley and are available 24 hours a day. The professional excellence of these physicians gets regular publicity in an annual reader survey in the healthcare issue of *Las Vegas Life* magazine, recognizing various FMC physicians for providing high quality healthcare. Patients appreciate

the FMC specialists' commitment to quality service and their strong backgrounds in Internal Medicine and/or Family Practice.

Some of FMC's newer patients arrive in the Las Vegas Valley after living elsewhere; others are born here. For the youngest valley residents, FMC offers Pediatric services at three Fremont Children's Clinics. From its inception in December 2002, with one physician and one office, FMC's Pediatric services has expanded to three locations and 14 physicians specializing in Pediatrics.

Whatever a person's age, fast times can wear down even the most fit valley resident. To care for conditions that require immediate or in-facility care, Fremont's In-Patient Team (FIT), established in 1999, consists of primary care physicians who maintain staff privileges at all major hospitals, rehabilitation clinics, and skilled nursing facilities in the Las Vegas area. FIT physicians provide patient care, teaching, research and leadership related to healthcare.

Fremont physicians also provide quality, specialty healthcare for women in a region where such care is more elusive than a good hand in blackjack. The only centers of their kind, FMC's two Obstetrics (OB) and Gynecology (GYN) centers offer full-time OB/GYN services providing the Las Vegas community with eight

dedicated and experienced physicians specializing in OB/GYN. FMC's two OB/GYN centers are located in Las Vegas and Henderson.

To increase the odds that everyone will stay healthy and avoid illness, FMC includes wellness departments in four of its centers. Medical staff in these departments supports wellness programs including comprehensive annual wellness exams and employer directed physical exams.

Other resources for employers and employees are the Worker's Compensation task specialists who provide round-the-clock services in four primary care centers. In 2003, more than one in twelve patients who sought medical help at FMC came in with work-related injuries.

With such diverse services offered through one company, the patient's experience of seeking and receiving health care is simplified. Today, many Healthcare Providers attempt to save costs by consolidating their services; FMC, however, is poised for growth and

J. Corey Brown, M.D., Founder — Fremont Medical Centers

continued specialization in all areas of healthcare. Now entering their 20th year, and treating over 1,000 patients per day, FMC's physicians and medical staff remain committed to the people of Southern Nevada.

For Dr. Brown, those first days and nights of his medical career are still in his thoughts. He remembers the young people in the emergency rooms of inner city Vancouver, BC who were dying or critically ill. Those memories remind him of what really matters. "People become afraid when something is very wrong with their bodies and they don't know what is going to happen to them. I tell my staff, don't worry about anything other than you and the patient."

North Vista Hospital

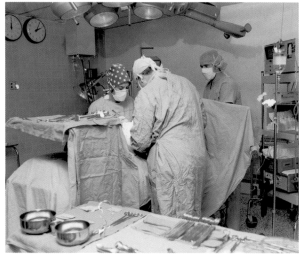

☐Once a small, single-story health care facility, North Vista Hospital in North Las Vegas has evolved into a tower of comprehensive medical and mental health services for the community.

The facility, which is accredited by the joint Commission on Accreditation of Healthcare Organizations, was recently acquired by Iasis Healthcare. The hospital sits on over 10 acres in downtown North Las Vegas and serves the greater Las Vegas metropolitan area.

Its roots date back to late 1959, when a local physician, Dr. Everett C. Freer, founded the Community Hospital of North Las Vegas. Several months later, the hospital opened with just five doctors, 15 employees and eight beds. At the time, it adequately supported the acute care needs of the area's 18,000 residents.

Over the next several decades, the population of North Las Vegas soared to 140,000. The hospital kept pace by growing its number of staff, programs and affiliated physicians. In 1991 it changed its name to Lake Mead Hospital Medical Center. The following year it built a three-story tower adjacent to its original structure to accommodate more patients, then added a fourth story in 1994.

Since then the hospital has joined the ranks as one of North Las Vegas' largest employers and taxpayers. Yet even its founders could not have envisioned how research and technology would dramatically change the type and quality of medical care it would offer.

Today the hospital provides the following services: prenatal and obstetrics, pediatrics, surgical, respiratory, cardiology, neurosurgery, critical care, progressive care, diagnostic imaging, laboratory, orthopedics, surgery, mental health, pharmacy, physical, speech and occupational therapy, radiology and chemotherapy.

Despite its dramatic advancements, the hospital continually explores ways to distinguish itself from other medical facilities and is building a national reputation as one of the hospitals that provides quality care. Part of its plan includes recruiting physicians in specialty areas, such as gynecologic oncology, bariatric and colorectal surgery, orthopedics, and beefing up its programs and services.

Examples are easy to find. For instance, its gastrointestinal program offers one of the latest methods of diagnosis and treatments, such as colonoscopy, upper endoscopy, ERCP and sigmoidoscopy. Its emergency

department includes an on-site laboratory, radiology department and birthing room. Also, the hospital's Intensive Care and Coronary Care Unit feature up-to-date monitoring equipment such as patient telemetry.

During the 1990s, the hospital's medical staff began demonstrating its vast capabilities by performing various surgical procedures, ranging from a simple tonsillectomy to more complicated operations, such as total joint replacements or pacemaker implantation.

The hospital soon added niche programs: mental health, maternal/neonatal, Women's Cancer Center and Baby Talk.

Its mental health services target adults 18 years of age or older and are designed to restore each patient's independence in a safe and structured environment. From diagnosis to treatment to discharge, care is tailored to the individual.

Services include intensive treatment interventions and psychological and drug treatments for those suffering from acute psychiatric conditions, such as anxiety, schizophrenia and psychophysiological and personality disorders. While the mental health unit provides comprehensive patient care, it also treats patients with serious substance abuse problems and eating disorders.

Likewise, the maternal/neonatal program provides a full range of services for newborns and their mothers, such as extra infant care education, IV therapy, sepsis work-ups, Bili-light therapy and transient increases of oxygen.

The 8,000-square-foot Women's Cancer Center opened in November 2000 and occupies the hospital's fourth floor. It treats women suffering from gynecologic cancer, including ovarian, uterine and cervical cancer. Women are screened for gynecologic malignancies through a combination of approaches like ultrasonography, cytology and tumor marker tests.

Since the cancer center is a member of the Gynecologic Oncology Group, a research organization funded by the National Cancer Institute, many patients are able to participate in clinical trials and receive treatments that aren't yet available to the general public.

Among the most popular of the hospital's programs is Baby Talk. Participating moms-to-be can enroll in free prenatal classes and receive free pregnancy consultation and financial application assistance or simply get help finding the right doctor.

Considering its comprehensive programs and medical expertise, it's not surprising that the hospital developed into a fertile training ground for medical students. In June 1999 it partnered with Touro University International, an osteopathic medical school based in Vallejo, California, to create an osteopathic residency program.

The growth spurt continued the following year. A 45,000-square-foot medical arts building was added on to its campus in February 2000. The facility supports family practitioners and specialists in internal medicine, cardiology, obstetrics and gynecology, otolaryngology, general surgery, oncology and radiology. Patients also benefit from its outpatient physical therapy and rehabilitation clinic, a linear accelerator for cancer treatment and magnetic resonance imaging services.

While the hospital's business philosophy focuses on excellence in heath care delivery, its culture emphasizes teamwork, community outreach and health education. Its mission extends beyond treating patients to meeting the health care needs of the community.

Every year it sponsors the North Las Vegas Hispanic Health Fair, various local charity events and health education seminars, such as those that teach heart healthy habits to patients at-risk for cardiac disease.

Another community program is Premier Advantage, which was launched in 2002. Aimed at adults in the community over the age of 55, members receive discounts on prescriptions, hearing aids, glasses and contacts, airfare, hotels, rental cars, legal and insurance services from participating retail stores and vendors.

After Lake Mead Hospital Medical Center was acquired by Iasis Healthcare, it was renamed North Vista Hospital, and it will continue adapting to new technologies and treatments that offer patents the highest quality medical care.

Lake Mead Hospital Medical Center (now North Vista Hospital) services more than 140,000 people in North Las Vegas.

Healthsouth Rehabilitation Hospital of Henderson

Healthsouth is the nation's largest healthcare services provider, with nearly 1,700 facilities nationwide and abroad. Its vast network of highly skilled physicians and therapists, along with the latest equipment and technology, guarantees that all patients have easy access to high-quality healthcare. Healthsouth is dedicated to providing expert, cost-effective care, producing excellent outcomes and getting people back...to work...to play...to living.

Healthsouth Rehabilitation Hospital of Henderson is proud to be part of this network. The beautiful new 60-bed acute rehabilitation hospital opened in December 2001 and is already an integral part of the healthcare community in Henderson. It is centrally located just west of St. Rose Siena Hospital, on St. Rose Parkway, west of Eastern Ave. They also have sister facilities in Las Vegas located on Valley View Blvd. and Tenaya Way.

Medicare, Medicaid and most Insurance Companies cover both the inpatient and outpatient services provided at Healthsouth Rehabilitation Hospital of Henderson.

Healthsouth Rehabilitation Hospital of Henderson specializes in Stroke Rehabilitation, Parkinson's, Multiple Sclerosis, Amputation, Joint Replacement, Hip Fractures, Orthopedic disorders/injuries, Spinal Cord Injuries, Wound Care, Spacticity Management, and other physical rehabilitation needs.

The hospital provides a complete continuity of care including Physical Therapy, Occupational Therapy, Speech Therapy, Respiratory Therapy, Aquatic Therapy in a large indoor pool, Modified Barium Swallow, Dysphasia Therapy utilizing VitalStim™ and compensatory strategies, Lee Silverman Voice Therapy, Case Management, Cognitive Therapy, Nutritional Counseling, Psychology, On-site Pharmacy, Rehab Nursing and Physical Medicine. In addition to the above inpatient services, it also provides

Healthsouth is dedicated to providing expert, cost-effective care, producing excellent outcomes and getting people back...to work...to play...to living.

complete Outpatient Therapy including Functional Capacity Evaluation, Day Treatment Program and Home Health services to complete the patient's recovery program upon discharge from the hospital.

Since Henderson has been one of the nation's fastest growing communities over the last 10 years, the city and its citizens have enthusiastically embraced this much-needed, new state-of-the art hospital in their community.

Healthsouth Rehabilitation Hospital of Henderson differs from other traditional inpatient facilities, such as nursing homes, in that it tracks patient outcomes, insists on a pristine clean environment and offers an intensive approach to rehabilitation, supervised by a physician. It is this approach that allows the hospital to achieve superior outcomes. Visitors are encouraged to tour the facility to observe the scope of services and the caring, highly-trained staff whose total focus is the acute rehabilitation of clients. The primary measure of success is to help the clients help themselves — to recover and care for themselves and return home as quickly as possible.

Medicare, Medicaid and most Insurance Companies cover both the inpatient and outpatient services provided at Healthsouth Rehabilitation Hospital of Henderson. The knowledgeable admission representatives can assist one in making the necessary arrangements to facilitate the registration and authorization process.

ScripNet

In 1997 Dennis M. Sponer founded ScripNet, a pharmacy management company that helps to mitigate an ignominious trend in the health care industry: the ever-increasing insurance costs that accrue to employers. Building upon his mother's health care management business, where he worked as in-house counsel prior to launching ScripNet, Mr. Sponer was galvanized by his experience on the managed-care side of the coin. Inefficiencies and inflexibility were rampant in the workers' compensation arena and from Mr. Sponer's perspective, this phenomenon illustrated the need to improve the pharmacy-end of health care management.

Mr. Sponer felt that inefficiency was trammeling the turnover rate of claims, endangering the health of patients who rely on quick access to quality medication for their recovery. So when Mr. Sponer launched ScripNet, he sought to marry cutting-edge technology with high-quality patient care. This idea has proven itself a redounding success: ScripNet ranked number 34 in *Inc. Magazine*'s annual listing of the 500 fastest-growing privately held companies in the nation. Under ScripNet's business paradigm, needy injured workers get access to their meds faster, pharmacies are paid more quickly and insurance companies are spared the headaches involved in ensuring that their injured workers receive the best possible care. All the parties involved are spared extraneous costs, either in the form of higher medical bills or lost work time.

ScripNet procures efficiency and impressive cost cutting via its state-of-the-art, electronic Point-of-Sale System. Connected to an online adjudication system, members of ScripNet's pharmacy-network verify coverage upon dispensing medication to injured workers. ScripNet's clients are assured immediate payment verification: as soon as drugs are dispensed, ScripNet is billed for them, whether or not an insurer has accepted these workers' compensation claims. Moreover, once the patient's information is downloaded to the ScripNet census, no further intervention from ScripNet, nor the payor, is required: the wheels of an automated process have been spun into motion.

Through its efforts, ScripNet has helped ensure that injured workers get back to work faster. Emblematic of ScripNet's efforts to center health care on employees, it takes risks that most managed-care companies avoid. ScripNet pays for an employee's first dose of meds, even if employers have not been contacted yet. In fact, before ScripNet arose on the workers' compensation scene, many injured employees were forced to pay out of pocket for meds while waiting for their claims to be processed.

ScripNet has debunked the broadly held myth that there is a tradeoff to be made between high-quality health care delivery and maintaining the cost of health care benefits at bay. ScripNet has been a trailblazer in the management of pharmacy benefits for workers' compensation claims. Now a budding niche in its own right, the managed care of workers' compensation has become, thanks to ScripNet, a must-have by insurance companies. ScripNet has managed to export the benefits of managed care to the workers' compensation arena in ways that make fledgling competitors green with envy.

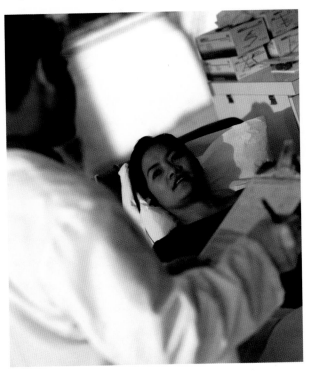

BIBLIOGRAPHY

Berman, Susan. *Lady Las Vegas: The Inside Story Behind America*. New York: TV Books, 1996

Denton, Sally and Morris, Roger. *The Money and the Power: The Making of Las Vegas*. New York: Vintage Books, 2002

Elliott, Gary E. *The New Western Frontier: An Illustrated History of Greater Las Vegas*. Carlsbad: Heritage Media Corp., 1999

Land, Barbara. *A Short History of Las Vegas*. Reno, Las Vegas: University of Nevada Press, 1999

Littlejohn, David. *The Real Las Vegas: Life Beyond the Strip*. Oxford, New York: Oxford University Press, 1999

McCracken, Robert D. *Las Vegas: The Great American Playground*. Reno, Las Vegas: University of Nevada Press, 1996

Moehring, Eugene P. *Resort City in the Sunbelt: Las Vegas, 1930-1970*. Reno, Las Vegas: University of Nevada Press, 1989

Rothman, Hal. *Neon Metropolis: How Las Vegas Started the Twenty-First Century*. New York, London: Routledge, 2002

Wilkerson, W. R. II. *The Man Who Invented Las Vegas*. Beverly Hills: Ciro's Books, 2000

INDEX

PARTNERS & WEB SITE INDEX